"We are probably familiar with the proverb ab
so heavenly minded he is no earthly good. Anc
that we don't even need a proverb for it—the carnal thinker who is so earthly minded
he is no heavenly good. And no earthly good either, as it turns out. The hardest thing to
achieve on this subject is *balance*, but it is a difficult feat that Rigney has accomplished.
Buy this book. Make it one of your earthly possessions. Read it to find out what that is
supposed to mean."

> **Douglas Wilson,** Senior Fellow of Theology, New St. Andrews College; Pastor,
> Christ Church, Moscow, Idaho

"Reading this will be a sweet moment of profound liberation for many. With wisdom
and verve, Rigney shows how we can worship our Creator through the enjoyment of his
creation. This is going to make a lot of Christians happier in Christ—and more attractively
Christlike."

> **Michael Reeves,** Director of Union and Senior Lecturer, Wales Evangelical
> School of Theology; author, *Delighting in the Trinity*; *The Unquenchable Flame*; and
> *Rejoicing in Christ*

"This book makes me want to watch the Olympics while eating a pumpkin crunch cake,
rejoicing in the God who richly provides us with everything to enjoy. But part of me is
a little wary of the indulgent pecan crunchiness and astonishing athletic feats. What if
my heart gets lost in these things? If you're familiar with that hesitation, this book is for
you. We were made to take in all the fullness of the intergalactic glory of the triune God.
This book is a trustworthy guide to help your gaze follow along the scattered beams up
to the sun."

> **Gloria Furman,** pastor's wife, Redeemer Church of Dubai; mother of four; author,
> *Glimpses of Grace* and *Treasuring Christ When Your Hands Are Full*

"It is not easy to understand how I can love God with all my heart, but also love the
world he has made. God's Word encourages us to love the creation (Psalm 19), but also to
love not the world (1 John 2:15–17). Rigney is really helpful to those wrestling with this
kind of question, and he helps us with a lively and engaging style. This book clarifies
and builds upon John Piper's Christian Hedonism. I heartily recommend it."

> **John M. Frame,** J. D. Trimble Chair of Systematic Theology and Philosophy,
> Reformed Theological Seminary, Orlando

The Things of Earth

THE

THINGS

OF

EARTH

Treasuring God by Enjoying His Gifts

JOE RIGNEY

FOREWORD BY JOHN PIPER

WHEATON, ILLINOIS

The Things of Earth: Treasuring God by Enjoying His Gifts

Copyright © 2015 by Joe Rigney

Published by Crossway
        1300 Crescent Street
        Wheaton, Illinois 60187

Cover design: Erik Maldre

First printing 2015

Printed in the United States of America

Unless otherwise indicated, Scripture quotations are from the ESV® Bible (*The Holy Bible, English Standard Version*®), copyright © 2001 by Crossway, a publishing ministry of Good News Publishers. 2011 Text Edition. Used by permission. All rights reserved.

Scripture quotations marked KJV are from the *King James Version* of the Bible.
All emphases in Scripture quotations have been added by the author.

Trade paperback ISBN: 978-1-4335-4473-6
ePub ISBN: 978-1-4335-4476-7
PDF ISBN: 978-1-4335-4474-3
Mobipocket ISBN: 978-1-4335-4475-0

Library of Congress Cataloging-in-Publication Data
Rigney, Joe, 1982-
   The things of earth : treasuring God by enjoying his
gifts / Joe Rigney ; foreword by John Piper.
      pages cm
   Includes bibliographical references and index.
   ISBN 978-1-4335-4473-6 (tp)
1. Hedonism—Religious aspects—Christianity.
2. Pleasure—Religious aspects—Christianity.
3. Happiness—Religious aspects—Christianity.
4. Gratitude—Religious aspects—Christianity.
5. God (Christianity)—Worship and love.
6. Piper, John, 1946–   I. Title.
BR115.H43R54   2015
233—dc23   2014020703

Crossway is a publishing ministry of Good News Publishers.

VP		28	27	26	25	24	23	22	21	20	19	18
17	16	15	14	13	12	11	10	9	8	7	6	

To my wife, Jen
You are a constant reminder that
the things of earth grow strangely bright
in the light of his glory and grace.

Contents

Foreword

If there is an evangelical Christian alive today who has thought and written more biblically, more deeply, more creatively, or more practically about the proper enjoyment of creation and culture, I don't know who it is. When I say "biblically," I mean that Joe thinks and writes under the authority of God's Word and with a view to answering all serious objections that arise from the Bible. I also mean that he writes as a persuaded Christian Hedonist—that is, with the pervasive conviction that God is most glorified in us when we are most satisfied in him.

But like all good students, he is not merely swallowing the teachings of Christian Hedonism; he is digesting them so that they turn into energies and insights beyond his teacher's. The fact that he asked me to write this foreword, and that I agreed to do it, is a sign that those insights are not contradictory, but complementary, to the teacher's efforts.

Joe has discerned that a strength of Christian Hedonism can also turn into a weakness. The strength is that Christian Hedonism, as I have tried to develop it, has a strong ascetic tendency (as the Bible does!). For example, I often add these words: "God is most glorified in us when we are most satisfied in him, *especially in those times when we embrace suffering for his sake with joy.*" Joy in affliction is a clearer witness that we treasure Christ more than comfort, than joy in comfortable, sunny days.

I also stress that it is more blessed to give than to receive and that giving is often painful. I have tried to make the tone of my ministry "sorrowful, yet always rejoicing" (2 Cor. 6:10). The very heart of Christian Hedonism, textually, is found in Philippians 1:19–23, where Christ is most magnified in our dying, because we treasure Christ so supremely that we call dying *gain*—because in it we get more of Christ. And we treasure Christ in our living by counting everything as loss because of the surpassing worth of knowing Christ Jesus our Lord (Phil. 3:8). The saltiness of the Christian life is tasted most keenly when, in the midst of being reviled and persecuted, we rejoice and are glad because our reward in heaven is great (Matt. 5:11–13).

The weakness of this emphasis is that little space is devoted to magnifying Christ in the right enjoyment of creation and culture. Little emphasis is given to Paul's words: "God created [foods] to be received with thanksgiving by those who believe and know the truth. For everything created by God is good, and nothing is to be rejected if it is received with thanksgiving" (1 Tim. 4:3–4). Or his words that God "richly provides us with everything to enjoy" (1 Tim. 6:17).

The trees of biblical wisdom in regard to savoring God in the savoring of his creation are not full-grown in what I have written about Christian Hedonism. I sowed some seeds, but I never circled back to tend those saplings, let alone grow them into a book. That's what Joe Rigney has done. And I am so pleased with what he has written that I feel no need to write that book. It needed to be written, and he has done it.

We are all shaped and motivated by our personal experiences. I have seen a side of biblical truth, and written about it the way I have, in large measure because of my experience of life and what I see as the needs around me in the church, in America, and in the world. I will probably keep my focus and my emphasis as long as I live. It's the way I see the Bible and the world at this time.

But my emphasis is not the whole truth. Joe has lived a different life and has faced different challenges and has felt the force of different needs in people's lives. This has given him a sensitivity to other dimensions of biblical truth and has enabled him to see them and write about them with depth, creativity, and intensely practical application.

This book has been very helpful to me. I mean that personally. I think I will be a better father and husband and friend and leader because of it. One reason is that Joe is undaunted by possible objections to what he emphasizes from the Bible. Does this emphasis fit with the biblical teaching on self-denial? Will it help when the child dies? Will it help us complete the Great Commission? Will it help us say, "Whom have I in heaven but you? And there is nothing on earth that I desire besides you"

(Ps. 73:25)? There are good answers to these questions—biblical answers. Joe is so devoted to Scripture that he is unafraid to face whatever it says without rejecting it in favor of his system or twisting it to make it fit. This is the kind of writer that gives me great help.

We are both aware that what we have written can be distorted and misused. But that puts us in good company, since all Christian heresies and sects distort and misuse the Bible. God evidently thought that the gift of the Bible was worth the distortions people would make of it. Joe has written a book that should have been written. It is a gift to the church and the world, not because it *is* the Bible but because it is pervaded by a passion to be *faithful* to the Bible. It is worth the distortions people will make of it. May they be few. He has not been careless.

My prayer for this book is the same as Joe's:

May the Father of Lights, who knows how to give good gifts to his children, teach you the secret of facing plenty and hunger, abundance and need, being brought low or being raised up. May he grant you the grace to do all good things, receive all good things, lose all good things, and endure all hard things through Christ who gives you strength. Amen.

John Piper

Acknowledgments

Much in this book focuses on the early chapters of Genesis. However, the passage about the four rivers flowing down to water the garden (2:10) receives short shrift (I don't think I mention it once). To rectify that omission, imagine that this book is the garden, and that there are four rivers flowing down to water it. The name of the first river is Jonathan Edwards, the second is C. S. Lewis, the third is John Piper, and the fourth is Doug Wilson (the latter two, like the Tigris and Euphrates, still being alive and well in our own day). These four rivers all have their distinctive characters, but they flow from one source. And, at least for me, they have all swelled together to produce this book.

Edwards has been a close friend ever since I plunged into his depths in seminary, and in many ways this book was hatched in a class on *The End for which God Created the World*. He helped me to see that we cannot speak of the glory of God without reference to God's triune being and that the world is crowded with images of divine things. I'm not sure how to describe Lewis's impact on me, other than to say that it's pervasive, as a quick skim through these pages will confirm. The clarity of his thought and the poetry of his prose have helped me to see that there is more in heaven and earth than is dreamt of in most books of theology.

I describe some of John Piper's influence on me in the introduction, so I won't rehearse it here. But it's no understatement to say that this book would not have been written without him. From the beginning, my hope has been that this book would be a little extension of the God-centered vision that he has faithfully preached and proclaimed for over thirty-five years. I'm profoundly grateful for his ministry, his mentorship, and his love and care for me and my family. From the moment that the book began to take shape, I knew there was no one else that I would want to write the foreword. His willingness to do so is a tremendous honor, and I still find myself stunned and humbled by his commendation.

If Edwards, Lewis, and Piper set the stage for this project, Doug Wilson was the catalyst. A handful of blog posts in 2010 led to a public conversation with Pastor John in 2011, which I had the privilege of moderating. It was that public conversation that finally convinced me of the need for this book, and Doug has encouraged me in the project along the way. Doug has indelibly shaped the way that I approach these questions, so much so that I find it impossible to remember all the things he has taught me. I have no doubt that there are many insights here that could be traced directly back to him, and I know I've not cataloged them all. Thankfully, Doug knows as well as anyone that a failure of memory does not signal a failure of gratitude. After all, that's what acknowledgments are for. So let me just say I am deeply thankful for Doug's ministry and friendship. The seeds he has sown have proven fruitful in my life, and I can only hope that my attempts at sowing will be as faithful and fruitful as his.

Beyond these four, there are a number of other authors that lurk in the pages that follow. Nate Wilson, in both his fiction and his prose, has regularly kindled in me a desire to soak up every ounce of reality that God throws my way and then to pour out what I have for the good of others. I like to think that this book is a kind of exegetical defense for the way that Nate sees and names the world. Andrew Peterson's songs have long ministered to my soul and awakened me to the freshness of the world God has made. If you want to understand what this book is all about, pick up one of his albums and listen to a song or two; that'll likely give you a deeper experiential knowledge of what I'm getting at than any number of expository paragraphs. Time would fail me to describe the impact that Augustine, Tolkien, Chesterton, and Leithart have had on this book; I've tried to detail some of that influence in the notes.

While writing this book I had the opportunity to teach and preach through the content a handful of times at Bethlehem Baptist Church. Shane Barnard and Shane Everett also invited me to teach a course on the material for the Worship Initiative. The questions and comments I received each time I worked through it only increased my desire to write it, and I hope have made the book substantially better.

A number of students at Bethlehem College and Seminary read various portions and marked up the manuscript with probing questions, critical reactions, and encouraging remarks. I'd like to particularly thank Justin Woyak, Scott McQuinn, Lance Kramer, Chris Powers, Dan and Emily Weller, Chris Robbins, Aaron Jameson, Jeff Lacine, Brian Tabb, and Brandon Bellomo. Other friends who encouraged me through the writing process include Clayton Luskie, Curt Steinhorst, Marshall Segal, Jonathan Parnell, Tony Reinke, and James Carr. My colleagues at Bethlehem College and Seminary regularly challenge and provoke my thinking, spurring me to new insights, many of which found their way into the book. I'm grateful to God for the partnership in ministry I have with Ryan Griffith, Johnathon Bowers, Josh Maloney, Ben Collins, Matt Crutchmer, Jason Abell, Jason DeRouchie, Andy Naselli, Travis Myers, and the rest of the faculty and staff at Bethlehem College and Seminary.

My good friend Alex Kirk carefully read the book and made some important connections that I was able to include in the final product. David Mathis read key portions and helped me navigate the world of evangelical publishing. My teaching assistant Zach Howard was invaluable in tracking down citations and helping me with formatting. Justin Taylor and the team at Crossway have proved that the back end of their publishing house is as Christ-exalting as the books they produce. Jill Carter, Amy Kruis, Erik Maldre, and the rest of the folks there have made this project a joy to work on. My editor, Lydia Brownback, caught my errors, cleaned up my prose, and clarified my thinking at a number of points.

My family has been a tremendous encouragement in this project. In particular, my grandfather Jim Reese; my father-in-law, Pete Smith; and my youngest brother, Daniel, all read drafts and made very perceptive comments, especially about how to make it accessible to nontheologians. Over the course of writing this book, my father, Bill Rigney, finished his earthly course after a long and painful fight with Alzheimer's and Parkinson's. Losing my dad over eight years helped me to realize just how significant the things of earth can be in revealing the character of God.

I acutely feel my dad's earthly absence, and yet the love and gratitude I bear to him and for him have only served to increase my sense of God's fatherly presence. In losing my dad, I found the substance to which he was but a shadow. And finding the substance—God the Father—only made me more grateful for my dad, who imaged him to me so well.

The chief arena where I apply everything I say in this book is my own immediate family. I have two wonderful sons, Sam and Peter, and I have learned more from them about the strange brightness of the things of earth than any book could possibly communicate. The kindling of this book may have been gathered in a seminary classroom, but the spark that ignited it and has sustained the flames was birthed in tickle fights in my living room.

Finally, my wife, Jenny, has supported, encouraged, and inspired me, long before this project was a twinkle in my eye. She has been a sounding board for my ideas for as long as we've been together, offering perceptive insights and helping me to practice what I preach. In highs and lows, in darkness and in light, she has been my constant companion for the last nine years. Grace has abounded to me through her, and words cannot express how privileged I feel to have her as my bride.

Introduction

What Are We to Do with the Things of Earth?

God is most glorified in you when you are most satisfied in him.

John Piper

He loves Thee too little, who loves anything together with Thee, which he loves not for Thy sake.

Augustine

Katherine is a college student who works twenty-five hours a week in order to pay her way through school. Though she tries to devote time to prayer and Scripture reading, she worries that she doesn't read her Bible enough. No matter how long her devotions are, the low-grade guilt seems to stay. After all, doesn't the Bible say to meditate on it day and night and to pray without ceasing?

Bob is in his late sixties and loves fishing, softball, and the Chicago Cubs. Last year, God used colon cancer to shake Bob loose and draw him to himself. Bob now wonders whether he can still enjoy his hobbies like he once did. After all, he doesn't want to waste his life.

Abby is a young woman who is engaged to be married. Two weeks ago her pastor preached a sermon on the danger of idolatry. Since then, she's been worried that she loves her fiancé, Dan, too much. She doesn't quite know what "too much" means, but whenever she's with him, her heart leaps, and then she immediately feels a sense of guilt.

Tim is a sophomore in college, and he is sold out for Jesus. He's tired of comfortable Christianity and wants to live a radically God-centered lifestyle. He thinks that so-called Christians who read fiction or watch movies or play sports are wasting their time because they're not finding their true satisfaction in God. Deep down, he struggles with whether he himself is fully satisfied in God in the way he should be. He lives with a constant sense of guilt because he knows he's too distracted by the things of earth.

Beth and Jake were recently married. Money is tight, and they find themselves regularly fighting over it. They are both sincere Christians, but they have different views of how to spend their limited budget. Jake insists that they live a "wartime" lifestyle, and while Beth agrees in principle, she's not so sure about the details. She's half-afraid that she'll come home one day and find that Jake has sold their bed and replaced it with sleeping bags and cots.

Sarah and her mom are best friends. Or at least they were until her mom died in a car accident two years ago. Sarah knows that her mom is in heaven with Jesus, and she trusts that God had good purposes for taking her from the family, but Sarah still cries almost every night. What's worse, she's started to feel guilty for her grief because she wonders whether God disapproves of the depth of her pain.

* * * *

If you recognize yourself in any of these snapshots, then this book was written for you. It was written for people who sincerely want to glorify God in all they do but find themselves wrestling with what the God-centered life actually looks like in practice. It was written for people who struggle with whether they love God's gifts too much and whether they love God enough. It was written for people who find themselves frustrated that the world seems designed to distract them from a single-minded pursuit of Christ alone. It was written for those who embrace a passion for the supremacy of God in all things but feel the tension between the supremacy of God and the "all things."

This book was written to answer a simple question: What are we to do with the things of earth? Embrace them? Reject them? Use them? Forget about them? Set our affections on them? Look at them with suspicious eyes? Enjoy them with a twinge or two of guilt?

Then again, perhaps this isn't a simple question. After all, the Bible itself seems conflicted on the issue. For example, Paul in his letter to the Colossians says the following:

> If then you have been raised with Christ, seek the things that are above, where Christ is, seated at the right hand of God. Set your minds on things that are above, not on things that are on earth. For you have died, and your life is hidden with Christ in God. When Christ who is your life appears, then you also will appear with him in glory. (Col. 3:1–4)

Where should you set your mind, your heart, "your affection" (KJV)? On things that are above—high things, holy things, spiritual things—*not* on earthly things. Why? Because you've been raised with Christ, and he is seated in heaven, and his worth far surpasses all earthly goods. Indeed, compared to him, the things of earth are so much trash and rubbish (Phil. 3:8).

Seems clear enough. But then in 1 Timothy, Paul seems to strike a different note about earthly things:

> For everything created by God is good, and nothing is to be rejected if it is received with thanksgiving, for it is made holy by the word of God and prayer. (1 Tim. 4:4–5)

So everything God made is good, including the things on earth. Therefore, we must not reject them, despise them, or keep them at arms' length. We must embrace them with thanksgiving. So which is it? Should we count everything as loss or receive everything with holy gratitude?

Or again, in his letter to the Philippians, Paul warns of the offense of setting one's mind on the things of earth:

> Brothers, join in imitating me, and keep your eyes on those who walk according to the example you have in us. For many, of whom I have often told you and now tell you even with tears, walk as enemies of the cross of Christ. Their end is destruction, their god is their belly, and they glory in their shame, with minds set on earthly things. (Phil. 3:17–19)

Be like Paul. Imitate him and those like him. Don't be an enemy of Christ's cross, one who turns his appetite into a god and who sets his affections on the things of earth.

Contrast that sentiment with Paul's charge to the wealthy at the end of his letter to Timothy. At first, it sounds similar, but Paul ends with a surprising twist:

> As for the rich in this present age, charge them not to be haughty, nor to set their hopes on the uncertainty of riches, but on God, who richly provides us with everything to enjoy. (1 Tim. 6:17)

Don't set your hope on uncertain riches. Don't set your mind on the things of earth. But don't forget that God richly provides you with everything to enjoy. How do we do this? How can we *enjoy* all that God richly provides without setting our *affections* on the things of earth?

The Battle of the Hymns

These two biblical threads have made their way into our songs and hymns. For instance, most evangelicals have sung Helen Lemmel's hymn "Turn Your Eyes upon Jesus." The chorus captures one half of the tension:

> Turn your eyes upon Jesus
> Look full in his wonderful face
> And the things of earth will grow strangely dim
> In the light of his glory and grace.

What happens to the things of earth when Jesus shows up? They grow dim. They fade. Compared to him, they are as nothing and less than nothing. So when we set our minds on things above, the things below lose their power and beauty.

But Hemmel's hymn isn't the only song we sing. In "This Is My Father's World," Maltbie Babcock gives voice to the other side of the tension, celebrating the goodness of God's creation:

> This is my Father's world:
> He shines in all that's fair;

In the rustling grass I hear Him pass;
He speaks to me everywhere.

So again, which is it? In the light of his face, do earthly goods grow *dim*? Or does he *shine* in all that's fair? Does the rustling grass disappear when Christ arrives? Or do we hear him speaking in it?

As I said before, what exactly are we to do with the things of earth?

Resolving the Tension by Fostering Greed or Guilt

One way of resolving the tension is essentially to choose one side and land there. Health, wealth, and prosperity preachers ostensibly celebrate the goodness of the things of earth, urging their congregations to "name it and claim it." Earthly blessings are the necessary sign of God's favor toward us, so we seek them above all and seek him for their sake. Such false teachers effectively encourage their people to set their minds on things below and to turn their eyes upon Jesus only when they want some earthly good from him. They imagine that godliness is a means of earthly gain, stoking the desire to be rich, which plunges people into ruin and destruction (1 Tim. 6:5, 9). This is the ditch of greed and sinful indulgence, and God hates it.[1]

On the other hand, we can so emphasize the necessity of setting our minds above that we effectively deny the goodness of God's creation, thereby falling into the other ditch. Isaac Watts, the author of "Joy to the World" and "When I Survey the Wondrous Cross," once wrote a hymn based on Colossians 3:2 entitled "How Vain Are All Things Here Below." The lyrics powerfully express the danger of rejecting the goodness of the things of earth. A brief walk through the hymn will highlight the sorts of impulses that I'm seeking to correct in this book.

How vain are all things here below;
How false, and yet how fair!
Each pleasure has its poison too,
And every sweet a snare.

Notice that *all* things below are vain. The things of earth are both false and fair. Husband, wife, children, food, hobbies, work—all of these are pleasures laced with poison. The sweetness of earthly joys are a snare and a trap, catching us in their destructive embrace.

> The brightest things below the sky
> Give but a flattering light;
> We should suspect some danger nigh,
> When we possess delight.

Given the falseness of earthly pleasures, we ought to be suspicious of them. When we savor a sirloin steak or delight in the playfulness of a child or marvel at a prairie thunderstorm, red lights ought to begin flashing in our minds: "Danger! Danger! Danger!"

> Our dearest joys, and dearest friends,
> The partners of our blood,
> How they divide our wavering minds,
> And leave but half for God!

Watts makes clear that even good gifts (such as friends and family) are at best distractions from a single-minded devotion to God. Delight in the giver and delight in his gifts are viewed as a zero-sum game in which the more love we give to the things of earth, the less love we have left for God himself (and vice versa). The implication is clear: if we are to be faithful to God and love him with *all* our heart, soul, mind, and strength, we must suppress and resist our delight in our dearest joys and friends.

> The fondness of a creature's love,
> How strong it strikes the sense!
> Thither the warm affections move,
> Nor can we call them thence.

Our feelings of delight in creatures are potent. They grab our attention and lead our affections away so that we can't call them back. Watts presumably wishes us to be on guard against growing fond of our family and friends, lest the strength of our joy pull us from God.

> Dear Saviour, let thy beauties be
> My soul's eternal food;

And grace command my heart away
From all created good.

Note again the dichotomy between the beauty of Christ and the beauty he created. Grace delivers us from created good. It mercifully draws us away from earthly pleasures. The grace of Christ makes the things of earth grow strangely dim.

To me, the theology in this hymn is sincere but misguided. When embraced, it produces a constant, joy-killing guilt, because try as we might, we still live in the world and enjoy earthly pleasures. If we adopt Watts's view, we erect an impossible standard and then constantly fall short of it. Is there another way? A better way? I believe there is.

Why Did God Make *This* World?

To ask our (not so) simple question in another way: Why did God make this world? Why did he make a world for his own glory in Christ and then fill it to the brim with pleasures—physical pleasures, sensible pleasures, emotional pleasures, and relational pleasures? Why did God make a world full of good friends, sizzling bacon, the laughter of children, West Texas sunsets, Dr. Pepper, college football, marital love, and the warmth of wool socks? This is the tension we experience, and I hope that this book can go some of the way in resolving it.

My aim is simple—I want to work with you for your joy. Your joy in your family. Your joy in your friends. Your joy in your pancakes and eggs, your steak and potatoes, your chips and your salsa. Your joy in your camping trips, workouts, and iPod playlist. Your joy in the Bible, in worship services, and in the quiet moments before you fall asleep. Your joy in your job, your hobbies, and your daily routine.

And in and through all these things, I want to work with you for your joy in the living and personal God who gave you all these things and delivered you from sin and death through the work of his Son and Holy Spirit that you might enjoy him and them, and him in them, forever. But before I explain how I'm going to do that, let me tell you a little about myself.

Christian Hedonism 101

I've been a Christian Hedonist for over a decade. *Christian Hedonism* is a term coined by a pastor and theologian from Minneapolis named John Piper. At its root, Christian Hedonism means embracing the biblical truth that God is most glorified in us when we are most satisfied in him. It means seeking to pursue your highest and deepest joy in Christ and Christ alone.[2]

In my case, I was a Christian Hedonist before I'd ever heard of John Piper. Of course, I wouldn't have used that term, but I was one nonetheless. You can check my journals from late high school. (On second thought, you can't; there's a lot of embarrassing stuff in there that should never see the light of day).

So I was a Christian Hedonist without the labels. I think it was the Psalms that did it. "Delight yourself in the LORD" (Ps. 37:4). "As the deer pants for streams of water, so my soul pants for you" (Ps. 42:1). "My soul thirsts for you; my flesh faints for you" (Ps. 63:1). Those were the prayers that I returned to again and again during my teenage years.

At any rate, when I encountered Christian Hedonism as a freshman in college, it found an eager home in my heart. I was primed for it. I still remember the first Piper sermon that I ever listened to. A friend had suggested it to me. The sermon was called "Boasting Only in the Cross," and, boy, did it throw me for a loop.[3] A good half of the sermon was over my head. I had never heard the word "exultation" before (I was convinced that Piper was mispronouncing "exaltation"). But there was something in what he said that resonated with me, way down deep where joint and marrow grow together. So I listened to it again. And again. And again.

And then I listened to other sermons. I read some articles. And I discovered that I am a Christian Hedonist and hadn't known it. Piper put deeper biblical foundations underneath my experience of the Christian life. More importantly, he fixed God at the center of my pursuit of pleasure.

I came to embrace Christian Hedonism in both experience and name. I had new categories for engaging with God, a new vocabulary in which words such as *affections* and *satisfaction* and, yes, *exultation* figured prominently. Here are some of the things that sank deep in those days:

1) All men seek happiness. Always.
2) God does not find our desires too strong, but too weak.
3) A passion for God's glory and a passion for my happiness are not at odds; in fact, they are the same passion.
4) Praise consummates our enjoyment of God.
5) Head and heart are both necessary to rightly worship God.
6) God is uppermost in his own affections.
7) And, of course, God is most glorified in me when I am most satisfied in him.

So I signed up. I went all in—God-centered, Christ-exalting, Bible-saturated, missions-mobilizing, prayer-driven, and a dozen more hyphenated words besides. I wanted to spread a passion for the supremacy of God in all things. The Bible broke open in ways that were unprecedented in my experience. I had never read the Scriptures so carefully or with that much enjoyment before. Connections were made between texts. The train of thought in key passages fell into place. I remember spending hours in the study room at the end of my hall with my Bible and a journal (and maybe an article or two). I devoured the Scriptures and was hungry for more. It felt like spiritual growth on steroids.

A Sovereign God and an Insufferable Student

This isn't to say that there weren't struggles. I distinctly remember feeling back-doored by the sovereignty of God in salvation. When it came to discussions of predestination, I had always been somewhere between hostile and aloof. The word *predestine* was in the Bible, so I was stuck with it, but that didn't mean I was all that happy about it or that I really understood what it meant.

But once I embraced the reality of a big God revealed in the authoritative Scriptures, it was only a matter of time before I had to really grapple with some of those hard texts. When I saw it coming, I geared up for a true battle royale in my head and heart. I expected a fight. But when I actually got into the Scriptures, the tension didn't feel nearly as intense. It was like I woke up one day and said, "T? Yep. U? Yep. L? A little tricky, but yep. I? Yep. P? Yep. Huh. Well, there you have it. I guess I'm a Calvinist."

Don't misunderstand me. I know there are tensions. I know there are challenging passages, more than I even realized at the time. But in those days, I was primed and ready to go wherever the Scriptures were going. I was in no mood to dispute with God about his power, authority, grace, and goodness. Who was I to talk back?

Like most freshly Reformed eighteen-year-olds, I was not always pleasant to be around. In fact, most of the time my zeal substantially outstripped my knowledge and maturity. Arguments fell like manna in the wilderness (or locusts in Egypt, depending on your point of view). The word *insufferable* comes to mind (and I'm not sure I was all that likable to begin with).

In my defense, it was enthusiasm for the things of God that drove most of it. I know there was pride and immaturity and downright stupidity mixed up in all of it. But I was genuinely and sincerely thrilled with God as he was revealed in the Scriptures. I wanted others to see what I saw, and I wanted it so badly that I was willing to push them just a little bit more.

You'd think that embracing our total helplessness in sin and the absolute sovereign goodness of God in salvation would make one humble. But no; in my case, the high-on-my-horse days initially outnumbered the humbled-to-the-dust days.

Years later, after the insufferability and wretched zeal was largely exorcised by the grace of God in the school of hard knocks, my friends and I dubbed the affliction "New Calvinist Syndrome." Symptoms include:

1) A strange fire in the eyes accompanied by a propensity to float three feet off the ground;
2) A distorted sense of proportion ("Just watch me make mountains out of those molehills");
3) A fanatical commitment to swallow any *reductio*, so long as it makes God big and man small;
4) Acquisition of just enough Greek to have no clue what one is talking about.

The only known treatment for NCS is to lock the afflicted Calvinist in a room with nothing but the Bible and a picture of John Wesley. When he stops throwing the Bible at Wesley's face, he's free to rejoin Christendom, but only under the close supervision of godly elders with the patience of Job and a sense of humor.

In any event, God's grace abounded to me, and my delight in him and my love and care for others grew with time and maturity. Suffering, doubts, and a season of depression tempered my zeal and turned it into something approaching "sorrowful, yet always rejoicing" (2 Cor. 6:10).

Theology with Legs

After graduation, I moved to Minneapolis with my new wife to participate in the vocational eldership program at The Bethlehem Institute, the leadership development arm of Bethlehem Baptist Church, where John Piper was the pastor. I came to TBI to see what a Christian Hedonist church looked like. I wanted to encounter all of those hyphenated words in action. I'd read the books; now I wanted to see the theology with legs on it.

The classes focused heavily on biblical Greek and exegesis of the Scriptures. We diagrammed sentences and "arced" whole chapters of Romans.[4] I loved my classes, the professors, and my fellow apprentices. The discussions were always lively, and the fellowship and camaraderie were sweet. But all was not sunshine and roses.

Though I didn't want to admit it, my spiritual vitality was languishing. Nothing dramatic. Just a low-grade dullness. Academically, I was flourishing, but actual engagement with God in prayer and worship was stunted. Mild spiritual apathy comes close to describing it. And then God surprised me with an eighteenth-century pastor and theologian.

When I first discovered that we would be devoting two full courses to the theology of Jonathan Edwards, I admit that I was a bit disappointed. I was eager for more biblical theology and Greek book studies. Edwards seemed distant and unimportant next to the Scriptures. What's more, I already knew what he was going to say. I'd read most of *The End for which God Created the World* in college and found it somewhat helpful. It sounded like an eighteenth-century version of Piper, and I'd been over that ground before. God is passionate about his glory. We should pursue our joy in him. Christian Hedonism 101. Reading *End of Creation* and *Religious Affections* didn't sound like my idea of fun.

But as my professor began to slowly and carefully walk us through Edwards's treatises, I realized that I had been absolutely naïve to think that I'd understood half of what Edwards had to offer. Through Edwards's writings, the reality of the living God came crashing in on me again in fresh new ways. The Trinity became central to everything I thought and felt. I don't mean the doctrine of the Trinity. I mean *God-as-Trinity*, the actual three-in-one. He became powerfully and beautifully real in ways that I hadn't dreamed of. My understanding of what it means for God to glorify himself was torn apart and rebuilt. I came to see that there are layers and depths to reality beyond what I'd imagined. Things were interwoven in surprising and thrilling ways, and my heart went soaring again to new heights.

Providentially, after I completed the apprenticeship, I was offered a job as an instructor in a new experimental undergraduate program at Bethlehem. What's more, I was asked to assist in teaching the Edwards courses at the newly expanded Bethlehem College and Seminary. This allowed me to work through Edwards's theology again and again, strengthening those roots and discovering new and fresh applications of a passion for God's supremacy.

Along the way, two other authors began to exert a formative influence on my theology and practice of the Christian life. C. S. Lewis, who appears in almost every chapter of this book, became a reliable friend and guide, pressing home the goodness of materiality and finitude and ordinary life. Pastor Douglas Wilson regularly provoked and challenged me by underscoring the centrality of gratitude in the Christian life. What's more, I credit Doug with sparking the idea for this book through a series of blog posts a few years ago.[5] Doug's musings prompted me to identify and wrestle with unstated questions I'd had for years as a Christian.

Questions such as, Given the very real danger of idolatry, how can we truly enjoy God's gifts in such a way that he is really honored as giver? Or, How can we integrate "spiritual" activities (like prayer, Scripture reading, and corporate worship) with our normal and mundane activities (like eating or working or playing with the family)? Or, How should we think about our love for God and our love for everything else, given our finitude and limitations?

In short, the questions and issues raised have to do with what it means to live the faithful Christian (Hedonist) life, and in my experience, we have work to do.[7] This, of course, is not surprising. As Wilson is fond of saying, "If you enroll in a math class, you're going to have math problems." If we enroll in a Christian Hedonist class, we're going to have Christian Hedonist problems. The trick is to press forward and seek God's help in solving them. That's what this book aims to do.

The Layout

The first five chapters are foundational. In them, we will explore God, God's relation to creation, creation itself, what it means to be a creature, and what it means to be a sinner saved by the gospel. Chapter 1 explores the doctrine of the Trinity through two theological models, drawing heavily upon the Gospel of John and Jonathan Edwards. We should labor to understand the glory of God in Trinitarian terms, as God's Trinitarian fullness. Out of love for his glory, the triune God creates the world in order to communicate and extend his fullness outside of himself, or, to use another image, in order to invite creatures to participate in his own triune life.

Chapter 2 is an extended reflection on one analogy summarized in these three statements: God is an author. This is his story. We are his characters. This analogy allows us to conceive of God's relationship to the world in a way that honors his exhaustive sovereignty as well as our responsibility for our actions. Reality is layered with intentionality, both divine and human. This analogy also provides a fruitful solution to the problem of evil and establishes another crucial Christian truth: in order to be faithful Christians, we must be willing to have our minds and hearts stretched by complementary biblical truths.

Bringing together the first two chapters, chapter 3 argues that creation should be understood as the constant and pervasive revelation of God. God communicates himself to us through creation. This is the glory of created reality, namely, that it is a fitting vehicle for communicating the divine life. As such, we can find "images of divine things" wherever we look. God's revelation in creation highlights the importance of analogy and metaphor through which we compare one thing to another so that both are mutually illuminated. Finally, C. S. Lewis will help us to "look along" creation, to experience tiny theophanies in even the simplest pleasures.

Chapter 4 moves from creation as a whole to an exploration of what it means to be a creature—bodily, finite, temporal, and, according to Genesis, very good. Creaturely limitations are not defects to be overcome. In fact, God in his wisdom has chosen to meet many of our needs and desires through created things. God's gifts are given to us for our enjoyment and so we can fulfill God's mission as his priests, kings, and prophets. Additionally, this chapter wrestles with various questions of *value*: do creatures have intrinsic value? Should we value all things equally? Should we value God infinitely? In response to these questions, I commend the biblical witness that our love for God ought to be supreme, full, and expanding.

Chapter 5 addresses two fundamental challenges to the vision of gift enjoyment set forth thus far—passages in the Bible that teach that we should desire *only* God; and the deep and abiding reality of human sin, rebellion, and abuse of God's gifts. To the first, the chapter explores two complementary ways that we approach the giver-gift relationship in Scripture. To the second, the chapter explores the nature of idolatry and ingratitude, the false and deadly solution of asceticism (in all its forms), and the alternative solution to idolatry set forth in the gospel.

Chapter 6 transitions to a more practical vision of what it means to live a God-centered life by stressing the need for rhythms of direct godwardness (such as prayer and worship) and indirect godwardness (all the other things we do). We are embodied and en-storied creatures, designed by God to make use of anchor points in our pursuit of God. Direct and indirect godwardness are mutually fruitful and beneficial, as our direct godwardness orients our daily lives, and our daily lives provide concrete categories with which to engage God directly.

Chapter 7 addresses the issues of culture making and culture enjoyment. Culture is the product of God's creation and man's creativity, and it is God's appointed means of maturing and glorifying his very good creation. Faithful naming provides a fruitful angle on culture making, and God's invitation to Adam to name the animals grounds our culture making and our culture enjoyment. Like creation, culture has the capacity to enlarge and expand our hearts and minds so that we can know God better. The presence of evil in culture and creation complicates the picture, so we must use wisdom and discernment in what and how we create and enjoy culture.

Chapter 8 continues the practical application of the earlier part of the book by providing concrete, personal examples from my own life that illustrate various dimensions of how we can genuinely enjoy all that God provides without committing idolatry. I certainly don't claim to have it all figured out, but I hope that my experience of solid joys in God and what he has given me can spur others on to love and good deeds.

Chapter 9 seeks to show how a robust emphasis on receiving all of God's gifts does not undermine the call to leave earthly comforts for the sake of the gospel among unreached peoples. Instead, it creates the kind of God-centered, creation-affirming, risk-taking missionaries that will lay a foundation for the completion of Jesus's command to disciple the nations. This chapter also explores the biblical call to self-denial against the backdrop of the goodness of those things that we leave and lose for the sake of Christ. This leads into a discussion of a right attitude toward wealth and, in particular, how gratefully receiving what God supplies ought to make us big-hearted and open-handed with it.

Chapter 10 continues the focus on wealth by exploring the nature and challenges of living a radical, "wartime" lifestyle. In particular, I try to highlight (from my own experience) the ways that wartime thinking in relation to wealth can go terribly wrong, harming relationships, squandering resources, and failing to be truly strategic in our use of time and treasure. I commend an expansive view of wartime, in which the "front" in the war is enlarged so that it begins at home and then emanates to the church, the local community (especially the poor), and the nations of the world.

Chapter 11 seeks to integrate suffering, pain, and the loss of good gifts into the picture. Suffering is a necessary check on our enjoyment of God's gifts, and the kind of integrated joy commended throughout the book is still possible, even in the absence of the good gifts. Most importantly, I seek to show how true, God-centered, integrated enjoyment of God's gifts faces the horrific loss of gifts and the ultimate loss of all gifts—death.

The book concludes in chapter 12 with an exhortation to revel in creaturely existence; to receive everything from God, good or bad, with gratitude; to reject false standards and expectations; and to marvel that we are being invited to participate in the triune life by receiving God's goodness in creation and beyond.

I won't lie to you. There will be some heavy theology in this book. And I can be a bit wordy at times (I'm a college professor, after all). But if you'll stick with me, I think that God might be pleased to do something wonderful in your life. The things of earth are all around you. What are you going to do with them?

1

The Glory of the Triune God

In the confession of the Trinity, we hear the heartbeat of the Christian religion.

Herman Bavinck

I should think that these things might incline us to suppose, that God has not forgot himself, in the ends which he proposed in the creation of the world.

Jonathan Edwards

Before getting to the practical and pastoral challenges, we need to get some things on the table. Some of it will be high theology, the kind that can make the head hurt and the eyes glaze over. Bear with me, and I'll try to keep it lively. The Scriptures provide us with tremendous resources to help us live the Christian life (everything we need for life and godliness, in fact), but drawing out those resources takes work. It's labor, but it's worth it.

My view is that we should begin with the Trinity. I'm tempted to say "*always* begin," but we'll leave that aside for now. I regularly tell my students that it's crucial that we be Trinitarian Christians, all the way down. The Trinity is the heart of the Christian religion, the great mystery that makes all other mysteries understandable. In fact, much of the content of this book might be viewed as an application of the Trinity to various aspects of practical theology and Christian living.

Let's begin with a definition of the Trinity. Wayne Grudem in his *Systematic Theology* distills the Trinity into the following three statements:

1) God is three persons.
2) Each person is fully God.
3) There is one God.[1]

In short, in the one God there are three separate, coequal persons.

Of course, the relative simplicity of this statement is actually a testament to the grand mystery of the Godhead. In what sense is God one and in what sense is God three? How does the three-ness and plurality of God relate to his absolute oneness and unity?

A Word about Models and Analogies of God

Theologians throughout church history have made use of models and analogies to better understand what it means that God is three and one. If creation is a reflection of the divine nature, and the divine nature is fundamentally triune, then we ought to be able to recognize aspects of the Trinity in what God has made. Of course, in making use of such analogies, we must never mistake our models for the reality. C. S. Lewis liked to say that our models are like maps—they can help us to understand the land, but they should never replace an actual visit to the countryside.[2] Put another way, the use of models and analogies ought never to become a way of "analyzing" God, as though we might actually be able to diagram him on the whiteboard.

Models of the Trinity can be roughly categorized into two types: oneness analogies and threeness analogies.[3] Oneness analogies emphasize the unity of the Godhead, as though one God "unfolded" into three persons. For example, I am one human being, but as one human being, I am a father, a husband, and a professor. This analogy is a kind of three-in-one, but it is fundamentally misleading because Joe the father isn't a distinct person from Joe the husband. Thus, the analogy tends toward modalism, an ancient heresy in which the three persons of the Trinity are treated as distinct modes of existence rather than full and coequal persons.

On the other hand, threeness analogies emphasize the distinctions between the persons, as though three persons came together into one God.

Thus, one family made up of three persons—a father, a mother, and a child—can provide an analogy of the Trinity, but again it is misleading because the family itself isn't personal, and each member of the family is only a part of the whole. Thus, whereas oneness analogies tend toward modalism, threeness analogies tend toward tri-theism, three distinct gods.

Despite the dangers of each type of analogy, together they can help us understand how God can be one and three. Using multiple analogies keeps us from emphasizing God's oneness over his threeness or his threeness over his oneness. Theologians throughout church history have recognized these dangers and therefore have employed various analogies to illuminate the Trinity while acknowledging that no analogy is sufficient to explain the triunity of God.[4]

The Psychological Model

Bearing in mind the limitations of Trinitarian analogies, we can now explore one or two of them as a way of better understanding the God who is three in one. First up is the psychological model. Dating back to Augustine and finding considerable expression in the theology of Jonathan Edwards, it holds that in the Godhead, there is God in his direct existence (Father), God's self-reflection or contemplation of himself (Son), and God's love and delight for himself (Holy Spirit). Or again, there is God, God's idea of God, and God's love for his idea of himself.

Now, when confronted with the psychological model, many people have the same reaction: Where is *that* in the Bible? And I realize that on first glance, it sounds a bit odd. I certainly thought so the first time I heard it. (Incidentally, if you want to go further into this than I will, find Edwards's "Essay on the Trinity." Or read the first chapter in Piper's *The Pleasures of God*.[5]) Suffice it to say, I think that the Bible does provide hints and pointers that our own existence as creatures with minds and hearts, understanding and will, knowledge and love, is a reflection of who God is in his own divine life.

First, the Bible regularly describes the Son of God as God's "image" or "representation" (Col. 1:15; 2 Cor. 4:4–6). The Son is the radiance of the Father's glory and the exact imprint of his nature (Heb. 1:3). The eternal Son of God is often connected to God's wisdom (1 Cor. 1:30; Prov. 8:30) and to his Word or self-expression (John 1:1). Jesus says that if you've seen him, you've seen the Father (John 14:7–11), as if he were simply an image, a replication of his Father's nature. What's more, the Son is the one who manifests and makes known the Father (John 17:24–26).

Drawing these biblical threads together, we can say that from all eternity God has had with him an image, a representation, a reflection of his own infinite perfection and beauty, and through this image has fully and completely known, understood, and expressed himself.

What, then, of the Holy Spirit? The Bible often connects the Holy Spirit to God's love and joy. It is striking that while the Father and the Son are repeatedly described as loving each other (John 3:35; 5:20; 14:31) and human beings (John 14:23; 16:27), the Spirit is never said to love the Son or the Father or us! Jonathan Edwards explains this strange omission by arguing that the Spirit *is* the very love of God, the love that flows between the Father and the Son and overflows to his creatures. He finds support for such a notion in the fact that God's love is poured into our hearts *by the Spirit* (Rom. 5:5) and that God's abiding, love's abiding, and the Spirit's abiding in us all seem to be different ways of describing the same reality (1 John 3:24; 4:12–13). What's more, when the biblical writers begin their epistles, they often say something like, "Grace to you and peace from God our Father and the Lord Jesus Christ" (e.g., 1 Cor. 1:3; 2 Cor. 1:2; Eph. 1:2; Phil. 1:2). The absence of the Spirit in these passages is again striking, given the fact that the Holy Spirit is fully divine. Edwards argues that this absence is explained by the fact that the Spirit *is* the grace and peace of God that flows to us from the Father and the Son. Finally, Edwards notes that at Jesus's baptism, the *Spirit* descends upon him like a dove as the Father expresses pleasure in his beloved Son (Matt. 3:16–17). What at first glance appears speculative actually turns out to have a fair bit of biblical foundation.[6]

Thus the trajectory of these passages is that from all eternity God has beheld his beloved Son with perfect clarity, and there has arisen between Father and Son a love so pure and deep, so matchless and limitless, so boundless and infinite that the love stands forth as a full third person in the Godhead, the Holy Spirit.[7]

In light of these two streams of biblical thought, Edwards concludes that one way for us to understand the Trinity is to see God existing in his direct existence as the Father, in his knowledge of himself in the Son, and in the mutual love flowing between the Father and the Son in the person of the Holy Spirit.[8]

Or to say it another way, the Father knows, loves, and delights in the Son by the Spirit.

The Family Model

The family model of the Trinity is in many ways more straightforward. In this model, the three persons of the Trinity are seen as members of a family or a society, bound together in a bond of love and overflowing with joy and delight in one another. The Bible explicitly endorses this model in that the first two persons of the Godhead are referred to as Father and Son, that is, as members of a family. The family model helps us to recognize the full equality of each person of the Godhead, because each member has a crucial and important role to play in the work of redemption. The Father *chooses* a people for himself and *sends* the Son. The Son *obeys* his Father and *accomplishes* the work that he is given to do, laying down his life in order to purchase God's people. The Spirit *is sent* by the Father and the Son (John 14:16; 16:7), is the *down payment* of our inheritance (Eph. 1:14), and indeed is *the sum of all the good things* that God has purchased for us (Matt. 7:11; Luke 11:13).

At this point, it is worth pausing to reflect on a key aspect of the Trinity that I'll come back to again and again. In the Gospel of John, when Philip asks to see the Father, Jesus responds:

> Have I been with you so long, and you still do not know me, Philip? Whoever has seen me has seen the Father. How can you say, 'Show us the Father'? Do you not believe that I am in the Father and the Father is in me? The words that I say to you I do not speak on my own authority, but the Father who dwells in me does his works. Believe me that I am in the Father and the Father is in me, or else believe on account of the works themselves. (John 14:9–11)

The Father is in the Son, and the Son is in the Father. Because of this, when we see the Son, we have also seen the Father. The Father dwells in the Son and does his works, works that testify to the reality that the Father and the Son are in each other. The theological term for this is *perichoresis*. It refers to the *mutual indwelling* of the members of the Godhead. This reality is what enables us to *distinguish* the Father, the Son, and the Holy Spirit from one another, without *separating* them from one another. The Father is not the Son, but he is *in* the Son. The Son is not the Spirit, but he is *in* the Spirit. The Spirit is not the Father, but he is *in* the Father. And this mutual indwelling is thorough and complete. All that the Father is, he is in the Son and the Spirit. All that the Son is, he is in the Father and the Spirit. All that the Spirit is, he is in the Father and the Son. There are no leftovers, no remainder, no excess divinity.

Perichoresis means that in the Trinity, the three persons exist as one God without crowding out the others. They overlap and indwell one another completely and totally without in any way compromising the personal distinctions among them. We'll return to perichoresis later in the book.

For His Glory

Pressing into the Trinity in this way will have huge implications for how we think about other fundamental truths of the Christian faith, such as God's goal in all that he does. Thanks to the recovery in recent years of a God-centered vision and theology, many Christians gladly affirm that God does all that he does *for his glory*. They embrace the biblical truth that God aims to glorify himself in the creation of the world and the redemption of his people. They love the truth that God is passionately committed to his glory, that God is uppermost in God's affections. However, many who embrace the truth would be hard-pressed to explain what exactly they mean by "the glory of God." Indeed, the phrase runs the great danger of becoming simply another buzzword, a slogan used to say something without meaning anything. One of the central aims of this book is to deepen and fill out our understanding of the glory of God by pressing into the Trinity, the Bible, and creation.

Put simply, because God is always triune, we must always conceive of his glory in Trinitarian terms. God's glory is his Trinitarian fullness, or the abundance of perfections and knowledge and love and joy and life that he has within the Godhead. Or, to put it another way, the Father, the Son, and the Holy Spirit knowing, loving, and rejoicing in each other from all eternity simply *is* the glory of God. It's why Jesus prays in John 17:5, "Father, glorify me in your own presence with the glory that I had *with you* before the world existed." This is the glory that the Father gave the Son because the Father loved him before the foundation of the world (John 17:24). So when you hear "the glory of God," think "Trinitarian fullness."

If God's glory is his Trinitarian fullness, then what does it mean to glorify God? Many define God's glorification of himself as the *display* or *manifestation* of his perfections. And while the display of God's attributes and perfections is certainly included in glorification, a Trinitarian vision of God pushes us to say more. Glorification includes not merely the display of God's attributes but also the knowledge of those attributes and love for and delight in those attributes. Remember the psychological model: God himself does not merely exist in his perfections as Father but also knows himself fully in the person of the Son and loves and delights in himself in the person of the Holy Spirit. Therefore, glorification must include more than mere display; it must also include the knowledge and love and joy that result from that display. In short, a triune God requires a triune understanding of glory and glorification.

Drawing together an understanding of the Trinity, the doctrine of perichoresis, and a fuller understanding of glory and glorification, we are now in a position to answer one of the pressing questions from the introduction: What does it mean to glorify God? Let's put it in terms of God's actions in seeking his glory.

> God glorifies himself by inviting us to participate in his Trinitarian fullness. Put another way, God glorifies himself by extending his glory so that his divine life comes to exist in creaturely form.

Those two statements represent different pictures of what happens as the triune God glorifies himself. In the latter, God's glory is depicted as flowing out from himself, emanating and overflowing to creatures who exist solely by his will. The other picture moves in the opposite direction. Instead of glory flowing out to us, we are invited into God. We are drawn in so that we come to share in divine knowledge, love, and joy, or as Peter says, we become "partakers of the divine nature" (2 Pet. 1:4). So the language of *display* is perfectly legitimate, provided that the display is always understood as an invitation to participate, to partake, to mingle. As Lewis writes in *The Weight of Glory*,

> If we take the imagery of Scripture seriously, if we believe that God will one day *give* us the Morning Star and cause us to *put on* the splendour of the sun, then we may surmise that both the ancient myths and the modern poetry, so false as history, may be very near the truth as prophecy. At present, we are on the outside of the world, the wrong side of the door. We discern the freshness and purity of morning, but they do not make us fresh and pure. We cannot mingle with the splendours we see. But all the leaves of the New Testament are rustling with the rumour that it will not always be so. Some day, God willing, we shall get *in*.[9]

The Upper Room Discourse in the Gospel of John (13–17) provides the fullest picture of the invitation to indwell, the promise of perichoretic participation in the Bible. Following the exit of Judas, Jesus launches into an extended reflection on his coming death, the tribulation to be faced by his disciples, the coming of the Holy Spirit, and the life that his followers should live in the midst of a fallen and broken world. In the process he provides glimpses into the divine life and into God's purposes for us (and I'd encourage you to have your Bible open to John 13–17 as we proceed).

In reading the passage, we can easily feel disoriented, like Jesus is taking us somewhere but doesn't want to be followed. Jesus moves along in one direction, only to double back and repeat himself, often with a slight modification. The simplicity of the individual words masks the complexity of the tangents, paradoxes, and wanderings. However, even amidst the apparent meanderings and confusion, we can sense a deeper structure at work, an order and purpose that is holding all of the commands, promises, and cryptic statements together. Perhaps it's akin to being in the midst of a tornado, a flurry of chaos and confusion governed by consistent laws of physics.

Fundamental to this entire passage is the reality that Jesus is about to leave his disciples. After his death, resurrection, and ascension, he will no longer be physically present with them. He says, "Where I am going you cannot come" (13:33). He is leaving them (14:18), going away to the Father, who sent him (14:25; 16:5, 28).

However, in leaving the world, he is not abandoning them (and us) as orphans (14:18). Because he is going to the Father, he will send the Holy Spirit (16:7), another Helper who will bear witness about the Son and give us peace (15:26; 14:26–27). The Father will send the Spirit to us (14:16), in the name of the Son (14:26), to be with us and in us forever (14:16–17). The presence of the Spirit with us means that we will see the Son (14:19).

What's more, the Son himself will come to us (14:18); in fact, both the Father and the Son will come to us and make their home with us (14:23). The Father is in the Son, and the Son is in the Father (14:9–11), and the Son is in us and we are in the Son (14:20). This mutual indwelling is also a mutual abiding (15:4). The Son has loved us in the same way the Father loves the Son, and therefore we should abide in the love of the Son. The Son also promises that his joy will be in us, and our joy will be full (15:11; 17:13).

Celebrations of triune glory are scattered throughout the discourse. The Son of Man is glorified, and the Father is glorified in the Son, and the Father will glorify himself in the Son (13:31–32). The Son will answer our prayers so that the Father will be glorified (14:13) and our joy will be full (16:24). The Spirit will glorify the Son when he comes, by revealing all that the Father has given to the Son (16:14).

These various threads come together in Jesus's final prayer. He prays that the Father will glorify him so that he can in turn glorify the Father through giving eternal life, which is knowledge of the Father and the Son, to all who have been given to the Son by the Father (17:1–3). The Son has glorified the Father on earth and now desires to be glorified with the Father with their original, precreation glory (17:4–5). We belong to both the Father and the Son, and the Son is glorified in us (17:10). Jesus's fundamental prayer for his immediate disciples (14:9) and the rest of us who believe because of their word (14:20) is that we would be one as the Father and Son are one (17:13).

However, this oneness transcends mere unity and agreement and is in actuality something more like union, as Jesus explains our oneness with God in terms of mutual indwelling: . . . "just as you, Father, are in me, and I in you, that they also may be in us" (17:21). Such oneness is possible because of the glory given to us by the Son, the same glory that was given to the Son by the Father (17:22).

The end of all of this is that we would be perfectly one in the Father and in the Son and that the world would know that the Father sent the Son and that the Father loves us in the same way that he loves the Son (17:21, 23). The Son's great desire is that we would be with him, to see the glory that he has from the Father because of the Father's eternal love for the Son (17:24). The Son will continue to manifest the name of the Father to us so that the love of the Father for the Son will be in us, and the Son will be in us (17:26).[10]

Sharing the Triune Glory

Again, this passage swirls, billows, and churns like a tempest on the high seas, and that's part of the point. The triune glory of the Father, Son, and Spirit is being extended to us so that we participate in their knowledge, love, and joy. We are being invited into the fellowship of the Godhead so that we have the same union with God that the Father and Son have with each other. Of course, as finite creatures, we will never and can never achieve the exact same relationship as the Father and Son. We never cease to be creatures; we never become God. However, the great promise, if Jesus's prayer is fulfilled, is that we will *approach* such a union of knowledge, love, and joy for all eternity, with ever-increasing speed. We finite beings are chasing the infinite, and therefore we'll never catch it (him!). But the increase of our knowledge of God and love for God and joy in God will continue, world without end, amen.

These sorts of theological explorations can tend to feel somewhat academic and abstract. However, the picture that emerges is anything but detached. Indeed, the biblical portrait of the triune God is potent and vibrant, if we just have eyes to see. So allow me to run through the same material again, this time wearing camel hair and with the smell of locusts and honey on my breath.

The triune God of Scripture lives! He is not static. He is not lifeless. He is not bored. He is not boring. He is the living God!

He is the Father of lights, fount of divinity, origin of origins, begetting yet unbegotten, deity prime, the almighty maker of heaven and earth.

He is the beloved Son, Word of the Father, God's sermon and song, his image and wisdom, very God of very God, begotten before all worlds.

He is the Holy Spirit, breath of the living God, the river of his delights, the oil on his beard, the glad bond of loving union, proceeding from Father and Son.

This is God: Father, Son, and Holy Spirit, knowing each other, loving each other, delighting in each other, from all eternity, with no needs, no wants, no lack. Complete and total and infinite happiness. This is who God *is*.

This is no abstract deity, no impersonal divinity. God *is* love—dynamic, alive, abundant, and overflowing. Relationship is at the heart of reality. The original Word of this God is God over again. His love for himself is so potent that he's a person.

Absentee landlord? Hardly. Generic watchmaker? Not a chance. He is a jealous husband, a consuming fire, a cloud of glory that outshines the sun. He is a thundering tornado of knowledge and love and joy and life.

And the Father, the Son, and the Holy Spirit so love the fullness of their shared life that they think it fitting and right that such glorious knowledge and love and joy overflow. So they make a world to contain it. They create vessels to hold the fullness of their divine joy.

The Father, the Son, and the Holy Spirit are like an indie rock band that loves their music so much that they decide to take the show on the road. Only this band creates an audience *from nothing*.

The triune God is like a husband and wife who love one another deeply and love their relationship and shared life so much that they decide to bring children into it. Only this triune couple creates children *from nothing*.

God created the world to get a bride for his Son.

And what this means is that when we think about the glory of God, we ought not think merely about the display of God's attributes, as though God were simply a big fireworks show, off in the distance. The glory and fullness of God includes the display of all of his perfections, but it also includes our *knowledge* of his perfections and our *love* for his perfections, and all the thoughts and affections and actions that flow out of that knowledge and love. In fact, our knowledge of God is simply God's knowledge of himself *in us*. Our love for God is simply God's love for God *in us*. Our delight in God is simply God's delight in God *in us*.[11] In a word, when God glorifies himself, he invites us to participate in his triune life. As Lewis said, "The whole dance, or drama, or pattern of the Tri-personal life is to be played out in each one of us: . . . each one of us has got to enter that pattern, take his place in that dance."[12] He invites us in, the Son welcoming us as his bride, the Father embracing us as his daughter-in-law, the Spirit as the bond that unites us all together in one big, happy, glorious family.

This is the origin and the finish line, the beginning and the end, the Alpha and Omega. This is God, the supreme harmony of all.

2

The Author and His Story

A story is a way to say something that cannot be said any other way, and it takes every word of the story to say what that means.

Flannery O'Connor

My point is that, if God does exist, He is related to the universe more as an author is related to a play than as one object in the universe is related to another.

C. S. Lewis

Our brief jaunt through the doctrine of the Trinity underscores the crucial truth that God is self-sufficient and happy. He has no needs or unmet desires. He suffers no lack or want. He is completely and totally independent and happy in himself. And yet he still freely and gladly creates the world. The present chapter aims to explore just how he relates to the world he has made.

The Scriptures teach that God created the world ex nihilo, from nothing. He did not use any preexistent, independent, or eternal matter to construct the cosmos. He simply spoke creation into existence. Genesis 1 repeatedly emphasizes that God said, "Let there be . . . ," and there was. Or in the words of Psalm 33:9, "He spoke, and it came to be; he commanded, and it stood firm." He is the God who "calls into existence the things that do not exist" (Rom. 4:17). John begins his

Gospel with a Trinitarian account of creation: "In the beginning was the Word, and the Word was with God, and the Word was God. He was in the beginning with God. All things were made through him, and without him was not any thing made that was made" (John 1:1–3). The last convoluted sentence contains a crucial point: if there is a "made" thing in the universe, it was made through the Word of God, who is himself God.

Not only did God create the world from nothing in the beginning, he also sustains it from nothing at every point of its existence. All things were created by the Son of God (Col. 1:16), and all things hold together in him (Col. 1:17). This too happens at the point of speech. "He upholds the universe *by the word of his power*" (Heb. 1:3). If he stopped speaking, we would stop being.

The fact that God creates and sustains everything through speech entails his omnipresence in the world he's made. Thus, if we ask, "*Where is God in relation to the world?*," we can answer with the Scriptures that he is in heaven (Ps. 115:3), that he is high and lifted up (Isa. 57:15), and that he is not far from any of us (Acts 17:27). But we must also insist that God is present everywhere, that there is no part of creation devoid of his presence. Psalm 139 celebrates this glorious truth:

> Where shall I go from your Spirit?
>> Or where shall I flee from your presence?
> If I ascend to heaven, you are there!
>> If I make my bed in Sheol, you are there!
> If I take the wings of the morning and dwell in
>> the uttermost parts of the sea,
>> even there your hand shall lead me, and your
>> right hand shall hold me. (Ps. 139:7–10)

No matter how high you go, no matter how low you go, no matter how far you go, God is present and active. Jonathan Edwards captures the extent of God's presence and activity in the world in his sermon "God Is Everywhere Present":

> God is present everywhere, whereas any other being is only so by His operation and influence. God is in the continual exercise of His

infinite power and wisdom throughout the whole creation. Every moment takes a continual act of infinite power to uphold things in being. When we look upon anything that we can behold, we see the present operation of infinite power; for the same power that made things to be the first moment that they ever were is now exercised to make them to be this moment, and is continually exercised to make them to be every moment that they are.

God's preservation of the world is nothing but a continued act of creation. We read that God created all things by the word of His power, and we read that He upholds all things by the word of His power (Heb 1:3). . . . As it is the continual operation of God to uphold things in being, so it is the divine operation that keeps them in action. Whenever a body moves or a spirit thinks or wills, it is infinite power and wisdom that assists it. God has established the laws of nature, and He maintains them by his constant influence. . . . With respect to ourselves, it is because God is in us that our blood runs, our pulse beats, our lungs play, our food digests, and our organs of sense perform their operation.

So when we look at the sun, moon, and stars above, or look upon the earth, or things below, if we look so much as upon the stones or under them, we see infinite power now in exercise at that place. If we look upon ourselves and see our hands or feet, these members have an existence now because God is there and by an act of infinite power upholds them. So God is not only everywhere, but He is everywhere working.[1]

The pervasiveness of God's active presence in the world helps to address a perennial theological question: How do we reconcile the biblical teaching on the absolute sovereignty of God over all things and the full and complete responsibility of man for his actions?

Divine Sovereignty and Human Freedom

Before addressing the *how* question, it's worth taking a moment to establish both sides of this tension from the Bible.

First, Scripture teaches that God knows and ordains everything that comes to pass. In other words, the Scriptures teach that God is absolutely, universally, and exhaustively sovereign over all things. There is not one square inch of reality that is not claimed, ruled, governed, and ordained by God.

- Our God is in the heavens; he does all that he pleases (Ps. 115:3).
- He works all things according to the counsel of his will (Eph. 1:11).
- No purpose of his can be thwarted (Job 42:2).
- He does according to his will among the host of heaven and among the inhabitants of the earth; and none can stay his hand or say to him, "What have you done?" (Dan. 4:35).
- He is God, and there is no other. He is God, and there is none like him. His counsel will stand, and he will accomplish all his purpose (Isa. 46:9–10).

His sovereignty extends to all things great and small:

- The weather (Ps. 135:7)
- The establishment of governments (Rom. 13:1)
- The appearance of the stars (Isa. 40:26)
- The falling of sparrows (Matt. 10:29)
- The life and death of all men (Deut. 32:39)
- The location of civilizations (Acts 17:26)
- The decisions of rulers (Prov. 21:1)
- The plans of human beings (Prov. 19:21)
- Even the sinful decisions of rebels (Gen. 20:6; Acts 4:27–28)

The Scriptures make clear from Genesis to Revelation, from top to bottom and front to back, that God rules, reigns, governs, and ordains all things.[2]

Second, the Bible teaches that human beings are really and truly responsible for their thoughts, intentions, and actions. Our choices and decisions are genuine and meaningful. They have real, actual effects on others, on the world, and even on God. Here is just some of the evidence:

- The Bible assumes that our choices are real and meaningful. "Choose this day whom you will serve" (Josh. 24:15).
- The Bible teaches that God will judge us for our actions (2 Cor. 5:10).
- The Bible teaches that God will judge us for our words (Matt. 12:36–37).

- In the Scriptures God issues commands, exhortations, and warnings and implies that we have some capacity to respond to them, if we choose to do so (Ex. 20:3; Rom. 8:13; Gal. 6:10).
- The Bible teaches that our actions are instrumental and necessary in the completion of God's purposes. "How are they to hear without someone preaching?" (Rom. 10:14).
- The Bible teaches that answered prayer depends in some measure on our asking with right motives (James 4:2).
- The Bible teaches that God responds to the persistent prayers of his people (Luke 18:1–8).

In sum, the Scriptures are clear that we are true moral agents, that we make authentic decisions that have real effects on the world, and that we will be held accountable for our thoughts, words, and actions.

Before returning to the *how* question, it's important to underline a key point. The Bible makes little attempt to reconcile the sovereignty of God and human responsibility. It simply teaches clearly and abundantly that both are true. The biblical authors appear to have the same mentality as Charles Spurgeon, who, when asked how he reconciled sovereignty and freedom, said, "I never try to reconcile friends."

The Author and His Story

Having said that, the Bible does seem to point in certain directions, giving us hints as to how we should think about the relationship of God's actions in the world to our responsibility in the world. Over the years, I have returned again and again to what I believe is a potent analogy of God's relationship to the world. Put simply it is this:

God is an author. This world is his story. We are his characters.

One of the strongest biblical hints in this direction is found later in Psalm 139: "In your book were written, every one of them, the days that were formed for me, when as yet there were none of them" (v. 16). God is an author, and our days are his story. Combining this passage with the earlier passages on God's creating and sustaining the world through speech, perhaps we can say this: God writes the book of history, and then reads it aloud into existence. He puts pen to paper and forms a plan for the ages, and then performs a dramatic rendering of his epic poem that is so potent that his words actually take on flesh.[3]

The analogy of an author and his story helps us to understand how God can be completely, totally, and exhaustively sovereign, and human beings can be responsible and their choices and actions can be meaningful and significant. It allows us to see layers in our understanding of causality.

Let's push the analogy a bit by reflecting on the relationship of C. S. Lewis to Narnia in *The Lion, the Witch, and the Wardrobe*.

- Why was it always winter and never Christmas in Narnia? *Because the White Witch enslaved the land.*
- Why was it always winter and never Christmas in Narnia? *Because that's the way Lewis wrote the story.*
- Why does Aslan have to die? *Because Edmund was a traitor.*
- Why does Aslan have to die? *Because Lewis wrote the story that way.*
- Who killed the White Witch? *Aslan did.*
- Who killed the White Witch? *C. S. Lewis did.*

Every aspect of the story—from plot to characters to background details—is under the sovereign control of the divine author. And the actions of the characters are real and necessary for the resolution of the plot.[4]

The Layered Causality of an Author and His Characters

At this point, someone might object that the analogy breaks down because we are more real than characters in a fairy tale. We are more than fiction, possessing *more* existence (if that's the way to put it) than Peter, Susan, Edmund, and Lucy. How helpful can this analogy be if it breaks down so readily?

Now I readily grant that we are more real than the Pevensies. In relation to us, fictional characters have less existence, less reality. But I'd also insist that the same holds true for God's relation to us. In relation to him, we are less real. And what's more, I'd suggest that the existential distance between us and the Pevensies is far less than the distance between C. S. Lewis and God Almighty, maker of heaven and earth. And it is the distance between the human authors and the divine author that makes the distance between fictional characters and real persons largely irrelevant.

For therein lies the uniqueness and might of God's creative power: when he invents a world other than himself, he makes it real and actual. Our fictional creations are phantasms, existing only in minds (or on pages or movie screens). But God's creations have substance, *really* living and moving and having their being in him. As N. D. Wilson has written:

> [We are made of] words. Magic words. Words spoken by the Infinite, words so potent, spoken by One so potent that they have weight and mass and flavor. They are real. They have taken on flesh and dwelt among us. They are us.[5]

It is because of God's infinite, reality-causing power that the author-story analogy retains its potency, despite the vast distance between God's creations and our own. More importantly, it's the sort of analogy that has a lot of explanatory power when applied to complex stories in the Bible.

For example, we see evidence of this type of authorial and layered causality in the story of Joseph in the book of Genesis. Out of jealousy, Joseph's brothers sell him into slavery in Egypt, clearly intending harm to him. When Joseph finally confronts them after he has been made vice-regent of Egypt, he clearly recognizes their responsibility for their actions. "I am your brother, Joseph, whom *you* sold into Egypt" (Gen. 45:4). But Joseph doesn't stop there; he goes on to say, "And now do not be distressed or angry with yourselves because you sold me here, for God sent me before you to preserve life" (v. 5). Later he says, "So it was not you who sent me here, but God" (v. 8). Notice the juxtaposition: you *sold* me here, but God *sent* me here (see also Ps. 105:16–17).

Lest we think that God's good intentions somehow cancel out or minimize the evil of his brothers' envy and jealousy, Joseph later speaks directly to this when he says, "You meant *evil* against me, but God meant it for good, to bring it about that many people should be kept alive" (Gen. 50:20). In other words, there were layers of intention involved in the sale of Joseph into slavery. The intentions of his brothers were for evil, and they were responsible to God for them. But God's intentions *in the exact same act* were for good, that the people of God might be preserved in the midst of a great famine.[6]

We see similar layers of causation at work in the story of Job. When Satan appears before God and questions Job's faith, God gives all that Job has into Satan's hand (Job 1:12). Immediately, Job's oxen are stolen by the Sabeans (v. 15), his flocks are destroyed by fire from God (v. 16), his servants are slaughtered by the Chaldeans (v. 17), and his children are killed in a tornado (v. 19). The flow of the narrative clearly indicates that we are to understand these disasters as the work of Satan. In addition, after God puts Job's health in Satan's hand (2:6), Satan strikes Job with sores. Thus, when asked who is responsible for Job's misery, the answer is layered. The Sabeans and Chaldeans are responsible. Natural disasters are responsible. Satan is responsible. But Job attributes ultimate responsibility to none of these; he attributes ultimate responsibility to God. "The LORD gave and the LORD has taken away; blessed be the name of the LORD" (1:21). And in saying this, Job is not blaming God or charging him with wrongdoing (v. 22).

Like the author of a novel, God can ordain that evil exist without himself being tainted by evil. No one condemns Tolkien because he put Sauron in Middle-earth. The treachery of Saruman does not defile Tolkien. He does not share in the corruption of the Nazgul. And yet all of these are under his sovereign direction and design.

In the last chapter, I noted that I would be returning to the notion of *perichoresis* (mutual indwelling) throughout this book. Consider this the first application. The layers of causality that I have in mind should be understood in a perichoretic fashion. The intentions of the author and the intentions of the characters mutually indwell each other. The fact that the Father dwells in the Son and the Son dwells in the Father doesn't abolish the personal distinctions between them. Similarly, the fact that God's good intentions exist alongside, above, and beside the evil intentions of his characters doesn't abolish the fundamental distinction between them. God remains God, and the creatures remain creatures. The author is the author, and the characters are the characters. At the same time, the characters and all their thoughts, intentions, and actions are the content and product of the author's creative will.

Crucifying the Old Man and Maturing the New Man

Some may not find the author-story analogy as helpful as I do. The tension between the sovereignty of God and human responsibility still feels too weighty and substantial. For those who feel this way, let me make a larger point about doing faithful biblical theology. Over the years, as I've wrestled through various biblical, theological, and pastoral problems and tensions, I've noticed that fidelity to the Scriptures regularly requires me to stretch, expand, and reorient my theological and emotional frameworks. And when I say stretch, I mean *stretch*. I mean that one biblical truth pulls me in one direction, and another biblical truth pulls me in the other direction, and it falls to me to live with the pain and discomfort of the stretching.

Here are examples of some of the truths I have in mind:

- God is one. God is three.
- God is transcendent and full of majesty. God is immanent and close at hand.
- Jesus Christ is fully God. Jesus Christ is fully man.
- Jesus is a Lion. Jesus is a Lamb.
- We are sinners. We are saints.
- We should enjoy God through feasting. We should enjoy God through fasting.
- We should know God fully and accurately with our minds. We should love God deeply and passionately with our hearts.
- We should weep with those who weep. We should rejoice with those who rejoice.
- God is sovereign over our actions. We are responsible for our actions.

This is God's way, the way of the cross. God intends to explode our pitiful little categories by insisting in the strongest terms that we be pulled in opposite directions. These are not contradictions. There may be paradox, and there is certainly tremendous mystery, but if we are going to submit our patterns and categories of thinking to the Bible, then we must allow them to be stretched and pulled (and sometimes put to death altogether) in order to remain faithful to what God has said. Think of it as simultaneously the crucifixion of the old man (with his passions, desires, and rebellion against God's truth) and the maturation and growth of the new man, created and governed by Christ. Or, as Augustine says, God's design in these theological mysteries is "to wear Adam down and let Christ's glorious grace shine through."[7]

Through this painful process, God grows and matures and draws us nearer to himself by expanding our minds to take in all the biblical truth and expanding our hearts to feel all that we should feel. He does this in order to remind us that he is holy, that he is unique, that there is none like him. Yes, we can probe and explore and make use of analogies and illustrations in order to understand how it all works, but our analogies will always break down, and they will generally break down for the same reason: we are dealing with the absolutely holy, unique, self-sufficient, and triune God of Scripture.

So if you can't seem to reconcile two truths that are clearly taught in the Bible, resist the impulse to compromise one or the other. Refuse to allow one truth to mute another truth. Labor to hold them in tension. Be willing to be stretched. Don't hold one biblical truth so closely that you refuse to let all of Scripture speak. Don't despair when your mind aches because of the tension. You should expect paradox; you should expect mystery; you should expect to have your categories blown, and your mind stretched, and your heart expanded so that you can take in more and more of God.

Pulling It Together

Let's pull together a number of the things we've seen.

First, we can see that God is meticulous in his attention to detail. Like Tolkien, every Ent has a genealogy. In fact, every ant has a genealogy. There are no rogue molecules. There are no random atoms. There are no wayward snowflakes. Everything has purpose. Everything has design. Everything has intent. We may not always know exactly what it is, but we can rest in the knowledge that God is working all things according to the counsel of his will, that his purposes are always for our good.

Sit at a busy intersection and watch the cars pass in all directions. Every driver has a story. Every passenger has a past. They are all coming from somewhere. And they all have a future. Watch them as they pass you and disappear out of sight, out of mind. The swirl of stories at one intersection on one afternoon in one city in one country on one planet in a mid-sized solar system exceeds your tiny mind's capacity. And yet God marks them all, and more. He knows every story because he wrote every story. And not just the human ones. There are squirrel wars that make the Hatfields and McCoys look like a pillow fight. And at some point every story intersects with every other one. This story is woven tighter than a Persian rug. There are no dropped plots, no aimless storylines. God is not the producer of a television drama that starts promisingly, can't find its way, and is cancelled after eleven episodes.

God is writing a true metanarrative, a master story, a grand drama that puts the director's cut of *The Lord of the Rings* to shame. And this A story—this history of redemption—contains B stories about nations and kingdoms, Babylons and Egypts; C stories about tribes and villages, clans and families; D stories about brave boys and terrible dragons, about petty bullies and slanderous cowards, about giants and princesses and honor students and back-bench soccer players. There are E, F, and G stories about animals, vegetables, and minerals; lions, tigers, and bears (oh my!). Somewhere in there are stories about stars and their wars, about atoms and their bonding, about black holes and black sheep and, if Tolkien is to be believed, a hobbit or two.

Second, understanding the world as God's story provides important categories for wrestling with the problem of evil.[8] If the world is a story, then the presence of evil is fundamentally an example of narratival tension. Thus, we can see more clearly God's reasoning in permitting and ordaining that evil exist. God ordains evil for the same reason that Lewis created the White Witch—so that Aslan would have someone to conquer. Evil exists so that Good can triumph. Death exists so that it can be thrown into hell (Rev. 20:14). And this does not in any way minimize the wickedness or horror of evil. God is sovereign, and evil is real.

This way of looking at the world allows us to view every part of the story through two lenses: a wide lens and a narrow lens.[9] The narrow lens keeps us from minimizing the reality of evil, as if pain and wickedness were simply illusions. We must never give in to the fleshly logic that says, "Because God ordains all things, there is really no such thing as evil." The Bible will have nothing to do with such reasoning. Christians do not shrink from calling evil "evil" (Gen. 50:20), or calamity "calamity" (Isa. 45:7), or disaster "disaster" (Amos 3:6). What's more, we are called to weep with those who weep, to fight the curse that hangs over this fallen world, and to rage against the darkness with all the power of the light.

At the same time, we must not elevate evil above its station. Nothing happens apart from God's wise and good decree. Therefore, we must not stop reading in the early chapters. The story does not stop, so our wide lens allows us to see, or at least to trust, that Judas's betrayal will not go unpunished, Wormtongue's lies will not stand, and the blood of the martyrs will in fact bear fruit. This is a happily-ever-after kind of story. This is the kind of story where dragons are slain and tears are wiped away and faithful death is always followed by resurrection. Sorrow may last for the night, but joy comes in the morning (Ps. 30:5).

Finally, though God is truly the author of this story of glory, there's one more piece to the puzzle, the place where God takes the author-story analogy, shatters it, and puts it back together in a way that bends our very brains.

God Is the Author, the Main Character, and More

Begin with God's revelation of himself to Moses in Exodus 3. God reveals himself in two ways: as "I AM WHO I AM" (3:14) and as "LORD" (Yahweh) (3:15), the name by which he is to be remembered throughout all generations.

"I AM WHO I AM" emphasizes that God is the independent, self-existent one. He is not ultimately defined by anything outside of himself. As we saw in the first chapter, he is self-sufficient, absolute, independent, autonomous. He has no needs or unmet desires. He existed before creation and apart from creation. As Paul says, God is not "served by human hands, as though he needed anything" (Acts 17:25). He is perfectly and infinitely and completely happy in the fellowship of the Godhead.

So when God says, "I AM WHO I AM," he is emphasizing his God-ness, his independent and self-sufficient existence.

The name Yahweh, on the other hand, stresses God's relationship to his creation, the reality that he is the God of Abraham, the God of Isaac, and the God of Jacob (Ex. 3:15). God's memorial name binds him to the world he's made and particularly to his covenant people. He is Yahweh, a God merciful and compassionate, slow to anger and abounding in stead-fast love (Ex. 34:6). What's more, some Hebrew scholars believe that the name Yahweh is actually based on the causative form of the Hebrew verb *hayah*, "to be." These scholars argue that we should interpret the name Yahweh as "The One Who Causes All Things to Be That Are," or "The Causer of All Things" for short.[10] Thus, the name Yahweh stresses the absolute sovereignty of God over all of creation.

Think of it this way: C. S. Lewis has existence apart from Narnia. Even if the Narnian chronicles were never written, C. S. Lewis would still exist. Thus, C. S. Lewis simply is who he is, apart from Narnia. However, in relation to Narnia, he is also the causer of all things that are. Narnia has no existence apart from him; therefore, were he to reveal himself in Narnia, Narnians could call him the Causer of All Things. So too with God. Apart from creation, he is God, I AM, the self-existent one. But in relation to creation, he is Yahweh, the causer of all things. Thus, "I AM" emphasizes God-as-God; Yahweh emphasizes God-as-author.

Now here's the amazing thing: how do we know that God is God? How do we know that God is the author, the causer of all things? We know because God reveals it to Moses in a burning bush, at a particular time, in a particular place. In other words, we come to know that God is self-existent and that he is the author because God reveals himself *as a character* within the story. God is not merely the one in whom we live and move and have our being. He is also the one who speaks to Abraham at Mount Moriah, who leads Israel through the wilderness as a pillar of cloud and fire, and who makes his presence to dwell in the temple in Jerusalem.

God-as-author and God-as-character mean that we can view God's relationship to the world in complementary ways. On the one hand, he is transcendent and high and lifted up, looking far down upon the children of man. He is the Alpha and Omega, relating to creation atemporally, outside of time. If history is a great river, he views the entire sweep of it—twists and turns and all—in one, simple, comprehensive glance from his heavenly mountain.

On the other hand, from the beginning, he enters into his story as a character, walking with his creatures and engaging with them as fellow characters, rejoicing over their successes and grieving over their losses. God doesn't merely survey the river from above; he also rides the rapids with us, hands waving wildly in the air. This is the God who weeps, the God who repents, the God who changes his mind. This is the God who, though unchanging, *becomes* flesh and dwells among us.[11]

This is what the incarnation is all about—the author of the story becoming not just a character, but a *human* character. In this narrative, God is the storyteller *and* the main character. He is the bard *and* the hero. He authors the fairy tale and then comes to kill the dragon and get the girl.

3

Creation as Communication

The world was no doubt made, that it might be a theatre of the divine glory.

John Calvin

And this our life . . . finds tongues in trees, books in the running brooks, Sermons in stones, and good in everything.

William Shakespeare

The world is charged with the grandeur of God.

Gerard Manley Hopkins

Any patch of sunlight in a wood will show you something about the sun which you could never get from reading books on astronomy. These pure and spontaneous pleasures are "patches of Godlight" in the woods of our experience.

C. S. Lewis

The previous two chapters have focused on God as he is in himself—infinitely happy in the fellowship of the Trinity—and God as he is in relation to creation—author of the story of his glory. Tying these two threads together, we are able to see just how God has chosen to communicate his glory. Creation is God's self-expression, the free overflow of his triune personality and life. Creation itself is revelatory, and this revelation is not sporadic, occasional, or restricted to one corner of reality. Rather, God's revelation of himself in creation is pervasive and constant. As the old hymn says, "He speaks to me everywhere."[1] Or, as C. S. Lewis said, "We may ignore, but we can nowhere evade the presence of God. The world is crowded with Him. He walks everywhere incognito."[2]

We'll expand on the limitations and finitude of creation in the next chapter. For now, it's enough to note that God created the world as a fitting overflow of his own love for and delight in the fellowship he enjoys within the Godhead. This fact must not be overlooked, as it's one of the fundamental arguments of this book. God's love for God led him to create the world from nothing. Therefore, our love for God, if it is to be an accurate reflection of God's love, must also lead us to a deep and profound and fitting love for creation. God's love for God pushes him into creation. So should ours.

Creation as Communication

If God reveals himself in creation, then every aspect of creation is communicative, from the smallest to the greatest. There is no area of reality that does not reveal the triune God. The heavens declare his glory (Ps. 19:1), and that is only the beginning. His invisible attributes, namely his eternal power and divine nature, are clearly perceived *in the things that have been made* (Rom. 1:20). Note this: creation makes invisible realities visible. We see the divine nature *in* the things that God has made, just as we see the skill, wisdom, and creativity of the artist in his painting, or the composer in his symphony.

The communicative nature of creation led Jonathan Edwards to regard the world and all it contains as a sort of language. Edwards writes,

> I am not ashamed to own that I believe that the whole universe, heaven and earth, air and seas, and the divine constitution and history of the holy Scriptures, be full of images of divine things, as full as a language is of words; and that the multitudes of those things that I have mentioned are but a very small part of what is really intended to be signified and typified by these things.[3]

The sunrise is not just a sunrise; it's a word. It has meaning, intent, communicative content. It bears a message. So do clouds and laughter and honey and pearls and chairs and soda. All of them are spoken into existence by the Word of God, making creation, as one of my friends says, "the Word's words." Or, as Ken Myers once said, commenting on Psalm 1, "Trees are audio-visual aids to help us understand righteousness."[4]

Edwards refers to creation-as-communication as "images of divine things" or "types." Most of us are familiar with discussions of typology in the Bible, as when we recognize that the Passover lamb was a type or image or picture of the sacrifice of Christ. King Solomon is a type of Christ (Matt. 12:42). The exodus of the Hebrews from Egypt is a type of our salvation from sin and death (Rom. 8:14). The Sabbath is a type of our ultimate rest with Christ (Heb. 4:9). The Scriptures are full of this sort of intentional foreshadowing and imaging of spiritual realities.

Edwards recognizes such images and types in the Scriptures, but goes further in identifying types and images in the natural world. God has constructed a system of symbols that continuously communicate his presence in nature and history. He writes, "Types are a certain sort of language, as it were, in which God is wont to speak to us."[5]

We learn this language the same way that we learn any other language: either through immersion from a young age or through education. Edwards believes that "God hasn't expressly explained all the types of Scriptures, but has done so much as is sufficient to teach us the language."[6] In other words, Scripture is the grammar textbook for the language of God, instructing us clearly in the patterns of meaning and the rules by which we are enabled to read everything else.

Indeed, Scripture commands us to read the world in this way. "Look at the birds" (Matt. 6:26). "Consider the lilies" (Matt. 6:28). "Go to the ant" (Prov. 6:6). There are divine lessons in seeds and fields, in sand and rocks, in wineskins and fig trees. In this way, we should, as Calvin said, seek to read creation with the spectacles of Scripture.[7]

Of course, because of human sin, our ability to interpret creation has been marred and corrupted. Our eyesight is poor, our minds are distorted, and our hearts are depraved. We can't see the light of the knowledge of the glory of Christ in the gospel, let alone in the natural world.

Only through the restoration accomplished by the new birth are we able to rightly interpret the Scriptures and thus rightly interpret the world. Unless we are born again, we cannot see the kingdom—in the mustard seed (Matt. 13:31–32) or in the leaven (Matt. 13:33) or in the priceless pearl (Matt. 13:45). But having been born again, and having immersed ourselves in Scripture and thus learned the basics of God's language, we are then free to seek to faithfully discern God's meaning everywhere else.

Typology, Analogy, and Metaphor

Typology operates on a principle of comparison. In fact, the kind of typology practiced by Edwards is roughly synonymous with analogy. Reading the created order involves recognizing patterns in God's world, identifying relevant similarities and differences between creation and God and between different parts of creation. Typology is thus closely related to metaphor and simile. In fact, we might think of types as divinely intended metaphors.

When using metaphor, we set one thing next to another in order to better understand both of them. Metaphor calls us to see one thing as another, to have two realities mutually illuminated by the comparison. When we say, "My love is like a red, red rose," we deepen our understanding of both our beloved and roses.

I've mentioned Psalm 19 already ("The heavens declare the glory of God"). As the psalmist David unpacks the meaning of this statement, he uses a number of lively analogies to help us see what he sees when he gazes at the heavens:

> The heavens declare the glory of God,
>   and the sky above proclaims his handiwork.
> Day to day pours out speech,
>   and night to night reveals knowledge.
> There is no speech, nor are there words,
>   whose voice is not heard.
> Their voice goes out through all the earth,
>   and their words to the end of the world.
> In them he has set a tent for the sun,

> which comes out like a bridegroom leaving his chamber,
> and, like a strong man, runs its course with joy.
> Its rising is from the end of the heavens,
> and its circuit to the end of them,
> and there is nothing hidden from its heat. (vv. 1–6)

There is much to see here, but I just want to focus on how David unfolds his vision of the sun in verse 5. The sun is like a bridegroom leaving his chamber and like a strong man who runs his course with joy. David looks at the sun as it moves across the sky and then looks at a groom on his wedding day and sees a connection. He looks at the sun again and is reminded of Josheb-basshebeth, one of his mighty men, running into battle with spear raised and eyes blazing (2 Sam. 23:8). The sun is like the groom, is like the mighty man. And, if we're paying attention to the entire Bible, we'll see in this swirl of images more than just the images. We'll see Yahweh, the great bridegroom who rejoices over his bride (Isa. 62:5). We'll see Jesus, his face "like the sun shining in full strength" (Rev. 1:16); the strong man who binds the Devil to plunder his goods (Matt. 11:20); the author and perfecter of our faith, who ran his race for the joy set before him (Heb. 12:2); the true warrior who kills the dragon to get the girl (Gen. 3:15; Rev. 21:2).[8]

Analogy and metaphor, whether in Scripture or in the natural world, are the primary ways that God has chosen to reveal himself to us. Created reality brings God's perfections home to us in ways that are visible, concrete, and particular. They keep God's attributes and characteristics from being mere abstractions, because it's impossible for us to love a list of qualities. God is a person, not an alpha-numeric list of attributes, and thus he reveals *himself* in and through his *mighty works*.[9]

The pages of Scripture overflow with creational analogies and metaphors to help us understand the glorious and ineffable mystery of the triune God. God is a Father, and so he gives us earthly fathers so that we'd know what he's like. God is a shield and a fortress. He is a roaring lion who devours his enemies. He hides his people under the shadow of his wings. To understand his anger, we must look to a consuming fire. To grasp his steadfastness, we plant our feet on a rock. To comprehend the surety of his protection, we witness the shepherd with his sheep in the valley of shadows. Such descriptions may indeed be symbolic, but they are divinely designed symbols, and their great variety and diversity aid us as we seek to know and understand the one who has called us into being.[10]

Looking At versus Looking Along

So then, if creation reveals God, how can we engage with the world so that we see him in it? Many Christians have been helped with this question by C. S. Lewis's "Meditation in a Toolshed":

> I was standing today in the dark toolshed. The sun was shining outside and through the crack at the top of the door there came a sunbeam. From where I stood that beam of light, with the specks of dust floating in it, was the most striking thing in the place. Everything else was almost pitch-black. I was seeing the beam, not seeing things by it. Then I moved so that the beam fell on my eyes. Instantly the whole previous picture vanished. I saw no toolshed, and (above all) no beam. Instead I saw, framed in the irregular cranny at the top of the door, green leaves moving on the branches of a tree outside and beyond that, 90 odd million miles away, the sun. Looking along the beam, and looking at the beam are very different experiences.[11]

John Piper calls this "the essential key to unlocking the proper use of the physical world of sensation for spiritual purposes."[12] Instead of merely "looking at" the beam of created glory (such as the heavens), we should "look along" the heavens. When we do, we won't merely see the glory of the heavens; we'll see the glory of God. Piper writes:

> All of God's creation becomes a beam to be "looked along" or a sound to be "heard along" or a fragrance to be "smelled along" or a flavor to be "tasted along" or a touch to be "felt along." All our senses become partners with the eyes of the heart in perceiving the glory of God through the physical world.[13]

In itself, the distinction between "looking at" and "looking along" can help us see divine glory in and through created glory. However,

Lewis's analogy, when applied to God and creation, is subject to certain shortcomings.

For example, in his meditation, Lewis is not primarily concerned with looking at creation or looking along creation *to God*. Rather, he is speaking of two different ways of viewing our *experience* of this world. When he speaks of "looking at" the beam, he means the attempt to get outside of an experience in order to objectively analyze it (usually for the purpose of debunking it). He gives the example of a scientist attempting to explain a young man's feelings of love for a young woman in terms of genetic predispositions and chemical reactions. Thus, for Lewis, "looking at" is the attempt to explain and analyze an experience from the outside, whereas "looking along" is the attempt to know an experience from the inside.

This is slightly different from the application that Piper makes of the analogy when speaking of God and the world. For example, while Lewis does seem to regard "looking along" as in some ways superior to "looking at," he also says that "one must look both *along* and *at* everything." In other words, both ways of seeing have value. However, on Piper's use of the analogy (in which we look along creation to the glory of God), it's unclear what value "looking at" creation would have at all. If "looking at" creation means seeing creation *without* being amazed at the God who reveals himself through it, then such "looking at" is worse than worthless; it's idolatrous and damnable. Instead, all of our looking should be a "looking along" creation to God so that we see him in and through it.

What's more, if creation is the beam, and by it we run our eyes up to God, who is the sun, then we're confronted with the problem of the disappearing beam. As Lewis said, when he looked along the beam, he "saw no toolshed, and (above all) no beam." But when we "look along" creation to the divine glory, creation remains. When we see divine glory in the heavens, we continue to see the heavens. When we recognize the beauty of Christ's love for his church in a husband's love for his wife, the marital love remains (and if anything, intensifies). This isn't to discount the value of "looking along" creation to the divine source. It simply means that we have more work to do when it comes to describing (and more importantly, experiencing) the relationship between creation and the glory of God.

Vessels of Glory

"Meditation in a Toolshed" isn't all that Lewis has to say on the subject. In *Letters to Malcolm* he writes:

> Creation seems to be delegation through and through. He will do nothing simply of Himself which can be done by creatures. I suppose this is because He is a giver. And He has nothing to give but Himself. And to give Himself is to do His deeds—in a sense, and on varying levels to be Himself—through the things He has made.[14]

In creation, God gives himself. And giving himself means that he does his deeds and in some sense *is* himself through the things he has made. This is not pantheism, the idea that God is everything and everything is God. But it is the notion that God is *in* everything, that creation really is the bearer of divine life and glory, so that (to quote Lewis again), when we look at any aspect of creation, we can say "This also is Thou: neither is this Thou."[15]

This is another example of having our theological framework stretched by being pulled in opposite directions. On the one hand, we never compromise the Creator-creature distinction. God remains God—infinite, absolute, and self-sufficient—and creation remains creation—finite, derivative, and dependent. Creator and creature are not to be identified with each other in pantheistic fashion. On the other hand, the divine presence is truly in the created stuff—really in the pizza and the wife and the music and the sunset. Creation is a fitting vehicle, or—to use the biblical term—vessel, for divine glory. To expand a Pauline analogy, the treasure resides in jars of clay.[16]

The idea of creation as a vessel for divine glory helps guard against any pantheistic tendencies, any blasphemous attempt to bridge the Creator-creature divide. At the same time, it can be misleading, as though created reality is merely a shell containing a divine pearl or a husk containing divine corn. Shells and husks are meant to be discarded when you reach their contents. But God does not intend for us to throw creation away once we've reached him. To borrow an analogy from Doug Wilson, we don't use the ladder of creation to climb up to God, and then kick the ladder away. Creation retains its value, even as it points us to the God of infinite value.

Shafts of the Glory

Thankfully, Lewis is not done with his reflections on the relationship between creation and divine glory. Toward the end of *Letters to Malcolm*, he describes minor earthly blessings (such as the coolness of a stream on a hot day) as "an exposition of *the* glory itself."[17] Or, most provocatively, "[Earthly] pleasures are *shafts of the glory* as it strikes our sensibility."[18]

This is no pearl in a shell. The beams of created glory participate in and communicate the eternal, divine glory. Lewis is worth quoting at length:

> I have tried, since that moment, to make every pleasure a channel of adoration. I don't mean simply by giving thanks for it. One must of course give thanks, but I mean something different. How shall I put it?
>
> We can't—or I can't—hear the song of a bird simply as a sound. Its meaning or message ("That's a bird") comes with it inevitably—just as one can't see a familiar word in print as a merely visual pattern. The reading is as involuntary as the seeing. When the wind roars I don't just hear the roar; I "hear the wind." In the same way it is possible to "read" as well as to "have" a pleasure. Or not even "as well as." The distinction ought to become, and sometimes is, impossible; to receive it and to recognize its divine source are a single experience. This heavenly fruit is instantly redolent of the orchard where it grew. This sweet air whispers of the country from whence it blows. It is a message. We know we are being touched by a finger of that right hand at which there are pleasures for evermore. There need be no question of thanks or praise as a separate event, something done afterwards. To experience the tiny theophany is itself to adore.
>
> Gratitude exclaims, very properly, "How good of God to give me this." Adoration says, "What must be the quality of that Being whose far-off and momentary coruscations are like this!" One's mind runs back up the sunbeam to the sun.[19]

This passage is packed with implications for how we relate to the things of earth. First, notice that Lewis is talking about *every* pleasure. He does not reserve this experience for special occasions or spiritual activities. Every enjoyment has the capacity to be a "tiny theophany," a touch from God's finger.

Second, notice how the distinction between the experience of the pleasure and the interpretation or reading of the pleasure almost collapses. The divine glory is so woven into the created enjoyment that to separate them is to do violence to both. In fact, later I will suggest that one of the central evils of sin is the attempt to create false dualisms, to separate what God has joined together, namely, the divine presence in the created world.

Third, the analogies that Lewis uses underscore what we've seen in Edwards about creation as communication. Created realities are the black marks on the page; once we've learned to read, they can never be anything but divine words. Creation doesn't just contain a message; it *is* a message. Sound and sense cannot be separated. They are indelibly intermingled. The vibrations of the air that carry sound to our ears are more than vibrations; they are the voice of the one who made heaven and earth, the one who holds our very life in being. The vast variety and diversity of created reality testify to his manifold perfections.

Finally, to return to "Meditation in a Toolshed," the earthly pleasures are sunbeams that we can chase back to the sun. But the beam doesn't get lost in looking at the sun. In fact, it becomes more itself, more potent, more the object of our attention. We, in some mysterious way, look along them *by* looking at them. However, the imagery of the mind running back to the sun can be profoundly misleading. For we are in no hurry. In fact, to hurry is to miss the point. If divine glory really *is* in creation, then ought we not linger in creation? Instead of blowing through the earthly pleasure at 90 mph, shouldn't we slow to a stroll and take in as much of creation as we can? Isn't hurrying through on our way to praise of God the equivalent of applauding after the first three notes of a symphony? Wouldn't it be better to attentively listen to the entire score and then let applause come thundering out of us (or perhaps be hushed into silence by the wonder of it all)? Shouldn't we linger over creation (even loiter), not as a way of avoiding God but as a way of knowing him and enjoying him more fully?

Creation is a message, an invitation to be drawn into the divine life, the ecstatic vibrance of the Father, the Son, and the Holy Spirit. As Lewis says, "We are summoned to pass in through Nature, beyond her, into that splendour which she fitfully reflects."[20] How closely, then, are we listening?

To the Law and to the Testimony

At this point, the natural and obvious questions are these: It's all well and good to quote Jonathan Edwards and C. S. Lewis, but is any of that in the Bible? Can you show me passages and verses that would lead us to this conclusion? Or are these simply the thoughts of fallible men, intriguing and suggestive, but less secure than a word from the Lord?

These are absolutely the right questions. The entire second half of the book will be devoted to applying these insights to our lives from the Scriptures. For now, I'll simply examine three passages that I believe support what we've seen about creation in Edwards and Lewis. First, a simple example of a created reality used as an analogy in order to help us know God more fully:

> My son, eat honey, for it is good,
>> and the drippings of the honeycomb are sweet to your taste.
> Know that wisdom is such to your soul;
>> if you find it, there will be a future,
>> and your hope will not be cut off. (Prov. 24:13–14)

Why did God make honey so tasty and sweet? So that we would have some idea what wisdom is like (at least, that's one reason). The sweetness of honey points beyond itself to the wisdom of God. Honey is "good," and we are exhorted in Psalm 34 to "taste and see that the LORD is good!" Our souls have taste buds, just like our tongues, and we can train the soul buds by exercising the tongue buds. We savor the sweetness of honey or sweet tea or pumpkin crunch cake and in the moment engage in a fancy bit of "reading," transposing the physical enjoyment of taste onto our souls and offering thanks to God, not only for the simple pleasures of food but for the spiritual pleasures to which the food is but a fitting echo.

But this means that we can't short-circuit the enjoyment of the honey. In order for us to gain the full *spiritual* benefit of honey, we must *really* enjoy its sweetness. There must be a savoring of honey *as honey* before there can ever be a savoring of honey as a pointer to divine wisdom. In short, if we are to obey the biblical exhortation to "*know* that wisdom is *such* to your soul," we must first "Know . . . such," that is, we must first eat honey. We must come to have a deep and real knowledge of honey's sweetness, the kind of experiential knowledge that can only come when we linger over the pleasant taste on our tongue.

Second, what about creation as shafts of the glory, the interweaving of created wonders with the divine presence such that the distinction almost disappears? Psalm 104 is a hymn to the God of creation, a meditation on God's work in Genesis 1.

It begins with an invocation: "Bless the LORD, O my soul"; and an exclamation: "O LORD my God, *you* are very great." The opening words suggest that this will be a psalm about God. The psalm continues by extolling God's activities: riding on the wind, making his ministers a flaming fire, setting the earth on its foundations, and rebuking the waters so that the mountains rise out of the deep. Here we see a subtle transition as the psalmist directs his attention to God's works in creation. The psalmist admires God's gift of water to donkeys, the song of birds in the trees, the growth of grass as food for livestock, and the provision of "wine to gladden the heart of man, oil to make his face shine and bread to strengthen man's heart" (v. 15).

The psalmist considers the dwelling places of storks, goats, and rock badgers. He extols the sun and the moon for their regulation of time and praises God for giving man the gift of vocation. He meditates upon the sea and the creatures that fill it, the ships that go upon it, and Leviathan, the great serpent, that sports in it. He marvels at the dependence of all living things on God for life and breath and everything and the power and wisdom of God in returning all his creatures back to the dust.

In short, in order to write this hymn of praise *to God*, the psalmist did a whole lot of thinking about creation. He considered it, he studied it, he marveled at it. He thought and he composed; he reflected and he wrote. The works of God in creation were the primary objects of his meditation. In many ways, creation dominates this psalm. And then, as he draws it to a conclusion, he says:

> May my meditation be pleasing to him,
> for I rejoice *in the* LORD. (v. 34)

This encomium to the wonder of creation has been, from start to finish, a rejoicing in the Lord, not merely a rejoicing in creation. The celebration of the birds and the sea, the sun and the trees, the ships and the beasts—all of it has been a (perichoretic, perhaps?) rejoicing in Yahweh, the one who created all these manifold works in infinite wisdom and whose glory is over all that he has made.

Finally, Isaiah's vision of God in his temple provides a striking addition to our understanding of God's relationship to creation. The words of the seraphim as they sing before the throne of God are familiar to us:

> Holy, holy, holy is the LORD of hosts;
> the whole earth is full of his glory! (Isa. 6:3)

The last phrase might suggest a kind of separation between the glory of God and the earth. The earth is full of God's glory the way a cup is full of water or a husk is full of corn. But the Hebrew in this passage actually points beyond such an understanding. In fact, a more literal rendering of the sentence would be, "The fullness of the whole earth is his glory."

A more provocative rendering to be sure. But what might it mean? Two possibilities seem likely. First, this passage may be depicting creation as God's clothing, his robe of glory. In the Scriptures, clothing is often an expression of glory, as in the case of the priestly garments and the royal robes of kingship. Jesus notes that not even "Solomon *in all his glory*" was arrayed or clothed like the lilies of the field (Matt. 6:29). Paul describes our glorification at the final resurrection in terms of being clothed (1 Corinthians 15; 2 Corinthians 5). Thus, God creates the world ex nihilo in order to wear it as a beautiful garment, a glory-robe fit for the King of kings.

The second possibility is that the passage indicates that creation is bridal. Paul, in speaking of the relationship between husbands and wives, says that "woman is the glory of man" (1 Cor. 11:7). And in the Old Testament we read, "An excellent wife is the crown of her husband" (Prov. 12:4). In a remarkable passage, Paul describes the church, who is the bride of Christ, as "the *fullness* of him who fills all in all" (Eph. 1:23). Thus, as we noted earlier, God created the world to get a bride for his Son.[21]

Conclusion

What, then, can we say about creation? Creation is communication from the triune God. God loved his Trinitarian fullness so much that he created a world to communicate that fullness *ad extra*, outside himself. And not just any world—a world full of fish tacos, tickle fights, afternoon naps, Cajun seafood, back rubs, wool house shoes, and church softball.

The infinite and eternal God created something that is not God but nevertheless really and truly reflects and reveals God. To bring in the earlier categories, God's relationship to creation is perichoretic: creation exists in God, and God exists in some sense in it, but the Creator-creature divide is never abrogated and never compromised.

As a result, creation is glorious, *created* shafts of *divine* glory. As the light of the sun is refracted by water droplets into a rainbow, so creation refracts the glory of God, allowing the full spectrum of his beauty to be displayed for the knowledge and enjoyment of his people. Created glory mediates divine glory so that when we chase the pleasures up the beam to the source, we arrive at the joy of joys, the river of delights, the person of persons, the living God and Father of Jesus Christ.

As Doug Wilson says, creation is thick, and its thickness does not prevent us from seeing God clearly.[22] In fact, the thicker creation is, the more clearly we see God, the more fully we know God, the more robustly we enjoy God (more on this in chapter 5).

Finally, the ultimate affirmation of the capacity of earthly things to reveal God's glory is the incarnation of Jesus Christ. "The Word became flesh and dwelt among us, and we have seen his glory, glory as of the only Son from the Father, full of grace and truth" (John 1:14). Creation has been magnificently glorified, united to the divine being in an unprecedented and decisive way. And as Lewis is so fond of reminding us, God's miracles, including the miracle of the incarnation, are simply "a retelling in small letters of the very same story which is written across the whole world in letters too large for some of us to see."[23] The incarnation—the fullness of deity dwelling bodily in the person of Jesus of Nazareth—awakens us to the reality of the "discarnation," the living and active presence of the triune God, silent but sounding in every corner of the cosmos.[24]

4

Created to Be
a Creature

There is no good trying to be more spiritual than God.

C. S. Lewis

We—or at least I—shall not be able to adore God on the highest
occasions if we have learned no habit of doing so on the lowest.
At best, our faith and reason will tell us that He is adorable, but
we shall not have found Him so, not have "tasted and seen."

C. S. Lewis

Thus far, we've considered the triune God of glory as he is in himself,
then God as author in relation to the story of creation, and then, in the
last chapter, creation as the communication of God's glory. Pulling these
threads together, we can make the following statement:

The triune God—Father, Son, and Holy Spirit—out of love for and
delight in his own fullness, freely chose to create the world as a fitting, narratival communication of his glory. It's fitting, because infinite wisdom conceived and directed it. It's narratival, because the
shape of the world is a story, a sequence of events with a beginning,
a middle, and an end. It's communication, because God speaks it into
existence and speaks himself through it at every point. And all of it
is glory, because the creator and author is the Lord of glory.

The present chapter expands on our role within this grand drama. What does it mean to be a creature, a character within God's play, called into existence out of nothing and somehow capable of relating to the author in a real, profound, and personal way? Put another way, what does it mean to be made in the image of God?

In the Beginning

We begin this discussion (appropriately enough) in the beginning. As God speaks, divides, assembles, and gathers the various features of his created world, he repeatedly assesses what he has done. He evaluates his work. He looks at the light (Gen. 1:4), the earth and seas (Gen. 1:10), the vegetation (Gen. 1:12), the heavenly lights (Gen. 1:18), the swarms of fish and birds (Gen. 1:21), and the beasts and livestock (Gen. 1:25). And every time, he recognizes the same thing: it was good. God approves of his work. He recognizes his wisdom and power and creativity and artistry and goodness and kindness in what he has made. And when he's finished with his work, after completing all his creative activity, he evaluates everything that he has made, and he starts using superlatives. "And behold, it was *very* good" (Gen. 1:31).

God surveys the world of matter and time, of trees and their branches, of seas and their waves, of signs and seasons, days and years, and he has one reaction: exceedingly good. Over-the-top good. Exclamation-point good. Spike-the-football-and-end-zone-dance good. It's finite. It's temporal. It's limited. And it's very, very good.

God is the true materialist. As Lewis said, "He likes matter. He invented it."[1] Of course, this doesn't mean that the material world is all there is. It simply means that the physical is in some sense "spiritual." How could it not be, given that anything physical is called into existence by an infinite and eternal Spirit who speaks in three dimensions? Or, as N. D. Wilson has written,

> Tree, God says, and there is one. But He doesn't say the word *tree*; He says the tree itself. He needs no shortcut. He's not merely calling one into existence, though His voice creates. His voice *is* its existence. That thing in your yard, that mangy apple or towering spruce, that

thing is not the referent of His word. It is His word and its referent. If He were to stop talking, it wouldn't be there.[2]

Temporal, Bodily, Finite, and Good

So creation is good because God made it and deems it so. But we can say more, because the Bible says more. When it comes to the creation of man, we have front-row seats and a level of detail that ought to be instructive for us. The story of human origins in Genesis 2 is worth some careful thought and attention:

> When no bush of the field was yet in the land and no small plant of the field had yet sprung up—for the LORD God had not caused it to rain on the land, and there was no man to work the ground, and a mist was going up from the land and was watering the whole face of the ground—then the LORD God formed the man of dust from the ground and breathed into his nostrils the breath of life, and the man became a living creature. And the LORD God planted a garden in Eden, in the east, and there he put the man whom he had formed. And out of the ground the LORD God made to spring up every tree that is pleasant to the sight and good for food. The tree of life was in the midst of the garden, and the tree of the knowledge of good and evil. (Gen. 2:5–9)

"*When* no bush." "*Formed* the man of dust from the ground." "*There* he put the man." Human beings are temporal, bodily, and finite creatures. We exist in time. We exist in bodies. We exist in space. We are embodied and en-storied beings. And notice that the physical body came first. God formed the man of dust from the ground (How does one even do that?) and *then* breathed into him the breath of life so that he became a living creature. Contrary to some schools of thought, man is not a spirit imprisoned in a body. God's intent was not for the soul to exist independently from the body. The separation of soul and body that we experience at death is alien to our design. To be a true and full human being is to be an embodied soul and an ensouled body.

From these observations we can conclude that temporality, limitation, and finitude are not defects to be overcome. Our existence in time, space, and bodies is not a bug; it's a feature, designed by infinite wisdom for the communication of the unfathomable riches of his glory. God is not frustrated by our finitude. He is not hamstrung by our bodies. Our limitations pose no barrier to him. "He knows our frame; he remembers that we are dust" (Ps. 103:14). *He made us this way*, and he thinks it was a grand idea.[3]

God's Provision and Our Labor

Continuing with the story:

> The LORD God took the man and put him in the garden of Eden to work it and keep it. And the LORD God commanded the man, saying, "You may surely eat of every tree of the garden, but of the tree of the knowledge of good and evil you shall not eat, for in the day that you eat of it you shall surely die." (Gen. 2:15–17)

Behold the lavishness of God in providing for our physical needs. Earlier we were told that God made to spring up every tree that is pleasant to the sight and good for food (v. 9). Now we're told that they're (almost) all for us, with divine endorsement. "Look at all of the plants yielding seed. Behold every tree bearing fruit. Beautiful, aren't they? That's why I gave you eyes: to see such beautiful sights. Wait until you taste them. It'll be a party in your mouth. You may eat of every one of them. All of them are yours for food. Except one. There's only one no in this world full of yes (and even it is temporary)! Eat, drink, and be merry."[4]

If we extend this divine endorsement of sight and taste, then here we see God enthusiastically endorsing our joy and delight in all sensible pleasures (that is, pleasures we receive through our bodily senses, pleasures that we see, smell, taste, touch, and hear), provided they are enjoyed within the boundaries established by the giver of every good gift. Perhaps God could have done it another way. He might have made an immaterial world populated by purely spiritual beings. Infinite wisdom preferred stomachs. And tongues. And every combination of sour, sweet, bitter, salty, and savory that the chefs on the Food Network can discover. Because that's what they are doing: discovering all the ways that God chose to communicate his goodness, his sweetness, even his bitterness to human palates. My guess is that it'll take a while.

The creation of food, tongues, and the human digestive system is the product of infinite wisdom knitting the world together in a harmonious whole. The symphony of glory that sounds from the triune being contains notes of corn salsa and Sour Patch Kids, of sweet tea and rye bread (the kind that fills the belly). The variety of tastes creates categories and gives us edible images of divine things. "Taste and see that the LORD is good!" (Ps. 34:8). Our sense of hunger and thirst are divinely designed to highlight the soul's hunger for spiritual food: "Whoever comes to me shall not hunger, and whoever believes in me shall never thirst" (John 6:35). And there's no shortcut. Apart from our experience of empty stomachs and parched throats, of full bellies, quenched thirsts, and the incredible variety of taste, our spiritual lives would be impoverished, and we would have no real vocabulary for spiritual desire, no mental and emotional framework for engaging with God.

So then, the provision and supply of food and drink, along with the corresponding senses and systems to receive them bodily, are a gift from God, a testimony to his approval of our finitude and embodiment. But God's approval of our limitations in Genesis 2 hasn't yet reached its apex.

First Words

> Then the LORD God said, "It is not good that the man should be alone; I will make him a helper fit for him." Now out of the ground the LORD God had formed every beast of the field and every bird of the heavens and brought them to the man to see what he would call them. And whatever the man called every living creature, that was its name. The man gave names to all livestock and to the birds of the heavens and to every beast of the field. But for Adam there was not found a helper fit for him. (Gen. 2:18–20)

Five and a half days of "And God saw that it was good," and now, "not good." God sees something missing, a gap in his creation that must be filled. But let's just start with the obvious: when God says that it's not good for man to be alone, it would have been entirely inappropriate for

Adam to say, "What do you mean 'alone'? I have you, God." That's absolutely true—and completely beside the point.

Adam's solitude (even with God as his companion) is a defect, and God in his goodness acts to remedy this lack. Note this: *God acts. God meets the need. God* gives life and breath and all things (including companionship). But God has designed us so that *he* would meet some of our needs *through other people*. We ought not dispute with God on this point. There's no virtue in being more spiritual than he is here. Infinite wisdom directed him to mediate his all-satisfying presence to us through suitable *created* companions.[5]

And note that word *suitable*. God is not content with any old companion. He will provide a helper "fit" for man. Elephants are impressive, but they aren't a good fit. Bunnies are cute but not as companions. A dog may be man's best friend, but God will not rest until he's exceeded loyalty and slobber. And if a suitable helper cannot be found among the living creatures, then God will build a new one:

> So the LORD God caused a deep sleep to fall upon the man, and while he slept took one of his ribs and closed up its place with flesh. And the rib that the LORD God had taken from the man he made into a woman and brought her to the man. (Gen. 2:21–22)

God put Adam into a deep, death-like sleep. And while in that sleep, Adam lost something, a rib from his side. But he awoke to the stunning reality that he had not lost anything at all. This was better. This was fitting. This exceeded all expectations. Being raised up, he had moved from one degree of glory to another.

And the glory of the creation of Eve was not lost on Adam. Genesis 2:23 contains the first recorded *human* words in the Scriptures. Adam had spoken previously (naming the animals and, presumably, conversing with God). But we have not heard his voice until now.

Then the man said,

> "This at last is bone of my bones
> and flesh of my flesh;

she shall be called Woman,
    because she was taken out of Man." (v. 23)

Adam is a poet, and his first recorded words are a poem, an encomium, a hymn of praise—*the object of which is another creature*. Don't
misunderstand me. I'm not suggesting that Adam is committing idolatry.
(May it never be!) But I think we should let the significance of this event
land on us. Adam beholds this helper, this other, this being who is like
him but not him, and out of the overflow of the heart, his mouth speaks.
He gazes on his bride in all her glory and without a shred of idolatry
composes an ode *to her*:

> You come from me, but you are not me. Your bones were built from
> my bones. Your flesh was cut from my flesh. We are alike, but differ-
> ent. We are the same, but sundered. God has torn me in two, only to
> put me together again. He removed from me a rib so that he might
> return it with interest. He has divided me from myself so that soli-
> tary unity might give way to complementary union. What name will
> express this? I am *Adam*, formed by Yahweh from the ground [Heb.
> *adamah*]. You then shall be Woman [Heb. *ishshah*] because you were
> taken out of Man [Heb. *ish*].

Adam is not turning away from his love for God; this is what love for
God looks like when it meets one of his gifts. Adam has found a wife.
He has found a good thing. This is favor from the Lord, and he must
express it. The shaft of the glory strikes his sensibility, and he (slowly
and deliberately) chases the beam back to the source, savoring the gift
for the sake of the giver.

Our Vocation and Mission

Thus far, we've seen that the creator God has lavished us with gifts for
our enjoyment and pleasure. Sight, sound, taste, touch, and smell—all
these are given for our delight. Friends and family, spouse and neighbor—given to us that we might not be lonely, that we might find divine
fulfillment in created companions. But if this was all that we saw, we
would be missing the full picture of God's wisdom and grace. In these

early chapters of Genesis, gifts are not merely for our enjoyment; gifts are provision for mission.

Before seeing the provision, we must first understand the mission. And we can grasp the mission by coming to understand what it means to be made in God's image. Some theologians argue that we should understand man's identity as God's image bearer in terms of our capacities and abilities. Thus, being made in God's image means that we have the ability to reason or speak or relate to God and others. While these capacities are no doubt important, I agree with those scholars who see bearing God's image fundamentally in terms of man's function and calling.[6] Being made in God's image is a vocation, something that we are called by God to do and to be. In the opening chapters of Genesis (and in line with the rest of the Scriptures), man's vocation consists in three primary roles: priest, king, and prophet.

In Genesis 2:15, the Lord God puts the man in the garden "to work it and keep it." These two words appear together again in Numbers 3:5–10, where they describe the duties of the Levites with respect to the tabernacle. In that context, working and keeping include the responsibility to minister and guard the sanctuary. Thus, we ought to see the call to work, keep, guard, and cultivate the garden as evidence of man's priestly vocation. Man is *homo adorans,* man worshiping, called to hear and obey the word of God and then to worship God rightly while guarding and protecting sacred space from unclean encroachments (say, for example, a dragon who tries to undermine the word of God).[7]

In addition to his priestly call, man is also called to be a king. God's commission in Genesis 1:28 highlights Adam and Eve's royal vocation:

> And God blessed them. And God said to them, "Be fruitful and multiply and fill the earth and *subdue* it and *have dominion* over the fish of the sea and over the birds of the heavens and over every living thing that moves on the earth."

The call to have dominion is a call to exercise wise rule over God's world as his vice-regent. Man is an under-king, a steward of God's creation, charged with establishing God's rule and reign over the unsubdued earth. Thus, not only is man called to protect sacred space, but man is called to extend sacred space, so that the earth is filled with God's glory through a glorious society of his image bearers. To accomplish this task, man will need God's wisdom, and thus man is *homo sapiens,* the wise man. Adam is a royal priest, a priestly king, and he must represent and reflect God's character and rule to the rest of creation.

Man's final vocation is prophet, as indicated by his call to name the animals and to name his wife (Gen. 2:19–20). Man is *homo loquens,* speaking man, and God has granted him authority to use his creativity and imagination to shape and mold the world in accordance with God's word and character. Therefore, as prophet, man is called to name God's world by first obeying and knowing God and then joining God in the ongoing construction of God's glorious temple-city.

Summing up, in the early chapters of Genesis, to be made in God's image is to fulfill our vocation as obedient priests, wise kings, and faithful prophets. This is our mission, given to us by our good and holy creator—to be fruitful and multiply and fill the world, to subdue the earth and exercise dominion over its creatures, to cultivate the land, work the ground, and keep and guard the garden from all evil and uncleanness, and to image God by obediently echoing his words and faithfully naming his world.

Gifts as Provision for Mission

Grasping man's original calling enables us to see more deeply into God's purposes in lavishing us with gifts. Yes, food is given to us for enjoyment, to enlarge our categories for knowing God. But food is also God's way of providing us with energy and strength for work. When we eat, our bodies transform what we've consumed so that we will have strength to fulfill our calling. As the psalmist says, God gives "bread to strengthen man's heart" (Ps. 104:15). Thus, when God grants Adam permission to eat from every tree (Gen. 1:29; 2:16), we should also hear him saying, "You have been called to subdue the earth. You have been commissioned to take dominion. You must work this ground and protect this garden. To do so, you will need strength. You will need power and energy to sustain your labors. In a word, you will need food. Therefore, eat from every tree."

The same is true of God's provision of a wife. Yes, God's gift of Eve meets Adam's need for companionship. But the woman is also necessary to complete God's mission. Adam cannot be fruitful, multiply, and fill the earth all by his lonesome. He will need help (Gen. 2:18). As every eight-year-old knows, "First comes love, then comes marriage, then comes the baby in the baby carriage." God has given us a mission to fill the earth with worshipers, so that his praise resounds from every corner of the globe. Therefore, he gives Adam a wife so that together they might produce godly offspring, and, extending the larger point, he gives all of us friends, family, and neighbors that we might aid one another in filling the earth with his glory as the water covers the sea.

In fact, the same is true of all of God's gifts. All of them have been given to us, not only that we might enjoy them but so that they might prove fruitful in our lives. This includes those capacities and abilities that we mentioned earlier. We have been given eyes that we might see God displaying his beauty in the world, ears that we might hear God singing his grace in the world, a nose that we might smell the sweet aroma of God's life in the world, a tongue that we might taste God's splendor in the world, lips that we might tell of God's triumphs in the world, hands that we might lift them in worship of God and service to others, feet that we might venture out into God's world and extend his dominion to the ends of the earth. We have been given minds and hearts that think and reason and feel and will that we might enjoy them and employ them in the greatest of causes.

Do We Have Intrinsic Value?

Recognizing the biblical value of creation for our enjoyment and for the fulfillment of God's mission is a glorious thing. But it's precisely the obvious value and worth of creation that creates some of the tensions we feel when it comes to valuing God. For if creation is valuable, then it has the potential to become a substitute for God—in biblical terms, an idol. Therefore, we must take some time to reflect on the question of creation's value and worth, especially in relation to the worth and value of the triune God. We'll begin with human beings. People often claim that human beings have intrinsic value. But is this a biblical way to think? Do we human beings have inherent and intrinsic value?

The answer depends on what we mean by *inherent* and *intrinsic*. If we mean autonomous value, value that exists independently of God, then the answer must surely be no. We have nothing apart from God. We are created ex nihilo, from nothing. He gives to all things, life and breath and everything else (Acts 17:25), including value. "What do you have that you did not receive?" Paul asks (1 Cor. 4:7). Therefore, we must reject any notion of autonomous human worth, worth that is unrelated to God and ignores the fact that we are created from nothing.

On the other hand, if by intrinsic value we mean having value as a permanent and essential characteristic, then it seems that we should say, "Yes, human beings do have inherent and intrinsic value." We are valuable *because* God values us. Our worth is wholly derived from God's creation of us ("Let us make . . .") and his approval of us ("And God saw that it was very good"). It comes from outside of us, but it really comes to us. Our value is really there because God really put it there (and continues to put it there as long as he speaks us into existence). So perhaps we can say that human beings (and every other part of creation) have derivative, inherent value. It's derived because it's a gift from God. And it's inherent because when God gives something, he really gives it.[8]

Value Things according to Their Value

The discussion of intrinsic value transitions nicely into the question of how much we should value creation in relation to God. Do we value all things—whether wife or food or God—equally? Most Christians would say, "No, we should not value all things equally. We should value things according to their worth." Theologians and philosophers call this the principle of proportionate regard. Put simply, it means that we should value, esteem, and regard things in proportion to their value, nature, and worth. Our *subjective* sense of something's value should accord with its *objective* worth.

We all recognize that something is amiss if a man neglects his wife in order to play golf all the time. Or if a mother considers the cleanliness of her kitchen of more importance than the health and happiness of her children. We correct children who value their toys more than their siblings. Jesus himself endorses this principle when he asks, "Are not two sparrows sold for a penny? And not one of them will fall to the ground apart from your Father. But even the hairs of your head are all numbered. Fear not, therefore; you are of more value than many sparrows" (Matt. 10:29–31).[9] All of us operate in terms of a scale of values, however vague and imprecise it may be. People are more important than property. Family is more important than hobbies. And, if we're seeking to be faithful to Scripture, God is more important than everything else.[10]

Jonathan Edwards articulates this principle as clearly as anyone has: "The moral rectitude of [the] heart consists in paying the respect or regard of the heart which is due, or which fitness and suitableness requires."[11] A right heart, a holy heart consists in valuing and treasuring things appropriately. Edwards's main concern is to evaluate how much we should value creation in relation to God.

> To determine, then, what proportion of regard is to be allotted to the Creator, and all his creatures taken together, both must be as it were put in the balance; the Supreme Being, with all in him that is great, considerable, and excellent, is to be estimated and compared with all that is to be found in the whole creation: and according as the former is found to outweigh, in such proportion is he to have a greater share of regard.[12]

Put all of creation on one side of a scale and put God on the other. Which is heavier? And by how much?

Edwards argues that holiness (both for God and creatures) consists in valuing God supremely above all other things, and that even God operates according to this principle.

> And therefore if God esteems, values, and has respect to things according to their nature and proportions, he must necessarily have the greatest respect to himself. It would be against the perfection of his nature, his wisdom, holiness, and perfect rectitude, whereby he is disposed to do everything that is fit to be done, to suppose otherwise. . . . Hence it will follow that the moral rectitude and fitness of the disposition, inclination or affection of God's heart does chiefly consist in a respect or regard to himself infinitely above his regard to all other beings: or in other words, *his holiness consists in this.*[13]

Or, put simply, "He values and loves things accordingly, as they are worthy to be valued and loved."[14]

Edwards expresses this principle again in terms of his aim in preaching:

> I should think myself in the way of my duty to raise the affections of my hearers as high as I possibly can, provided that they are affected with nothing but truth, and with affections that are not disagreeable to the nature of what they are affected with.[15]

Piper concurs with Edwards on this point and restates it in this way:

> Some truths are worth a little bit of emotion like, "We are going to have one amazing meal in a minute!" That's worth a little emotion. That "God rules over your life and loves you and gave his Son to die for you and will take you into his everlasting fellowship forever and ever," is worth ten thousand times more emotion than what this meal will produce for us.[16]

The Challenge of the Principle of Proportionate Regard

Now, I wholeheartedly affirm the principle of proportionate regard. I believe that God *does* operate according to it, and that we *must* operate according to it.[17] I've taught it for years in my classes and sought to apply it in my own life in relation to God, my family, my job, and my hobbies. But we must not be unaware of the practical problems that the principle of proportionate regard can cause for us as creatures.

Here is the fundamental challenge: if we believe that we should value things according to their value, and if we know that God has infinite value and everything else has finite value, then we begin to feel that, if we are to be faithful Christians, there must be an infinite gap between our love for God and our love for everything else. Our enjoyment of God must infinitely surpass our joy in his gifts (in our family, for example).

But notice the practical result of this reasoning. When we experience deep joy in an evening out with our spouse or a fun day at the park with the kids, and we compare it to the joy that we have in direct communion with God, then a subtle sense of guilt arises because we know that our joy in Christ (however great it may be) is not *infinitely* greater than our joy in our family. We're not even sure what infinite joy would feel like, but we know that we fall short. The result is that we may seek to distance ourselves from our family and minimize our enjoyment of creation *all in the name of holiness.*

We may never even articulate the problem in these words. But embracing the principle of proportionate regard can lead us to operate primarily in terms of a comparison of our delight in God and our delight in other things. And given our experience, we always come up short.

Now there are a number of false and unbiblical notions in this application of the principle of proportionate regard. The first is viewing love for God and love for creation exclusively in comparative terms. Might there be another way to relate God and creation? I'll return to this in the next chapter. For the moment I want to address a more fundamental question: Should we seek to love God infinitely?

Should We Seek to Love God Infinitely?

For some, the logic of an affirmative answer is obvious. God has infinite value. We should value things according to their value. Therefore, we should value God infinitely. But the simplicity of the logic masks a fundamental misunderstanding of what it means to be a creature.

As creatures, we never do *anything* infinitely. To be a creature is to be finite and limited. We have no infinite capacity for anything. To seek to love God infinitely is to place upon ourselves an impossible burden. And the impossibility is not owing to our sinfulness but to our creatureliness. If failure to love God infinitely is a sin, then we are condemned, not as sinners but as creatures. And one of the primary aims of this book is to put to death all false guilt flowing from our existence as creatures.[18]

The burden of this chapter is to impress upon our minds the reality that finitude and limitations are not defects; they are designed. Meeting needs and giving joy *through creation* was God's idea, and despite the ways that we've misused and abused his good gifts, he hasn't rescinded the offer or the gifts.

Harping on this point is no minor thing. False guilt kills true joy and ruins us for fruitful ministry. Impossible obligations lead to constant failure and incurable guilt, which only serve to breed greater sin. Read that again. Impossible obligation. Constant failure. Incurable guilt. Greater sin.

In fact, to feel guilty for something that God does not regard as a sin is itself a sin. We ought to repent of our rebellion against our creaturely limitations. To erect a false standard of holiness is legalism, and the fact that we're failed Pharisees doesn't mitigate the sin.

What's the Alternative?

So what's the alternative to loving God infinitely? A few foundational Scriptures can show us the way. First, the first of the Ten Commandments.

> I am the LORD your God, who brought you out of the land of Egypt, out of the house of slavery. You shall have no other gods before me. (Ex. 20:2–3)

Next, the Great Commandment.

> And you shall love the Lord your God with all your heart and with all your soul and with all your mind and with all your strength. (Mark 12:30)

The first passage teaches that we should love God *supremely*;[19] the second, that we should love God *fully*. To love God supremely is to love him above all else, to place him at the pinnacle of our affections. "Thou, and Thou only, *first* in my heart."[20] God will brook no rival in our affections. He must be supreme. To love God fully is to max out our capacity with love for him. Whatever capacity we have to love, be it with heart, soul, mind, or strength, we should give God our all.[21]

This is no minor distinction. Finite creatures are naturally incapable of loving God infinitely. But we do have the natural ability to love him supremely and to love him fully. We can place him at the center of our affections, and we can value him with everything we've got. Our sin and depravity may prevent us from loving God in these ways, but our existence as creatures does not.

What's more, a supreme and full love for God does not negate our love for other people. The Great Commandment (Love God *fully*) leads straight into the second greatest: love your neighbor as yourself. Much more can be said, but for the moment it's enough to note that according to Jesus, love for neighbor is not at odds with full love for God. In fact, love for neighbor is what love for God looks like when it meets neighbors.

And I believe this principle can be extended beyond neighbors to every other good thing that God provides. What does full and supreme love for God look like when it meets one of his gifts? Glad reception and enjoyment of his gifts. Delight in Eve is what full and supreme love for God looks like when it meets Eve. Grateful enjoyment of fish tacos is what supreme love for God looks like when it eats fish tacos. Robust pleasure in church softball is what supreme love for God looks like when it plays church softball. Delight in people and love for people is what supreme and full love for God looks like when it meets people.

But we can say more about the biblical call of love for God. Our love for God should be supreme, full, *and expanding*. Paul prays for the Philippians that their "love may abound *more and more*" (Phil. 1:9). Paul prays for and commends the Thessalonians for their increasing love for each other. "May the Lord make you *increase and abound in love* for one another and for all" (1 Thess. 3:12). "We ought always to give thanks to God for you, brothers, as is right, because your faith is growing abundantly, and the *love of every one of you for one another is increasing*" (2 Thess. 1:3). How much more should our love for God be increasing and expanding.

Edwards expresses his belief in our ever-increasing capacity to know, love, and enjoy God.

> There are many reasons to think that what God has in view, in an increasing communication of himself through eternity, is an *increasing* knowledge of God, love to him, and joy in him.[22]

This ever-increasing knowledge, love, and joy solves the problem posed by our need to love God infinitely because of his infinite worth. The only way for a finite creature to fulfill any kind of infinite obligation is to fully fulfill it *forever*. In other words, eternity can resolve the problem of infinite love. Edwards leads us in this direction. Taking his cue from Jesus's prayer in John 17:21–23, he argues that our union with

God will increase and grow more and more strict throughout eternity. Jesus prays,

> I do not ask for these only, but also for those who will believe in me through their word, that they may all be one, just as you, Father, are in me, and I in you, that they also may be in us, so that the world may believe that you have sent me. The glory that you have given me I have given to them, that they may be one even as we are one, I in them and you in me, that they may become perfectly one, so that the world may know that you sent me and loved them even as you loved me. (John 17:20–23)

Here is Edwards on this remarkable passage (it's worth the effort it takes to read it, so take your time):

> And it is to be considered that the more those divine communications *increase* in the creature, the more it becomes one with God; for so much the more is it united to God in love, the heart is drawn nearer and nearer to God, and the union with him becomes more firm and close, and at the same time, the creature becomes more and more *conformed* to God. The image is more and more perfect, and so the good that is in the creature comes forever nearer and nearer to an identity with that which is in God. In the view therefore of God, who has a comprehensive prospect of the increasing union and conformity through eternity, it must be an infinitely strict and perfect nearness, conformity, and oneness. For it will forever come nearer and nearer to that strictness and perfection of union which there is between the Father and the Son. So that in the eyes of God, who perfectly sees the whole of it, in its infinite progress and increase, it must come to an eminent fulfillment of Christ's request, in John 17:21, 23. *That they all may be ONE*, as thou Father art in me, and I in thee, that they also may be ONE in us; I in them and thou in me, that they may be made perfect in ONE.[23]

The final quotation of John 17 reinforces what we saw in chapter 1 about God's goal in creation. God intends to extend his perichoretic indwelling to us. We are being ushered into a union with God that will come ever closer to the perfect union of the Father and the Son. The pattern of our union with God is the Father's perichoretic union with the Son (the Father is in the Son, and the Son is in the Father). Indeed, the goal is that we would be *in* them in the same way—the Son in us and the Father in the Son—and that this union would increase until it is perfect.

This is what it means to be a creature: finite, temporal, limited, but very good, with needs met both directly by God and through the manifold gifts that he supplies. We are God's priests, his kings (and queens), and his prophets, and he has lavished us with gifts beyond our imagining, both for our glad-hearted enjoyment and for the fulfillment of his great and glorious mission. We are valuable because God values us, and we ought to value him according to his value. Nevertheless, we banish every form of false guilt that condemns us for being creatures and for failing to love God infinitely. Instead, our love for God should be supreme, full, and expanding forever.

5

The Gospel
Solution to Idolatry

Every breath we take, every time our heart beats, every day
that the sun rises, every moment we see with our eyes or hear
with our ears or speak with our mouths or walk with our legs
is, for now, a free and undeserved gift to sinners who deserve
only judgment.

John Piper

To this point, I've been largely ignoring two great challenges to the vision of the Christian life that I'm commending in this book. No doubt,
thoughtful and attentive readers have had pressing questions since chapter 1, the kind of questions with Bible verses attached to them. It's time
to address some of those questions head-on.

The first challenge to this vision of the triune God, the world, and
human beings is the glaring reality of sin, rebellion, and idolatry. It's all
well and good to celebrate God's original design for human beings and
his good gifts, but we live east of Eden, on the far side of the fall, the side
where abuse and misuse of God's good gifts are pervasive and rampant.
It's true that our hearts are desire factories by God's design, but we have
turned them into idol factories, churning out false worship like it's our
job. We are rebels to our back teeth, and we don't receive one good thing
from God that we don't erect into a monument of false worship.

Because of our pervasive sinfulness, the Bible contains numerous warnings and exhortations about the danger of creation, the world, and God's good gifts. For instance:

> *Do not love the world or the things in the world.* If anyone loves the world, the love of the Father is not in him. For all that is in the world—the desires of the flesh and the desires of the eyes and pride of life—is not from the Father but is from the world. And the world is passing away along with its desires, but whoever does the will of God abides forever. (1 John 2:15–17)

> For Demas, *in love with this present world*, has deserted me and gone to Thessalonica. (2 Tim. 4:10)

> You adulterous people! *Do you not know that friendship with the world is enmity with God?* Therefore whoever wishes to be a friend of the world makes himself an enemy of God. (James 4:4)

> If then you have been raised with Christ, seek the things that are above, where Christ is, seated at the right hand of God. *Set your minds on things that are above, not on things that are on earth.* For you have died, and your life is hidden with Christ in God. (Col. 3:1–3)

The second challenge arises from certain absolutist passages in the Bible, passages that indicate that we should desire *only* God.

> *One thing* have I asked of the LORD,
>   that will I seek after:
> that I may dwell in the house of the LORD
>   all the days of my life,
> *to gaze upon the beauty of the LORD*
>   and to inquire in his temple. (Ps. 27:4)

> *Whom have I in heaven but you?*
>   *And there is nothing on earth that I desire besides you.*
> My flesh and my heart may fail,
>   but God is the strength of my heart and my portion forever.
>   (Ps. 73:25–26)

The *one* thing we ask is to gaze upon God's beauty. The *only* thing we desire, on earth and in heaven, is God, who is our portion forever. Of course, these exclusively God-centered passages are complicated by other sections of Scripture:

> As for the rich in this present age, charge them not to be haughty, nor to set their hopes on the uncertainty of riches, but on God, *who richly provides us with everything to enjoy.* (1 Tim. 6:17)

> So let no one boast in men. For *all things are yours*, whether Paul or Apollos or Cephas or the world or life or death or the present or the future—all are yours, and you are Christ's, and Christ is God's. (1 Cor. 3:21–23)

How then should we relate to God's gifts? Should we enjoy *everything* that God richly provides? Or should we desire *only* God? Wrestling with these questions is at the heart of living the faithful Christian life.

Two Ways of Viewing God's Relationship to His Gifts

My suggestion is that the Bible provides us with two complementary ways of viewing God's relationship to his gifts. The first is a comparative approach, in which God and his gifts are separated and set next to each other to determine which is more valuable. In the comparative view, we put God on one side of the scales and his gifts on the other to see which is weightier, more valuable, more glorious. When we do, we say with Isaiah:

> Behold, the nations are like a drop from a bucket,
>   and are accounted as the dust on the scales;
>   behold, he takes up the coastlands like fine dust . . .
> All the nations are as nothing before him,
>   they are accounted by him as less than nothing and emptiness.
>   (Isa. 40:15–17)

Compared to God, the entire creation is nothing but dust. Called into existence out of nothing, its value, as we saw in the last chapter, is nothing apart from God's valuing of it. In his treatise on God's ultimate goal in creation, Edwards asks what an infinitely wise judge would determine if the creator was set on one side of the scale and the rest of creation was set on the other side of the scale:

> To determine then, what proportion of regard is to be allotted to the creator, and all his creatures taken together, both must be as it were put in the balance; the Supreme Being, with all in him, that is great, considerable, & excellent, is to be estimated and compared with all that is to be found in the whole creation: And according as the former is found to out-weigh, in such proportion is he to have a greater share of regard. And in this case, as the whole system of created beings in comparison of the creator, would be found as the light dust of the balance (which is taken notice of by him that weighs) and as nothing and vanity; so the arbiter must determine accordingly with respect to the degree in which God should be regarded by all intelligent existence, and the degree in which he should be regarded in all that is done through the whole universal system.[1]

Because the whole system of creation is as nothing and vanity compared to the infinitely glorious creator, if we are thinking comparatively, then we should *desire only God* and not his gifts. He is worthy of all regard, all value, all love and delight and affection.

Paul clearly expresses the comparative approach in Philippians 3:

> But whatever gain I had, I counted as loss for the sake of Christ. Indeed, I count everything as loss because of the surpassing worth of knowing Christ Jesus my Lord. For his sake I have suffered the loss of all things and count them as rubbish, in order that I may gain Christ and be found in him, not having a righteousness of my own that comes from the law, but that which comes through faith in Christ, the righteousness from God that depends on faith—that I may know him and the power of his resurrection, and may share his sufferings, becoming like him in his death, that by any means possible I may attain the resurrection from the dead. (Phil. 3:7–11)

Compared to the worth of knowing Christ, every benefit that Paul had—his ethnicity, upbringing, moral efforts, and every other good thing—was considered loss and rubbish. Elsewhere Paul highlights the advantages of the Jews (Rom. 3:1), makes use of his Roman citizenship (Acts 22:25), and, as we've seen, commends the enjoyment of God's gifts (1 Tim. 6:17). But abstracted from the triune God and considered comparatively, they are in effect worthless.

The second approach is the integrated approach. We've explored aspects of it in the previous chapters, so I'll simply summarize it here. When we love God supremely and fully, we are able to integrate our joy in God and our joy in his gifts, receiving the gifts as shafts of his glory. Supreme love for God orients our affections and orders our desires and integrates our loves. When we love God supremely, we are free to love creation as creation (and not as God). Because the divine excellence is really present in the gift, we are free to enjoy it for his sake. God's gifts become avenues for enjoying him, beams of glory that we chase back to the source. We don't set God and his gifts in opposition to each other, as though they are rivals. Instead, in the words of Charles Simeon, we "enjoy God in everything and everything in God."[2] Or as Augustine prayed, "He loves thee too little, who loves anything together with thee, which he loves not for thy sake."[3]

Integrated Lives, Comparative Tests

It's not enough to distinguish these two ways of relating God to his gifts; we must also know how to relate the two approaches to each other. My contention, based on the overwhelming biblical evidence for the goodness of creation and its capacity to lead us deeper in the knowledge of God, is that the integrated approach is how we should live the bulk of our lives, and the comparative approach is a test to ensure that we maintain supreme and full love for God.

The comparative test often takes the form of self-denial or suffering. The loss of good gifts, whether willingly given up in the cause of love or painfully taken in some tragedy, is a test of where our ultimate treasure truly lies (more on this in chapters 8–10). The problem comes when we become permanent test takers, refusing to receive all that God richly provides out of fear of committing idolatry.

Perhaps an illustration can make the distinction clear. My favorite dessert is pumpkin crunch cake, an autumn delight that my wife makes. It's the kind of dessert that can become a meal replacement—breakfast, lunch, or dinner. I'm normally a fairly open-handed person when it comes to sharing what's mine, but pumpkin crunch cake is an exception. The words "Get your own" come to mind.

Now in extolling the sweetness of the pumpkin filling, or the crispiness of the topping, or the crunchiness of the walnuts mingled throughout, it's possible that I could come to love the dessert more than my wife. The cake and my bride could be rivals, competing for my affection. However, sweets versus spouse is not the only option. If my enjoyment of the cake is real and deep and satisfying, and if it issues forth in praise of my wife, appreciation for her efforts, and acts of love (like doing some dishes), then my love for the cake is no threat to my love for her. She wants me to enjoy the pumpkin goodness; that's why she made it! In fact, my enjoyment of the dessert serves and increases my love for her. The enjoyment of one doesn't cancel out the other; instead, they overlap and mutually indwell one another (there's perichoresis again), and my wife is honored as a fantastic cook and a wonderful spouse in my enjoyment of her culinary creation.

Thus, it's entirely appropriate, when confronted with tremendous gifts, to periodically compare love for the gifts and love for the giver. It's good to be reminded that the giver—God—is ultimate. But then, once the supremacy of the giver is settled, the right and fitting response is to dive back into the pumpkin crunch cake and enjoy every last bite.

Where Should We Set Our Minds?

This movement—from comparative test to integrated life—is precisely how we should resolve the tension created by biblical passages that command us not to set our mind on the things of earth. In the introduction, I highlighted Colossians 3:1–4 and Philippians 3:19 as two such passages. We're now in a position to consider them more fully.

> If then you have been raised with Christ, seek the things that are above, where Christ is, seated at the right hand of God. Set your minds on things that are above, not on things that are on earth. For

you have died, and your life is hidden with Christ in God. When Christ who is your life appears, then you also will appear with him in glory. (Col. 3:1–4)

Given the objective reality that God has united us to the risen Christ, how should we live? What should we seek? Where should we set our minds? On "things that are above, *not* on things that are on earth." Heavenly things. High things. Holy things. Not earthly things. But here's the key question: in this passage, what are these earthly things? The next verses tell us:

Put to death therefore what is *earthly* in you: sexual immorality, impurity, passion, evil desire, and covetousness, which is idolatry. On account of these the wrath of God is coming. (Col. 3:5–6)

Earthly here means something like "sinful" or "fleshly." It refers to idolatry and all the rebellious acts that flow from it. The key to grasping Paul's meaning perhaps lies in the word translated "set your mind upon." It's the Greek word *phroneo*, which means to direct your ultimate attention and affection to something. When you set your mind on something, you orient your life by it. Your mind-set guides and governs everything else you do, whether in thoughts or words or deeds.

Therefore, to set one's mind on the things that are below is to elevate the gifts above the giver.[4] It is to have our lives oriented by something other than the triune God. This is essentially to fail the comparative test. But once we put to death these sinful things, once we set our minds on Christ above, what should we do? In other words, what does a heavenly mind-set actually look like?

Paul's exhortations in the rest of Colossians provide a beautiful portrait: put on humility and meekness like a new robe (3:12); be patient and forgive each other (v. 13); wear your love on your sleeve and watch it compose a symphony (v. 14); put peace on the throne of your heart; be thankful (v. 15). Make the Scriptures at home in your soul. Teach and sing them to each other with thankfulness in your heart (v. 16); do everything in the name of Jesus. And did I mention give thanks to God (v. 17)?

Wives, submit to your husbands (v. 18); husbands, love your wives

(v. 19). Children, obey your parents; it makes God happy (v. 20). Fathers, don't provoke your children; that doesn't make God happy (v. 21).

Are you under authority? Then obey those over you sincerely because you fear God (v. 22). Do your work with gusto, because God will reward you (vv. 23–24). Are you in authority? Then be just and fair to those in your care, because you have a boss in heaven (4:1). Pray without ceasing. And, seriously, did I mention be grateful (v. 2)? Pray that the missionaries would be fruitful and bold (vv. 3–4). Show the world how the wise walk by taking time away from the Devil (v. 5). Use salty language, the kind that gives grace (v. 6).

A mind that is set on the things above spends an awful lot of time thinking about things on the earth. Family, neighbors, church, job, earthly responsibilities—the person governed by heavenly things intentionally and deliberately considers and engages them. The heavenly mind-set is profoundly earthy, but it is fundamentally oriented by the glory of Christ.

So then, in Colossians 3 and 4, Paul is teaching us that we must not orient our lives by earthly things. This is idolatry and produces all manner of sinfulness. Instead, we must orient our lives by the things above, by Christ, by the hope of glory. But once we've oriented our lives by Christ, then we spend considerable time and attention on living in the world and engaging with the things of earth. We set our minds on things above, and then we live integrated, earthly lives. We aim to love God supremely and fully, and then we love our neighbors as ourselves, as an expression of our highest love. As a result, our lives are suffused with gratitude, with music, with truth, and all of it governed by affections that are set on Christ, who is seated at God's right hand above.

Considering the Things of Earth from a Heavenly Mind-Set

We see this same pattern in Paul's letter to the Philippians. At the end of Philippians 3, Paul encourages us to follow his example and the example of those like him. He explains this by contrasting his own life with those who "walk as enemies of the cross of Christ" (v. 18). He describes them as those who are governed by their appetites ("their god is their belly") and whose minds are set on earthly things (v. 19). Paul again uses the word *phroneo* to describe this fundamental life orientation.

We've already seen that Paul passes the comparative test earlier in Philippians 3. His life is oriented and governed by the surpassing worth of knowing Christ Jesus. His mind is set on Christ, and therefore everything else is trash, comparatively speaking. This is the example that he calls us to follow.

Strikingly, however, even here in Philippians, he doesn't leave us merely with the comparative approach. In Philippians 4 he exhorts us to rejoice in the Lord (v. 4) and to pray with thanksgiving (v. 6). But his final exhortation wonderfully expresses the integrated life that flows from a heart and mind that is set on Christ:

> Finally, brothers, whatever is true, whatever is honorable, whatever is just, whatever is pure, whatever is lovely, whatever is commendable, if there is any excellence, if there is anything worthy of praise, think about these things. (v. 8)

Paul commands us to think about the good, the true, and the beautiful, wherever we find it. The word translated "think" is *logizomai*, and it often means "consider" or "regard." Putting the whole picture together, we ought to set our mind (*phroneo*) and orient our affections by things above, by Christ, and not by the things of earth. But with the supremacy of God firmly established in our hearts, we then move out to consider (*logizomai*) and think and engage with everything true and honorable and pure that God has made. We *set our minds* on things above and then *consider* what is good and lovely in things below.[5] The world is filled with excellent and praiseworthy things, and Paul unleashes us to pay attention to them, provided we do so from hearts and minds that receive their fundamental guidance from Christ on high.

Back to Idolatry

We're now in a position to grapple with the problem of human sin and idolatry. Idolatry begins with a false separation of gift and giver. Rather than a momentary comparison for the sake of testing our affections, idolatry is a permanent separation for the sake of false worship. God divides things in order to gloriously reunite them. Heaven and earth, male and female, Trinitarian glory and its created beams—all of these are separated in order to bring about a more perfect and glorious union.

On the other hand, sin just separates. It divides in order to destroy. It tears asunder and leaves the fragments scattered on the ground. The separation of gift from giver ruins our enjoyment of both. Lewis was fond of noting that if we put first things first, we get second things thrown in. If we put second things first, we lose both first and second things. Idolatry is insane precisely because it ruins the enjoyment of the gift that we've turned into a god.

Romans 1 is the paradigmatic passage in the Scriptures on idolatry. It's one of the fundamental reasons that I'm a Christian, since it describes and dissects my own heart and the world around me with such penetrating clarity. It's one of those passages that just rings true:

> For the wrath of God is revealed from heaven against all ungodliness and unrighteousness of men, who by their unrighteousness suppress the truth. For what can be known about God is plain to them, because God has shown it to them. For his invisible attributes, namely, his eternal power and divine nature, have been clearly perceived, ever since the creation of the world, in the things that have been made. So they are without excuse. For although they knew God, they did not honor him as God or give thanks to him, but they became futile in their thinking, and their foolish hearts were darkened. Claiming to be wise, they became fools, and exchanged the glory of the immortal God for images resembling mortal man and birds and animals and creeping things. Therefore God gave them up in the lusts of their hearts to impurity, to the dishonoring of their bodies among themselves, because they exchanged the truth about God for a lie and worshiped and served the creature rather than the Creator, who is blessed forever! Amen. (vv. 18–25)

God's wrath falls on unrighteous people because they suppress the obvious. The world resounds with God's excellence, testifying to his glorious reality. The created world makes God's invisible attributes visible. Not only are they overwhelmingly displayed in what God has made, they are clearly *perceived* by human beings. God has shown it to us; therefore, it is plain to us, so that we have no excuse for our rebellion.

There are two great sins at work in the world and in human hearts: idolatry and ingratitude. We refuse to honor God as God, and we refuse to say "thank you" for the abundance of goodness and kindness that he lavishes on us. Instead of thanksgiving, we turn God's gifts into gods, making a good thing into an ultimate thing.[6] We engage in a series of trades, exchanging God's glory for images and God's truth for a lie.

God's response is to give us exactly what we want, turning us over to our futile minds and lustful hearts. He delivers us up to our dark exchange, so that we now trade natural relations for unnatural, as we are filled up with all manner of wickedness, folly, and sin. Having been offered divine glory in and through God's good gifts, we worship and serve creation and plunge further into debauchery, disobedience, and destruction.

Edwards saw the destructive effects of this idolatrous exchange as clearly as anyone. Few passages have shaped my view of sin more than the following from his sermon "The Spirit of Charity the Opposite of a Selfish Spirit." I've broken it up to allow for clearer understanding.

> The ruin that the fall brought upon the soul of man consists very much in his losing the nobler and more benevolent principles of his nature, and falling wholly under the power and government of self-love. Before, and as God created him, he was exalted, and noble, and generous; but now he is debased, and ignoble, and selfish. Immediately upon the fall, the mind of man shrank from its primitive greatness and expandedness, to an exceeding smallness and contractedness; and as in other respects, so especially in this. Before, his soul was under the government of that noble principle of divine love, whereby it was enlarged to the comprehension of all his fellow creatures and their welfare. And not only so, but it was not confined within such narrow limits as the bounds of the creation, but went forth in the exercise of holy love to the Creator, and abroad upon the infinite ocean of good, and was, as it were, swallowed up by it, and became one with it.[7]

Before the fall, man was exalted, noble, and generous. Because he was governed by a supreme love for God, his heart was great and enlarged and expansive, so that he was able to take in all of God and all of his fellow creatures and their welfare. He was able to receive and enjoy all that God provided for him.

> But so soon as he had transgressed against God, these noble principles were immediately lost, and all this excellent enlargedness of man's soul was gone; and thenceforward he himself shrank, as it were, into a little space, circumscribed and closely shut up within itself to the exclusion of all things else. Sin, like some powerful astringent, contracted his soul to the very small dimensions of selfishness; and God was forsaken, and fellow creatures forsaken, and man retired within himself, and became totally governed by narrow and selfish principles and feelings. Self-love became absolute master of his soul, and the more noble and spiritual principles of his being took wings and flew away.[8]

Man's sin shrunk his soul. His heart shriveled and contracted under the influence of that powerful astringent. His capacity to know and love and enjoy God and his capacity to know and love and enjoy all of creation for God's sake was hopelessly lost. He gained the forbidden fruit but forfeited his soul, and with it the ability to enjoy anything rightly and fully.

Dealing with Idolatry

The heart of idolatry, then, is that we receive creation not as a gift but as a god. We set the creator and his creation in the scale of values and worship the gifts over the giver. Creation, rather than being a means of enjoying the creator, becomes his rival. We become fixated and entranced on God's good gifts, seeking in them something that we will never be able to find. Sex, food, approval, wealth, family, friends, job, nature, government—all of these become God's rivals. The potency and pleasure present in the world, cut off from its vibrant connection to the triune origin, becomes God's enemy and our death. Its power and capacity to delight us remains, but it now leads us down the wide road to destruction.

The idolatrous potential of God's good gifts remains even after we are born again. The warnings against false worship and worldliness in the New Testament give ample evidence of the abiding danger of idolatry for Christians. And the more wonderful the gift, the greater the danger.

Given the persistence of this threat to true worship of God, one way to address idolatry is to seek to thin out creation, to hold it loosely like a hot potato, and to be wary of its delights and pleasures. We recognize the potency of God's gifts, so we tread lightly, sticking to the shallows and refusing to plunge into the ocean of earthly pleasures.

This suspicion of creation can grow into an outright rejection of creation, a call for full abstinence from God's gifts (or at least certain gifts, usually those centered on bodily pleasures). Paul addresses this type of asceticism directly in Colossians 2:

> If with Christ you died to the elemental spirits of the world, why, as if you were still alive in the world, do you submit to regulations—"Do not handle, Do not taste, Do not touch" (referring to things that all perish as they are used)—according to human precepts and teachings? These have indeed an appearance of wisdom in promoting self-made religion and asceticism and severity to the body, but they are of no value in stopping the indulgence of the flesh. (vv. 20–23)

To pursue holiness by stiff-arming created pleasures appears wise. Ascetic religion and severity to the body may impress lots of people. But their value in promoting godliness is null. The reason should be obvious: sin is not in the stuff. Sin resides in human hearts, and thinning out creation just makes us thin idolaters. We exchange indulgent sins for ascetic ones, but rearranging the deck chairs on the Titanic doesn't alter the ship's path. The flesh is still steering the boat, and a true course correction will require something more fundamental than a rejection of God's gifts.

Paul's indictment of this approach to holiness is even stronger in 1 Timothy 4:

> Now the Spirit expressly says that in later times some will depart from the faith by devoting themselves to deceitful spirits and teachings of demons, through the insincerity of liars whose consciences are seared. (vv. 1–2)

Devoted to deceitful spirits. Embracing demonic teaching. Believing the lies of those whose consciences have been numbed and dulled to death. Sounds terrible, right? Like there might be sacrifices of goats and chicken blood involved? Perhaps some cultic prostitutes and Kool-Aid? What exactly would these false and demonic teachers say?

> . . . who forbid marriage and require abstinence from foods that God created to be received with thanksgiving by those who believe and know the truth. For everything created by God is good, and nothing is to be rejected if it is received with thanksgiving, for it is made holy by the word of God and prayer. (vv. 3–5)

Forbidding marriage (presumably because of the physical intimacy involved). Rejection of foods. This, Paul says, is demonic. Why? Because, as John Calvin wrote, "In despising the gifts, we insult the Giver."[9] Because God made chicken fried steak and Caesar salad and mashed potatoes and boiled lobster and dinner rolls and organic strawberries and Big Macs and fresh basil and Twinkies to be received with gratitude by those who embrace the truth.[10] Every bit of it is good, and none of it should be rejected, provided that thanksgiving, Scripture, and prayer are somehow involved in sanctifying it (more on this in the next chapter).[11]

The demonic scheme that Paul describes in this passage is as old as dirt. Demons love to depict God as miserly. In the last chapter we saw that God had endorsed Adam and Eve's enjoyment of every tree in the garden, except one. One no in a world full of yes. But when Satan approached Eve, he turned this reality on its head. "Did God actually say, 'You shall not eat of any tree in the garden'?" (Gen. 3:1). One no becomes a universal restriction. In the Serpent's mouth, God is not a father, but a forbidder, a cosmic killjoy who creates pleasures and then denies their indulgence.[12] The mark of the Serpent's lying theology is this denial and asceticism, and Paul teaches that we haven't seen the last of such deceitful doctrine. This is why he encourages Timothy to put such warnings and endorsements before the people. Christians need to be reminded of the goodness of creation and God's approval of it for our joy. Otherwise, we believe the Devil's lies and succumb to low-grade guilt every time we encounter the things of earth.

Examining Ourselves for Seeds of False Guilt

So we can't solve the sin and idolatry problem by rejecting the gifts outright. If we do, we simply move from being sensuous idolaters to foolish lackeys of the Devil. But most of us aren't about to become hermits living in the desert, far away from all possible temptations to indulge our appetites. We have no interest in becoming monks, and, therefore, the warnings in these two passages don't hit home.

However, while we may not be taking vows of celibacy or renouncing all food except moldy bread, I wonder if we haven't adopted a more subtle and insidious form of the same mentality. We still enjoy our hamburger and french fries, but we do so reluctantly, and perhaps with a tinge of guilt (especially if it really tastes good). We may not be actual monks, but have we adopted some sort of monastic standards, and then, because we fail to live up to them, we suffer from low-grade guilt that plagues us like, well, the plague?

If a rejection of God's goodness in creation is demonic, then might there not be more subtle forms of this temptation, schemes of the Devil that we should not be ignorant of? Ask yourself the following questions and probe the reasons for your answers:

1) Do I feel a low-grade sense of guilt because I enjoy legitimate earthly pleasures?
2) Is this guilt connected to any particular, concrete sinful attitude or action? Or is it rooted in a vague sense that I'm not enjoying God "enough" (whatever that means) or that I'm enjoying his gifts "too much"?
3) Am I attempting to detach from creation and God's gifts out of fear of idolatry, lest my love for them surpass my affections for him?
4) Am I overly suspicious of created things, looking at my delight in ice cream and sunny spring days and hugs from my spouse with a wary and skeptical eye, perpetually unsure whether they are too precious to me?
5) Do I have the sense that as I progress in holiness, my enjoyment of fresh raspberries and hiking in the mountains and an evening of games and laughter with old friends ought to diminish because I am becoming increasingly satisfied with God *alone*?

6) Do I regard certain activities such as prayer, worship, and Bible reading as inherently more holy and virtuous than other activities such as doing my job or listening to music or taking a nap?

My point is *not* that you shouldn't worry about the danger of idolatry. Far from it. Good gifts really can become distractions that keep us from communing with God. Idolatry isn't a game; it's a suicidal reality that wrecks our souls and awakens the wrath of a jealous God. My concern is that, in general, thinning out the gifts and rejecting the stuff, and suppressing our delight in created things, actually hinders our growth in grace and our ability to resist the pull of the Devil's lies. There is a crucial place for renunciation and self-denial in the Christian life, but before we get to it (in chapter 9), we must recognize that our sin problem is far deeper than the glory of God's gifts.

Thankfully, the gospel shows us a better way.

The Right Time to Reject the Fullness of the Lord

Before we look at the gospel answer to idolatry, it's important to note one type of situation in which abstaining from one of God's gifts is absolutely necessary. In 1 Corinthians 8–10 Paul addresses the question of whether Christians can eat meat that has been previously sacrificed to a pagan idol. Does the pagan ritual contaminate the food, rendering it unclean and unfit for saints to eat?

Paul's answer is an emphatic no! He says,

> Eat whatever is sold in the meat market without raising any question on the ground of conscience. For "the earth is the Lord's, and the fullness thereof." If one of the unbelievers invites you to dinner and you are disposed to go, eat whatever is set before you without raising any question on the ground of conscience. (1 Cor. 10:25–27)

Eat whatever is set before you because everything belongs to God. As Paul noted earlier in his letter, idols are nothing (8:4), and therefore they have no true ability to claim what has been made by God the Father and the Lord Jesus Christ (v. 5). Therefore, "food will not commend us to God. We are no worse off if we do not eat, and no better off if we do" (v. 8).

However, despite the carte blanche to eat whatever is put on your plate, Paul does envision two circumstances in which abstention is not merely encouraged but required. First, if, as a result of previous association with some idolatrous lifestyle, you're unable to disconnect the good gift from the evil practice, then you should abstain out of concern for your conscience (v. 7). Keeping gifts at arm's length is appropriate when a Christian has a particular weakness, a particular area of theological or moral immaturity. Such artificial boundaries are wisdom for the weak.

Of course, God's goal is that the weak grow stronger in grace and maturity, internalizing his standards, eating and digesting them so that they're written deeply on the heart and thus freeing us to celebrate the Lord and all of his fullness. Nevertheless, in the meantime (and it may be a lifetime), there may be circumstances where a weaker brother should not eat certain foods, drink certain beverages, listen to certain types of music, or enjoy some other legitimate pleasure because the created good is too bound up in their hearts with something wicked and idolatrous.

The second circumstance flows from the first. A stronger brother, who is fully convinced of the legitimacy of enjoying all of creation with gratitude to God, should gladly give up his right to partake of some good thing if he knows that his partaking will contribute to the defiling of a weaker brother's conscience (8:10–13; 10:28–30). Thus, the two things that can, in specific circumstances, trump enjoyment of legitimate, God-given pleasures are a concern for the integrity of one's own conscience and a sincere, sacrificial love for a weaker brother.

The Gospel, Creation, and Idolatry

Setting aside such particular circumstances, we turn now to see how the gospel addresses the challenge of creation, given that we are finite creatures in a world full of gifts, and rebellious sinners in a world full of potential idols.

First, the incarnation of Jesus Christ is the greatest endorsement of the abiding goodness of creation and its capacity for amplification, transformation, and glorification. "In him the whole fullness of deity dwells *bodily*" (Col. 2:9). Jesus did not come to deliver us from earthly existence. He didn't arrive to liberate us from sensible and physical realities. He came to destroy the works of the Devil, one of which (as Paul said) is the insinuation that God's good creation is hopelessly and irredeemably corrupted.

Second, Jesus succeeds where Adam fails. He is the true man, and unlike the first man, he stands against the Dragon's lies. He resists the siren song of the Serpent and comes out of his wilderness temptation filled with the Spirit and ready to launch the invasion of Canaan. Adam was the head of the human race, and his failure wrecked all his descendants, plunging them into legal guilt, corrupting sin, and unholy conduct. Jesus, as the head of the new humanity, passes the test and demonstrates what it means to be fully human. His faithful life of full and supreme and expanding love for God is essential for the salvation of sinners.

Third, on the cross, Christ draws to himself all of our idolatry and ingratitude, all of our glory exchange and sin, all of our guilt and rebellion, and he swallows it whole. And he swallows it by letting death swallow him. Christ is crucified so that we might be crucified with him (Gal. 2:20), so that we might be crucified to the world (Gal. 6:14). When Jesus died on the cross, all of those united to him by faith died to the old way of being human, the way of separating the gifts from the giver and worshiping and serving the creatures rather than the creator.

We died to the world through the cross of Christ so that we could live again by faith in the Son of God, who loved us and gave himself for us. He died so that we could live and that all of our enjoyment of God and his gifts might be a glorying, an exulting, a boasting in the cross (Gal. 6:14).[13]

Fourth, the resurrection of Jesus from the dead is the transformation of his humanity, the transition in his experience from living as a human being "according to the flesh" (Rom. 1:4) to being a human being glorified according to the Spirit. Jesus's perishable, human, natural body was sown in dishonor, in weakness. And it was raised imperishable, in glory, in power, as a spiritual body, that is, as a physical body transformed and enlivened by the Spirit of God (1 Cor. 15:42–44).[14]

Picture the scene in Jesus's tomb on that glorious morning. As his mangled body lay there, filling the small cave with the stench of death, in a moment, in the twinkling of an eye, the Spirit of the living God blew through that hall of corruption, and something happened that had never before been seen in human history. A new kind of life energized and transformed the fleshly body of Jesus of Nazareth. This was more than creation out of nothing; it was creation out of death. In that moment, God inaugurated his new creation. In that moment, the life and power and glory of the age to come invaded the present age of sin and flesh and death. In that moment, humanity was forever changed. There was now a new way to be human.

Fifth, after his resurrection, he walked with his disciples. He showed them his wounds. He broke bread and ate fish with them. And then he ascended into heaven in that glorified resurrection body, forever to dwell with God. There is a man on the throne of the universe. The mediator between God and man is "the *man* Christ Jesus" (1 Tim. 2:5). Fully man, fully God, and fully glorified. The resurrection and ascension of Jesus in a real, physical, human body proclaims not only that creation is good but that it is capable of being glorified. The physical is now deeply and irrevocably spiritual.

Sixth, through the preaching of the gospel, spiritually blind sinners are awakened to the glory of Christ in the gospel and to the glory of Christ everywhere else. Whereas in our fallen state we willfully suppress the truth and therefore are limited to seeing only created reality, when we are born again, our eyes are opened so that we now see beyond the created things to the divine glory that comes in and through them. We are liberated from our idolatrous enslavement to created things so that we can now freely and gladly and gloriously enjoy created things as the images and echoes and sensible shafts of divine glory that they really are.

Seventh, like Jesus, our ultimate hope is not a disembodied, immaterial existence in an invisible realm. We look and wait and long for the resurrection of the dead and the liberation of creation from its bondage to decay. Creation itself groans as it yearns to obtain the freedom of the glory of the children of God (Rom. 8:19–21). Our final destiny is the resurrection of our very physical but transformed bodies in a new heavens and a new earth. Heaven is earthy, and though we can't fully comprehend what God has in store for us, we can by the Spirit of God, through the Scriptures and God's gifts, have a foretaste of the goodness and power of the age to come.

Once again, Lewis gets it exactly right:

> To shrink back from all that can be called Nature into negative spiri-
> tuality is as if we ran away from horses instead of learning to ride.
> There is in our present pilgrim condition plenty of room (more room
> than most of us like) for abstinence and renunciation and mortifying
> our natural desires. But behind all asceticism the thought should
> be, "Who will trust us with the true wealth if we cannot be trusted
> even with the wealth that perishes?" Who will trust me with a spiri-
> tual body if I cannot control even an earthly body? These small and
> perishable bodies we now have were given to us as ponies are given
> to schoolboys. We must learn to manage: not that we may some day
> be free of horses altogether but that someday we may ride bareback,
> confident and rejoicing, those greater mounts, those winged, shin-
> ning and world-shaking horses which perhaps even now expect us
> with impatience, pawing and snorting in the King's stables. Not that
> the gallop would be of any value unless it were a gallop with the
> King; but how else—since He has retained His own charger—should
> we accompany Him?[15]

This then is the gospel's way of dealing with idolatry. Yes, there is
renunciation, but the pitch and goal of the gospel is the restoration of the
whole human being, including our engagement with God and his magnificent gifts. And this restoration of created joys in heaven reverberates
to our enjoyment now. In all of our present enjoyment of God's glorious
gifts, our hearts echo with the knowledge that the best is yet to come.

God has called us to love him supremely and fully and expansively.
He aims to fatten our souls that we might receive more of his glory and
fullness. And one of the main ways that he does this is through the divine
grace and glory mediated to us through his gifts. Every good and perfect
gift comes from the Father of lights (James 1:17). God knows how to give
good gifts to his children (Matt. 7:11).

But these gifts are dangerous, and the threat of idolatry is real, so we
say with Augustine,

> He loves Thee too little, who loves anything together with Thee,
> which he loves not for Thy sake.

But because these gifts are really and truly created shafts of divine glory, intended by God and restored in Christ as the necessary means for growing in our love and delight in God, we add an addendum, a sequel to Augustine's profound confession:

> He loves Thee too little, who enjoys not Thy gifts, which Thou hast given to enlarge our minds and expand our hearts and enrich our souls and increase our strength, that we might love Thee fully and supremely and expansively forever.

6

Rhythms of
Godwardness

You say grace before meals.
All right.
But I say grace before the play and the opera,
And grace before the concert and the pantomime,
And grace before I open a book,
And grace before sketching, boxing, walking, playing, dancing;
And grace before I dip the pen in the ink.

G. K. Chesterton

He's a hedonist at heart. All those fasts and vigils and stakes and crosses are only a facade. Or only like foam on the sea shore. Out at sea, out in His sea, there is pleasure, and more pleasure. He makes no secret of it; at His right hand are "pleasures for evermore." . . . He's vulgar, Wormwood. He has a bourgeois mind. He has filled His world with pleasures. There are things for humans to do all day long without His minding in the least—sleeping, washing, eating, drinking, making love, playing, praying, working. Everything has to be twisted before it's any use to us. We fight under cruel disadvantages. Nothing is naturally on our side.

Screwtape

Christian Hedonism is at war with all forms of stoicism. God is not honored by a duty-driven approach to the Christian life, unless we include the duty to delight in God. One of the main burdens of this book is to extend the war against duty-driven stoicism into the arena of God's gifts. We ought to be Christian Hedonists all the way down, reveling in the triune God himself and gladly receiving everything that he richly provides for our enjoyment.

Thus far, this book has sought to set some theological foundations for honoring the giver by enjoying his gifts. God is glorious in his self-existent tri-unity and invites us to participate in his Trinitarian fullness. He is the creator of this world, author of the story of his glory, and therefore he communicates and reveals himself in every part of it. Creation is a fitting vehicle for God's exhibition of his triune worth, and we are fitting vessels to receive his fullness: finite, limited, bodily, and perfectly suited for the reception of his goodness in and through his very good creation. Sin and idolatry wreck this free flow of infinite, pulsating divine life by separating the giver from his gifts and shattering the union between the sun and its beams. But, in Christ, God is restoring what has been lost and reintegrating our love for him and our enjoyment of his gifts so that they do not compete with each other but instead mutually serve and enhance each other for his glory and our joy.

But now we're left with the fundamental question of how we ought to actually live out such glorious, biblical truths. What does this kind of integrated, God-centered, Christ-exalting, gospel-driven, creation-affirming, gift-receiving life look like on the ground? The remaining chapters will explore some of the dynamics of such a life, beginning with what it means to live a godward life.

What Is Godwardness?

Godwardness is the attempt to faithfully live out the famous biblical exhortation in 1 Corinthians 10:31: "So, whether you eat or drink, or whatever you do, do all to the glory of God." To go forward is to move intentionally in the direction in front of us. To go backward is to move in the direction behind us. Thus, godwardness is the movement of the soul toward God such that our thoughts, affections, and actions ultimately terminate upon him.

But this raises questions about how we should engage with all the things that aren't God. How can we retain a godward focus when our attention is occupied elsewhere? Is godwardness lost if we direct our focus to the food and drink in front of us rather than to the God who gave it to us? What did Augustine mean when he said that we should love everything "for Thy sake"? What exactly does it mean to "do all to the glory of God"?

To answer, we must remind ourselves of some fundamental dimensions of our existence. The command to do all to the glory of God, to always direct our souls godward, is given to human beings, to creatures. And as we saw in chapter 4, fundamental to creaturely existence is finitude, limitation, and temporality. We do not experience reality all at once but rather in a succession of moments. We are indelibly and permanently en-storied creatures, living our entire existence within time, both in this age and in the one to come.

We never transcend our existence in time. We will never live atemporally, viewing all of reality from some sort of God's-eye perspective. We will be creatures, forever and always, and this creaturely, temporal, finite existence will be glorious, and increasingly so. Even God, who stands above and outside of our temporal, finite reality, engages with us within time, within space, within the story.

For example, God creates the world in six, sequential days, performing his forming and filling activity in the same way that a human artist and craftsman would. He separates and rearranges, divides and reunites, speaks and sings, declares and evaluates, dirties his hands and exhales his breath, and he does so by performing one work after another. On the seventh day, he rests from his creative labor, sitting down enthroned over his very good temple-kingdom, delegating the remaining work of multiplication, expansion, and dominion to his image bearers.

God's rhythm of work and rest sets the 6+1 pattern for human flourishing:

> Remember the Sabbath day, to keep it holy. Six days you shall labor, and do all your work, but the seventh day is a Sabbath to the LORD your God. On it you shall not do any work, you, or your son, or your daughter, your male servant, or your female servant, or your livestock, or the sojourner who is within your gates. For in six days the LORD made heaven and earth, the sea, and all that is in them, and

rested on the seventh day. Therefore the LORD blessed the Sabbath day and made it holy. (Ex. 20:8–11)

In other words, God endorses and approves of our temporal existence by modeling proper rhythms of work and rest. He builds such rhythms into the fabric of creation, delegating the regulation of times and seasons to the heavenly lights. The rhythm of summer, fall, winter, spring is original to creation and with it the expectation of different seasons of human activity and life: seedtime and harvest, sowing and reaping, planting and gathering. What these seasons might have looked like if Adam and Eve had not fallen remains a mystery to us, but the biblical testimony is clear: rhythms and seasons are divinely designed and regarded as very good.

After the exodus from Egypt, God sets Israel's calendars based on the seasons of the year and his great acts within history. Israel's feasts established the rhythms of life for the people. The Sabbath, Passover, Firstfruits, Weeks, Trumpets, Day of Atonement, and Booths all served to order and structure the rhythms of Israel's life. Some feasts were celebratory and festive; others were sorrowful and solemn. The variety of the feasts allowed for the experience and expression of a fuller range of emotions and worship.

And, of course, as the Byrds reminded us, "To everything (turn, turn, turn) / There is a season (turn, turn, turn)."[1] The origin of that song and the great passage on time and rhythms is found in Ecclesiastes 3:

For everything there is a season, and a time for every matter under heaven:

a time to be born, and a time to die;
a time to plant, and a time to pluck up what is planted;
a time to kill, and a time to heal;
a time to break down, and a time to build up;
a time to weep, and a time to laugh;
a time to mourn, and a time to dance;
a time to cast away stones, and a time to gather stones together;
a time to embrace, and a time to refrain from embracing;
a time to seek, and a time to lose;
a time to keep, and a time to cast away;

a time to tear, and a time to sew;

a time to keep silence, and a time to speak;

a time to love, and a time to hate;

a time for war, and a time for peace. (vv. 1–8)

Varieties of Godwardness

What do these reflections on temporality have to do with the question of godwardness? I'd like to suggest that we should distinguish between two different types of godwardness, what I'll call direct godwardness and indirect godwardness. Both of them are truly godward, meaning that the soul's object and end is ultimately God himself, but the manner of the soul's movement godward is different in each.

Direct godwardness involves our conscious, intentional focus on God himself. Included within it are activities such as the devotional reading of Scripture, private prayer, corporate worship, thanksgiving, saying grace before meals, confession of sin, and so on. The mark of direct godwardness is that our thoughts and intentions are focused *particularly* and *directly* on God himself as we address him and commune with him.

Indirect godwardness involves a subconscious focus on God himself while actively engaging with the world that God made, the world that reveals him at every point. Included within indirect godwardness are eating meals, mowing the lawn, playing soccer, washing the dishes, memorizing Greek vocabulary, love making, computer programming, flying an airplane, reading a novel, and so on. The mark of indirect godwardness is that our thoughts and intentions are focused *primarily* and *fundamentally* on God's world and all that it contains.[2]

Some might think that the difference between these is that indirect godwardness is mediated godwardness whereas direct godwardness is unmediated. In other words, indirect godwardness moves through some created reality as a means of arriving at God, whereas direct godwardness dispenses with means in order to go to God directly. But conceiving of the difference in this way is misleading.

In some sense, all of our access to God is mediated through some means or other. This mediation is obvious in indirect godwardness, since we're dwelling on the heavens or our children or smoked salmon or our computer or the task in front of us. But the mediation is no less real in direct godwardness. We still rely on some mediating reality to bring us to God, whether it's Scripture or a worship song or human language in petitionary prayer and thanksgiving. Psalm 43 recognizes the role of mediation in Scripture and worship:

> Send out your light and your truth;
>   let them lead me;
> let them bring me to your holy hill
>   and to your dwelling!
> Then I will go to the altar of God,
>   to God my exceeding joy,
> and I will praise you with the lyre,
>   O God, my God. (vv. 3–4)

God sends forth his light and his truth, whether in the Scriptures or in the heavens. These precious means lead us and guide us to his dwelling place, where we find God, who is our exceeding joy. Scripture is not an end in itself. The Bible brings us to God, and when we arrive, we praise *him*, using instruments and human words as means of expressing our hearts.

In short, mediation is inescapable, and therefore we shouldn't try to avoid it or transcend it. God knew what he was doing when he designed the world and the Bible and human beings to function in this way. The Scriptures and human language may speak more directly and specifically to God's reality than the heavens or the laughter of a child or lightning or a cool glass of water on a hot day, but all of them are communicating from God about God, and therefore all of them provide avenues for bringing us to God, our exceeding joy.

Finding a Rhythm

So then, we can distinguish acts of the soul that move directly godward and those that take a more circuitous route through the world in which we live. How then should these two types of godwardness relate? In line with what we saw earlier about God's endorsement of temporality and rhythms, my suggestion is that we should structure our lives around regular rhythms of direct and indirect godwardness, engaging with God's world fully and then frequently focusing our thoughts, intentions, and affections on the triune God in a direct and purposeful way.

A simple example can illustrate this sort of rhythm. When we sit down to eat a meal, whether it's a holiday feast or fast-food, we engage with God directly, thanking him for the daily bread and fellowship around the table and commending our eating and drinking and conversing to him in the name of his Son. Then we turn our attention to the food and the friends and the family and the conversation, enjoying the flavors and smells and directing our thoughts and attention to those around us. In other words, we pray before the meal, then really enjoy the meal, and then, perhaps at the end, we thank God again for such a delightful time.

Contrast this with the attempt to go godward directly at every point in the meal. Imagine someone interrupting the conversation to bow his head and say a short prayer after every bite. "Hold on a minute, Jim. Let me praise the Lord for the spice in this salsa. Now, what were you saying about your mom's surgery?" This might have the appearance of piety but would actually be rude to the others at the table. Could we really say that this is what it means to consider others more important than ourselves?

Now, of course this example is an exaggeration and a caricature. No one actually attempts to go directly godward after every bite as a means of obeying 1 Corinthians 10:31. But while we might not actually practice such poor mealtime manners, many of us do have a subtle sense of guilt that we don't do something like it when we eat. We're not sure what a God-centered mealtime ought to look like, which is what creates the low-grade condemnation in our soul when we simply give thanks to God for the meal and then enjoy the food and the fellowship.

Instead of rebelling against our temporality, we ought to thank God for his provision and then receive it and enjoy it gladly while seeking to love our neighbor. We ought to be fully engaged with others, asking them questions, offering encouragement, giving a listening ear. Such love for your dinner and your dinner companions is what supreme love for God looks like when it eats dinner and meets companions. In one sense, to be truly godward is to be manward in the moment.[3] Of course, it's entirely appropriate to offer short, spontaneous, silent prayers to God throughout the meal (perhaps, "Thank you for this wonderful time," or "Help my words give grace"), but the bulk of our attention ought to be on the people in front of us and the food that God has given us.

This is what Paul means in 1 Timothy when he contrasts Christian enjoyment of food and fellowship with demonic asceticism:

> [They] forbid marriage and require abstinence from foods that God created to be received with thanksgiving by those who believe and know the truth. For everything created by God is good, and nothing is to be rejected if it is received with thanksgiving, for it is made holy by the word of God and prayer. (4:3–5)

The food is good. The spouse is good. The friends are good. The earth is the Lord's and the fullness thereof. We shouldn't reject them. We ought to receive them gladly, giving thanks to God for them and setting them apart with biblical prayers. People who orient their lives through direct godwardness over the Scriptures and in prayer are free to gratefully receive God's goodness in what he has made and given.

The great Puritan preacher Richard Baxter expresses the need for such rhythms of direct and indirect godwardness:

> The intending of God's glory or our spiritual good, cannot be distinctly and sensibly re-acted in every particular pleasure we take, or bit we eat, or thing we use: but a sincere Habitual Intention well laid at first in the Heart, will serve to the right use of many particular Means.[4]

The intending of God's glory *cannot be* distinctly and sensibly re-acted in every pleasure (presumably because of our finitude and limitations). It would distract us from receiving all that God has for us *in the pleasure*. Instead, we lay a habitual intention deep in our heart (through our direct godwardness), and then the habitual intention orders our affections and desires so that we rightly use and enjoy whatever God supplies.

Rhythms of Fasting and Feasting

The biblical teaching on fasting and feasting nicely illustrates the way that rhythms of godwardness ought to work. The Bible assumes that we will *regularly* fast (Matt. 6:16–18), but it does not command us to *perpetually* fast. That is, the Bible assumes that we will break fast, that our abstinence from food is only temporary. There ought to be times when we forgo food so that we might devote ourselves to seeking God in prayer and worship (in 1 Corinthians 7 Paul suggests that a similar fast can occur with sex in marriage). In other words, we temporarily give up a means of indirect godwardness (food) so that we might take advantage of an extended time of direct godwardness.

Of course, as we saw earlier, even our feasting ought to be anchored by prayer, thanksgiving, and the Scriptures. However, fasting provides a particularly potent way of focusing our full attention on the triune God, whose love is better than food.[5] Recognizing the rhythms of feasting and fasting keeps us from elevating one over the other, as if one was inherently more holy. Taking our cues from Ecclesiastes 3, there is a time to feast and a time to fast. It is precisely in the godward rhythm of the two that we experience and express the fullness of God's grace in our lives.

Knowing the World So That We Can Know God Better

In chapter 5 we discussed the integrated approach to relating God and his gifts. Adding the notion of rhythms of direct and indirect godwardness helps to fill out how the enjoyment of God's gifts and a supreme love for God can be mutually beneficial and fruitful. If we are properly (and perichoretically) integrating our joy in God and our delight in his gifts, then our enjoyment of the gifts ought to enhance and increase our love for God himself, and our love for God himself ought to enhance and increase our enjoyment of his gifts. Or, to put it in rhythmic, temporal terms, direct godwardness enhances our indirect godwardness, and indirect godwardness enhances our direct godwardness. Each serves the other by providing something and guarding against something.

Indirect godwardness and a robust enjoyment of God's gifts serves and increases direct godwardness by creating new mental, emotional, and spiritual categories for our enjoyment of God. It keeps God from being vague and indistinct in our minds. As we saw earlier in Proverbs 24:13–14, our enjoyment of honey (because it is good) creates new ways of experiencing God and his wisdom in the soul. Being alive to the sweetness and potency of honey *as honey*, sends me back to God with a renewed understanding and appreciation and experiential knowledge of what God is like. As Lewis says, "Almost every day furnishes us with, so to speak, 'bearings' on the Bright Blur."[6]

The same could be said about my experience as a husband. Glorious biblical truth came alive to me on my wedding day as I waited for my wife to walk the aisle. "As the bridegroom rejoices over the bride, so shall your God rejoice over you" (Isa. 62:5). Indirect godwardness guards us against a truncated and impoverished direct godwardness. The created analogies enable my limited and finite mind to comprehend more of God's ineffable and incomprehensible fullness. The result is that we seek to love God with all of our *expanded* mind and all of our *enlarged* heart and all of our *fattened* soul and all of our *increased* strength.

In this sense, we carry our indirect godwardness into our direct engagement with God. The delight of fatherhood, the solidity of rocks, the safety of fortresses, the majesty of thunderstorms, the comfort of a good friend, the intensity of sexual pleasure, the colorful variety of autumn leaves—all these infuse and shape and inform our engagement with God directly. Which means that we need not necessarily fear the intensity of our joy in created things. Provided we are anchored in a supreme love for God, then, when our love for one of the gifts shoots through the roof like a rocket, it carries our love for God along with it, lifting it to new, unforeseen heights. In this sense, we rob ourselves of potent worship if we detach from the gifts or rush through our enjoyment of creation.

The Effect of His Face on the Things of Earth

Similarly, direct godwardness serves and increases our enjoyment of the seasons of indirect godwardness. Worship, prayer, devotional reading—all of these anchor our soul and shape the way that we engage with God's world and the people within it. Such anchor points are absolutely necessary so that sinful tendencies don't lead our heart to drift from supreme love for God. Direct godwardness thus serves, protects, and guards our enjoyment of God's gifts by orienting our affections.

And what's more, direct communion with God increases our enjoyment of God's gifts and God's world, which is why I've always been puzzled by the lines of Lemmel's hymn:

> Turn your eyes upon Jesus
> Look full in his wonderful face
> And the things of earth will grow strangely dim
> In the light of his glory and grace.[7]

Now, I'm sure that Mrs. Lemmel means "things of the world" or "sinful things" grow dim in the light of Jesus's face. But that's not what she says. She says "things of earth," which makes it sound like, in the light of his face, my wife and my kids and my Chipotle burrito get dim and dull and dusty. And that's not my experience *at all*. In the light of his face, they get brighter and better and more potent. A full look at Jesus makes his gifts *come alive*. She's more beautiful, they're more delightful, the burrito tastes better. Now I know what the gifts are *for*.

In this way, direct godwardness infuses and colors all of my other activities, from enjoying my food to completing my tasks to dating my wife to taking a nap. If I'm truly anchoring myself in the Scriptures and in prayer and in communion with the triune God, then the seasons of indirect godwardness are haunted by the Holy Spirit. Jonathan Edwards describes this kind of haunting in his *Personal Narrative*. After God granted him the new birth, he wrote:

> The appearance of every thing was altered; there seemed to be, as it were, a calm, sweet cast, or appearance of divine glory, in almost every thing. God's excellency, his wisdom, his purity and love, seemed to appear in every thing; in the sun, and moon, and stars; in the clouds and blue sky; in the grass, flowers, trees; in the water, and all nature; which used greatly to fix my mind. I often used to sit and view the moon for a long time; and in the day, spent much time in viewing the clouds and sky, to behold the sweet glory of God in these things; in the mean time, singing forth, with a low voice, my contemplations of the Creator and Redeemer.[8]

Elixirs and Anchor Points

While Edwards emphasizes the contemplative and private dimensions of these rhythms of godwardness and their effects, the poet George Herbert celebrates the active and vocational dimension of godward rhythms:

> Teach me, my God and King,
> In all things Thee to see,
> And what I do in anything,
> To do it as for Thee.
>
> Not rudely, as a beast,
> To run into action;
> But still to make Thee prepossest,
> And give it his perfection.
>
> A man that looks on glass,
> On it may stay his eye,
> Or, if he pleaseth, through it pass,
> And then the heav'n espy.
>
> All may of Thee partake;
> Nothing can be so mean
> Which with this tincture (for Thy sake)
> Will not grow bright and clean.
>
> A servant with this clause
> Makes drudgery divine:
> Who sweeps a room as for Thy laws,
> Makes that and th' action fine.
>
> This is the famous stone
> That turneth all to gold;
> For that which God doth touch and own
> Cannot for less be told.[9]

It is not difficult to detect 1 Corinthians 10:31 in the background of the poem, along with Colossians 3:17 and 3:23 ("Whatever you do, in word or deed, do everything in the name of the Lord Jesus," and "Whatever you do, work heartily, as for the Lord and not for men"). Herbert first asks God to teach him to see God in everything and, echoing Colossians 3:23, to do everything "as for thee." So what does it mean to do something "as for the Lord"? To begin, it means not to do something "rudely, as a beast." Beasts run into action without thinking, without deliberation or intent. Instead, faithful labor must include a prepossession of the Lord, a resolve to carry God into the work and thus to "give it his perfection" (this aligns well with Baxter's "habitual intention" well laid in the heart).

Herbert, anticipating Lewis's meditation in a toolshed, which we looked at in chapter 3, then explores what it means to see God in all things. The world is a window through which we espy heav'n. To look at the world and see only the world is like looking at a window instead of looking through the window to what's beyond it. Windows were made to be transparent, to unveil to our eyes something other than windows. So too the world, which exists to reveal God to us. Thus, we must labor to see beyond our families and food and nature and labor and instead recognize the revelation of God in them.

Herbert then underscores the universal nature of God's presence. No activity can be so mean that adding "for thy sake" to it cannot make it grow bright and clean. There is a kind of godwardness (encapsulated in that little phrase) that acts as a tincture, a dye that colors (or in this case brightens) the activity with holiness.

"This clause" ("for thy sake") in the mouth of a servant "makes drudgery divine." It turns menial tasks (sweeping rooms, changing diapers, and working the checkout counter) into noble vocations.[10] This is the famous "philosopher's stone," the legendary substance that can turn base metals into gold and in some accounts, be an elixir of life (thus the title of the poem). "This" in the final stanza appears to refer to the clause "for thy sake" from stanza 4, as well as the disposition of the heart that stands beneath it. But the final two lines of the poem indicate that this clause is more than a magic word. It is an invocation that draws God into action. It is *he himself* who touches all that we see and do, our sight and our labor, our vision and our drudgery, and in doing so makes it his own and elevates it far beyond what we could ask or think.

Herbert's poem shaped B. B. Warfield's approach to his own calling as a theologian and professor. "Religion," he writes, "does not take a man away from his work; it sends him into his work with an added quality of devotion." After reflecting on Herbert's poem, he writes about the integration of direct godwardness (prayer) and all of our other activities (such as studying):

> Sometimes we hear it said that ten minutes on your knees will give you a truer, deeper, more operative knowledge of God than ten hours over your books. "What!" is the appropriate response, "than ten hours over your books, on your knees?" Why should you turn from God when you turn to your books, or feel that you must turn from your books in order to turn to God?"[11]

What would "ten hours over your books [or under the hood of a car or on a computer or in the kitchen or in the classroom] on your knees" actually look like in practice? It's clear from the rest of Warfield's address that it doesn't mean a solitary direct godwardness that cancels concerted and focused effort on the subject of study or vocation. Nor is it a perpetual ping-pong match where we read a word, go heavenward, read another, then back to heaven, and then snap back to earth.

My suggestion is to think in terms of what Doug Wilson calls "anchor points." You pray before you study (or cook or clean or help the customer or write the e-mail), asking for God's help and blessing and orienting yourself to God and his kingdom and purposes. Then you throw yourself into whatever task is in front of you, working heartily, as for the Lord and not for men (Col. 3:23). If you run into a tough sentence in your studies or a difficult pastoral situation or a belligerent customer or a tricky computer problem, you take a moment and offer a brief prayer for help, and then you dive back into the work, confident that our God is a prayer-hearing God. Or you punctuate your efforts with brief prayers of thanksgiving and adoration, as the Spirit moves your soul. When it's all done, whether the specific task or the day's labor, you thank God for his grace and commend yourself to his keeping while you sleep.[12]

Seeing the Whole Horizon

Perhaps an analogy may help clarify the rhythms of communion with God and indirect godwardness. When it comes to seeing with my physical eyes, I find that I can really intensely focus on only one thing at once. While there may be a lot within my field of vision, my eyes truly focus only on one thing. My eyes may move around frequently and rapidly—from the computer in front of me to the book on the desk to the picture of my dad on the shelf to the lamp by the door—but I'm always looking at essentially one thing at a time. This is a fundamental feature of creaturely vision: if I am looking to the left, then I can't simultaneously be looking to the right, and vice versa.

Moreover, while I can see a lot of what's in front of me because of the quickness of my eyes and the reality of peripheral vision, the one thing I can't see is what's behind me. As a creature, I will never see the whole horizon at a glance; I can only stand on the prairie and spin in circles to take all of it in (you should try it some time). And again, this is not a defect. *God made us this way and approves of it.*

Applying these principles of physical vision to mental and spiritual vision, we might say that we can mentally and intentionally focus on one thing at a time, even as we dart our mind's eye around our mental sky. My spiritual eyes can focus specifically on the triune God (direct godwardness) and they can gaze around at everything else in front of me (indirect godwardness). The goal, however, is that God always remain in front of me. Even when he's not the direct object of my attention, he is ever in my field of vision. I never turn my back to him.

So I can be diligently engaged in a task—say, putting together a puzzle with my boys—and so I'm fully engaged with them, but I'm also capable of quickly "glancing" at God in order to connect and commune with him and thank him for wonderful moments such as these. Frequent spiritual glances anchor me and help me to receive my sons as gifts and not gods.

Of course, the analogy is imperfect since it seems to artificially compartmentalize God and everything else. So perhaps we can modify a quotation by C. S. Lewis: "I believe in God like I believe in the sun, not only because I see him, but because by him I see everything else."[13] The sun's rays fall upon the world and enlighten it. "When anything is exposed by the light, it becomes visible, for anything that becomes visible is light" (Eph. 5:13).[14]

Of course, even this modification falls short, since it shows how direct godwardness enlightens and enhances indirect godwardness, but not vice versa. So maybe we should change the analogy from light and vision to people and presence. I can sit in the living room and have a conversation with my wife. Or we can sit in the same room and each read a book. In the latter case, I'm aware of and glad for her presence (she's within my field of vision), even if she's not the direct object of my attention. Eric Liddell was aware of God's pleasure as he ran, even as his thoughts were occupied with his breathing, posture, and the finish line.

Despite the imperfection of the analogies, the point remains the same. We focus our primary attention on one thing at a time, whether God himself or the incredible diversity of the world. However, we never lose sight of the other, so that our communion with God enlightens our vision and engagement with the world, and our engagement with the world prevents God from remaining a vague and indistinct blur. Direct and indirect godwardness haunt one another so that the experience of each illuminates the other.

Pray without Ceasing

These types of rhythms of godwardness help us to imitate biblical examples such as the blessed man of Psalm 1, who meditates on God's law day and night, as well as to understand and obey biblical exhortations such as "Pray without ceasing" (1 Thess. 5:17). This is not a command to do nothing but pray (in which case Paul, David, and Jesus are all failures). Rather these examples and exhortations encourage us to pray and meditate on the Scriptures regularly, frequently, attentively, and with perseverance. We should devote time and effort to communion with God directly, much as Jesus went away to a solitary place to pray (Mark 1:35).

Then we enter our days anchored in the gospel and rooted in the love of God with our heart and mind tuned to his presence and reality in what he has made. In other words, we seek to enter our daily tasks *alive*, both to God and to the wonders of his world (and the needs of others). We carry the effects of our communion with God with us, as when Jesus descends the Mount of Transfiguration and casts out the unclean spirit that defied the efforts of his disciples (Mark 9:2–29). Jesus notes that their attempts failed because "this kind cannot be driven out by anything but prayer." However, the text doesn't record any prayer of Jesus's during the exorcism. The point seems to be that the effects of his earlier prayerful communion with God gave Jesus power and fruitfulness in his ministry. Direct godwardness hung with him, even as his attention was occupied by the needs of those in front of him.

Throughout our day, wherever we are, we seek to be all there, fully present to the people around us and to the tasks at hand. We punctuate our day with moments of direct godwardness—before meals, during solitary commutes, in the midst of breaks in the action, before and after difficult tasks, and a thousand other possibilities.

Additionally, we orient our weeks by gathering with God's people in worship, collectively singing praises, confessing sins, hearing the Word preached, and sharing fellowship at the Lord's Table. Our worship on the Lord's Day leads us to an encounter with the grace of God in Christ, rooting us and grounding us in the love of God and the cross of Christ and then sending us out into the world as salt and light, ready to proclaim and portray the gospel in our words and works.

Testing Our Rhythms

The great danger of distinguishing direct and indirect godwardness in this way is that they can become compartmentalized. Rather than being anchored by our communion with God, we simply check devotions off the list and then drift freely through the day wherever our sinful hearts will take us. Instead, we want our rhythms to actually tether us, to actually root us so that we don't turn from God as we turn to the business of our lives. But how do we ensure that we're anchoring ourselves and not merely giving God a high-five on our way to idolatry? Here are a number of tests to evaluate whether communion with God is having its proper effect.

How often does direct godwardness (however brief) spontaneously erupt? As you go about your day, do you find yourself regularly going godward with prayers and supplications and requests and thanksgiving and adoration? Is God always in your field of vision, so that no matter how intently you're focusing on the task at hand, direct communion with him is never far away? Is he always present, even when he's not being addressed?

Is there an increasing awareness of God's presence in everything you do? In other words, is there a growing sense that you're never far from God, that he is always close at hand, that he is always marking you and speaking to you in the thousand shafts of glory that bombard you?

Do you find yourself desiring to linger in prayer or song or Scripture reading? When life thrusts itself upon you again, and you must put down your Bible in order to make breakfast for your kids or head off to work, do you find yourself wishing you had a few more minutes? More importantly, do you eagerly look forward to the next time that you can be alone with God?

Do you find your times of devotion and meditation enriched by your daily life? In addition to the burdens and anxieties and cares that you bring to God, do you also bring the fruit of your active engagement with his world? Are his attributes and characteristics more concrete and productive in your heart, less abstract and impersonal?

Is the Word of God fresh in your heart? Or is it a dead letter, a sign that you've been merely checking the devotional box on your to-do list?

Finally, and most importantly, is there fruit in your life? Are you making progress in holiness? Can you see evidence of growth in godliness over the past six months, twelve months, two years? Not that there aren't still struggles or setbacks. But are you slowly and steadily becoming a more loving, joyful, caring, patient, and humble person? Are you less angry, proud, boastful, and anxious?

The Bible is silent when it comes to *mandating* how often and how long our times of direct communion with God should be. The Bible does give us a number of worthy examples—examples that we ought to take seriously and seek to imitate according to our ability, calling, responsibilities, and place in life.[15] However, the Bible's unwillingness to command specific times is intentional. We don't want to measure the value or fruitfulness of our direct godwardness purely by the number of pages we've read or the length of our prayers. Instead, the primary evidence is qualitative—a changed life, good fruit, gracious words, deeds of love. This isn't to say that discipline and quantity are irrelevant. Regular times of extended prayer and Scripture reading are essential. But the test of whether we are reading and praying enough is the quality of our lives. The proof, as they say, is in the pudding.

7

Naming the World

And in your Physics, if you gloss it well,
You'll find, not many pages from the start,
That your art strives to follow, as it may,
Nature—you are the pupil, she the teacher.
So we might say that human industry
Is the grandchild of God.

Dante Alighieri

Man is a poetical animal and touches nothing which he does
not adorn.

C. S. Lewis

Attentive readers may have had a question lurking in the back of their
minds as they've digested the previous chapters. Thus far, most of my
examples of the proper enjoyment of gifts have been drawn from nature—witnessing the heavens declare God's glory, savoring the sweetness
of pumpkin crunch cake, eating honey because it's good, delighting in
children because they're, well, delightful. These examples might have
given the impression that the primary (if not only) gifts that we are to
enjoy are those given directly by God.

But what about culture? It's one thing to talk about enjoying the
things that God makes. But what about enjoying the things that we
make? Can we apply this paradigm to our enjoyment of literature, art,
music, television, and movies (as well as furniture, clothing, and archi-
tecture)? And what about other forms of human activity? Is receiving

food as a gift from God any different from playing baseball (or watching baseball)? That's what the present chapter seeks to address.

The first thing to note is that the difference between creation and culture isn't as neat and tidy as we'd like to think. For example, we might think of enjoying creation as "delighting in the things that God makes" and enjoying culture as "delighting in the things that people make." However, when we begin to think about enjoying food, for example, we have to recognize that most (if not all) of the food that we enjoy is a mixture of human and divine effort. God may have made sugar sweet, pecans crunchy, and pumpkin creamy, but it's my wife who blends them together into pumpkin crunch cake.[1] The culinary arts are true *arts*; they require technical skill, a discerning palate, and creative imagination. Anyone who has ever had a glass of orange juice after brushing their teeth knows that you just don't throw flavors together. Some combinations simply don't mix.

The same mixed quality applies to other gifts as well. God has given me a wife and children, friends and neighbors. He made them and blessed me with them. At the same time, my reason for enjoying them certainly involves the things that they do as well—their thoughts, feelings, and actions. So, from the outset we should be aware that the distinction between creation and culture is not always as clear as we might like to think.

Defining Culture

In an earlier chapter, we noted that God created human beings in his image, after his likeness (Gen. 1:26). I argued that we ought to understand image bearing in terms of man's three vocations of priest, king, and prophet. A key part of man's vocation is found in Genesis 1:28, a passage that is often called the "cultural mandate."[2]

> And God blessed them. And God said to them, "Be fruitful and multiply and fill the earth and subdue it, and have dominion over the fish of the sea and over the birds of the heavens and over every living thing that moves on the earth."

The call to subdue the earth means that the earth, as originally given to man, was unsubdued, undomesticated. This implies that creation has unrealized potential, latent dimensions that lie beneath the surface. In the words of one author, God has embedded within creation "a rich array of potentialities," qualities and characteristics that he intends for man to discover and activate.[3] Solomon refers to this process of discovery when he says, "It is the glory of God to conceal things, but the glory of kings is to search things out" (Prov. 25:2).

Thus, with the cultural mandate, God gives divine endorsement to the development of the earth's natural resources through science and technology ("Let's go discover all the cool things that hydrogen can do") as well as to the identification of metaphorical and analogical relationships, which man should develop through the arts ("Some days, writing feels like trying to herd a pack of wet cats"). Culture, therefore, encompasses more than just "the arts"—painting, sculpting, literature, and music. Indeed, it incorporates all facets of human activity—from the mundane to the skilled, from the lowest to the highest. Both the fry cook at McDonald's and the conductor of the Boston Symphony are engaged in culture, each in his own way. In both cases, they are developing and transforming the world as they find it.

Culture, then, is a kind of cultivation, a drawing out what God has put in. Or, to change metaphors, culture is an adornment of creation, the further beautification of an already beautiful world. It refers both to the developmental activity of man—or culture making—and to the cultural products that result. In the words of Henry Van Til, culture is "the secondary environment which has been superimposed upon nature by man's creative effort."[4] In a word, Creation + Man's Creative Efforts = Culture.

This definition of culture has two crucial components. First, all our culture making is carried out in a world whose boundaries are absolutely defined by God. There is an objectivity to reality—a givenness—that renders the world as God made it unavoidable and inescapable. We'll call this the "reality principle." But, as Chesterton reminded us, the reason that order and structure exist is so that good things can run wild. The reality principle alone would result in stagnation, and, thus, we add to it the "creativity principle," the contribution we make as God's image bearers to the transformation of his world. If the reality principle establishes both a starting point and a direction, the creativity principle takes us beyond what's presently there toward the ultimate destination established by God. This notion of the blending of the reality principle with the creativity principle, of the transformation of God's world through human culture making, is ably captured by Robert Farrar Capon:

> Why do we marry, why take friends and lovers, why give ourselves to music, painting, chemistry, or cooking? Out of simple delight in the resident goodness of creation, of course; but out of more than that, too. Half of earth's gorgeousness lies hidden in the glimpsed city it longs to become. For all its rooted loveliness, the world has no continuing city here; it is an outlandish place, a foreign home, a session in via to a better version of itself—and it is our glory to see it so and thirst until Jerusalem comes home at last. We are given appetites, not to consume the world and forget it, but to taste its goodness and hunger to make it great.[5]

This is what culture does—takes the rooted loveliness of the world and makes it lovelier, tastes the goodness of the earth's givenness and makes it greater.

Completing Creation

The previous discussion of culture poses a puzzle for us. Recall that during the six days of creation, God regularly announces his approval of his ongoing work. Again and again, we're told, "God saw that it was good." And, of course, after God completes his work of creation, "God saw *everything* that he had made, and behold, it was *very* good" (Gen. 1:31). Thus, the movement within the creation week is from good to very good.

But now, given the cultural mandate, we're left with a world that is "very good" and yet still requires subduing. God's work is completed, but man's work has only just begun. How then ought we to think about *improving* upon God's very good world? Perhaps we can take another lesson from Paul in 1 Timothy 4:1–5.[6] We've already seen how this passage decisively undermines false forms of asceticism, which deny the goodness of God's gifts. But it may also hold a further key for helping us to think about culture. The final two verses are worth quoting again:

> For everything created by God is good, and nothing is to be rejected
> if it is received with thanksgiving, for it is made holy by the word
> of God and prayer.

In the first part of the verse, Paul celebrates the truth that we've seen in Genesis 1—that creation is good. But a good creation is not enough. We need a "made holy" creation, a *hallowed* creation, a *glorified* creation. God's goal is that his very good creation would be sanctified and that this sanctification would happen *through the activity of human beings*. In order for creation to be what God designed it to be, it must be received with thanksgiving ("by those who believe and know the truth," 1 Tim. 4:3) and hallowed by God's Word and prayer. Thus, the mingling of human creativity with God's good world must be a sanctified mingling. It must be a mingling that is guided, governed, and ordered by God's Word. It must be a mingling that is intentionally dependent upon God in prayer. It must be a creativity that is fundamentally receptive and grateful to the God who made the good world and gives the good gifts. Gratitude *to him* and prayer *to him* and the Word *from him* must orient and infuse all our creation enjoyment and culture making.

In *Reflections on the Psalms* C. S. Lewis famously said, "I think we delight to praise what we enjoy because the praise not merely expresses but completes the enjoyment."[7] Praise is the appointed consummation of joy. Likewise, perhaps we can say that by God's design, God-exalting, Scripture-guided, prayerful culture is the appointed consummation of God's very good creation. We gladly receive what God gives and thankfully return it to him, sanctified by his Word and prayer. Just as "delight is incomplete until it is expressed," so creation is incomplete until it is faithfully subdued, cultivated, and sanctified by thankful people. Or again, a gift is incomplete until it is thankfully received and glorified in and through the delight of God's people.

Maturing World, Maturing People

Thus far, we have seen that faithful creation enjoyment and culture making involve both the givenness of creation and man's creative labor. Our creativity must be a Scripture-guided, gratitude-infused, prayerfully dependent receiving and sanctifying of God's good world. In this way, we fulfill our calling as God's image bearers, as his priests, kings, and prophets. What's more, recognizing culture as world transformation and maturation allows us to see something more about the biblical understanding of man's threefold vocation, which we introduced in chapter 4. In short, I'd contend that we ought to see a progression in these three callings, a process of maturation from priest to king to prophet. This progression becomes evident when we reflect on the responsibilities of each of these roles in the Bible.

Priests are palace servants who accomplish relatively simple tasks in God's temple-house. They inspect the sacrifices, aid the worshiper in offering them, check for leprosy and other uncleanness, clean the temple and its vessels, and perform basic rituals. The priest's tasks require simple obedience, responding in faith and applying the words of God in straightforward situations. As Steve Jeffery argues, "Training to be a Priest was a matter of learning long lists of detailed rules. . . . None of the details of the Tabernacle's furnishings or the Priestly garments were left to chance; every detail was specified. . . . A Priest didn't have much creative thinking to do."[8] While the priest does perform an authoritative teaching role, it is primarily the transmission and basic exposition of God's law to the people.

Kingship requires an additional level of maturity. Whereas priests are servants in God's house, a king is a son of God, ruling over God's house as his representative (2 Sam. 7:14; Heb. 3:5–6). While Israel's king is required to know God's law (Deut. 17:18–20), he is also expected to rule in wisdom, applying the Word of God to new and unforeseen circumstances.[9] Solomon is the paragon of kingly virtue, exercising his wisdom in surprisingly complicated decisions (there was no verse in Leviticus to guide him when two harlots approached him with a dead baby). Whereas the priest simply has to decide between good and evil, blemished and unblemished, the king must discern between good, better, and best, or between the lesser of two evils. The ability to make wise decisions is rooted in the internalization of God's law. Thus wisdom builds on law, or, to use the biblical proverb, "the fear of the LORD is the beginning of wisdom" (Ps. 111:10; Prov. 9:10).

Prophets surpass both kings and priests in that they not only receive or apply God's law but also actually stand in God's council as his advisor. If priests are God's servants and kings are God's sons, prophets are God's friends, and he consults with them before acting ("For the Lord God does nothing without revealing his secret to his servants the prophets," Amos 3:7).[10] Moreover, whereas the king is charged with ruling over God's kingdom, the prophet is charged with tearing down kingdoms and then building new ones through his visionary words (Jer. 1:9–10). He is a world maker (and a world ender), creating new contexts and situations in which the law can be applied. If the fundamental priestly virtue is obedient service, and the fundamental kingly virtue is wise rulership, then the fundamental prophetic virtue is transformative imagination.[11]

Faithful Naming

So, then, God has designed the world to mature from one degree of glory to another, from good to very good to sanctified. Likewise, he has designed his image bearers to grow up into maturity, from obedient priests to wise kings to faithful prophets. With these two progressions on the table, we're now in a position to examine culture from another biblical angle—naming.

Earlier in the book, I linked naming with man's prophetic vocation. As prophet, man is called to faithfully name the world God has made. However, naming is also an expression of the other two vocations. Naming, as we'll see, is a kind of cultivation, a calling forth of what lies beneath the surface of the world, much like a farmer faithfully cultivates the ground to bring forth crops. Likewise, naming is a way of taking royal dominion, of subduing the untamed earth to the rule of God and man. However, naming transcends the priestly transmission of God's word and the kingly application of God's word to new situations. Naming requires creativity and imagination, the ability to see the as-yet-unseen and shape it in accordance with God's word and character.

With that background, we turn to examine the foundational biblical passage on naming:

> Then the Lord God said, "It is not good that the man should be alone; I will make him a helper fit for him." Now out of the ground

the LORD God had formed every beast of the field and every bird of the heavens and brought them to the man to see what he would call them. And whatever the man called every living creature, that was its name. The man gave names to all livestock and to the birds of the heavens and to every beast of the field. But for Adam there was not found a helper fit for him. So the LORD God caused a deep sleep to fall upon the man, and while he slept took one of his ribs and closed up its place with flesh. And the rib that the LORD God had taken from the man he made into a woman and brought her to the man. Then the man said,

> "This at last is bone of my bones
>   and flesh of my flesh;
> she shall be called Woman,
>   because she was taken out of Man." (Gen. 2:18–23)

In this passage, God gives Adam the privilege of naming the animals and naming the woman. Naming appears to involve both the reality principle and the creativity principle. In other words, naming involves God's design, purpose, and intent in creation, on the one hand, as well as man's recognition of God's design *and* advancement of God's reign through his act of naming, on the other.

In Genesis 1 the first human pair is given a fivefold blessing and mandate: "Be fruitful and multiply and fill the earth and subdue it, and have dominion over the fish of the sea and over the birds of the heavens and over every living thing that moves on the earth" (v. 28). The repetition of beasts and birds in Genesis 2:19 implies that one of the ways that man is to exercise dominion over creation is through naming them. Moreover, the fact that beasts and birds are distinguished ("every beast . . . every bird") implies that Adam was to recognize the distinct kinds that God had established by his creative fiat (vv. 21, 24–25) and classify and name them accordingly. However, his naming was to go beyond mere labeling. Adam's naming sees what's there, but it then sees more than what's (presently) there. Naming is a way of moving forward, of making progress. It includes both recognition of what God has done *and* development beyond what God has done. It includes both discovery *and* invention.[12] Thus, naming involves the reception of God's acts (that is, the contemplation and consideration of what God has done), as well as the development of God's acts (that is, the creativity and imagination to build upon what God has done). Or better, human naming is actually *God's* way of developing (subduing) creation, enlisting *man* as colaborer in the work of bringing the world from one degree of glory to another.[13]

While we are not told exactly how Adam chose the names for each kind of animal and bird, it seems warranted to infer that the poetic account of his naming of woman provides a kind of model for all his naming activity. In Adam's naming of the woman we see this interplay of God's design and man's creativity. Adam gives *reasons* for his naming choice, implying that there ought to be a propriety, a fitness, between the world as God made it and the world as man names it. Thus, woman (*ishshah*) is a fitting name for the female sex because ("for") she was taken out of man (*ish*). *Ishshah* was taken out of *ish*. This principle extends after the fall as Adam gives his wife a personal name (Eve) "because she was the mother of all living" (3:20).[14] In sum, Adam names the woman (and presumably the animals) on the basis of observed characteristics and relationships.[15]

Additionally, based on the flow of the biblical text, when Adam names the animals and the woman, he appears to be imitating God. In Genesis 1, we watch as God divides (e.g., waters from land), names (e.g., seas and earth), assesses ("And God saw . . ."), and approves (". . . that it was good."). Similarly, man divides ("Short, bushy-tailed creatures over there; tall, long-necked creatures over there"), names ("squirrel" and "giraffe"), assesses ("she was taken out of man"), and approves ("at last . . ."). Additionally, Adam names the woman on the same basis that he received his name from God, namely, origin. Man comes from the ground (Heb. *adamah*) and is thus named *adam*. Woman comes from man (*ish*) and is thus named *ishshah*. Adam, the son of God, does just what he sees his Father doing.[16] To put it another way, Adam *observes* and *understands* what woman is ("bone of my bones and flesh of my flesh; . . . she was taken out of Man"), *evaluates* rightly and *feels* intensely about the gift God has given him ("This *at last* . . ."), and then *applies* wisely and *expresses* clearly what he has observed, understood, evaluated, and felt by giving woman an appropriate name ("she shall be called Woman, because . . .").[17]

We Live in Language

Naming is thus a way of embracing the reality that as human beings we live in language. As we saw in chapter 3, the world is God's speech act: God calls it into existence out of nothing and then sustains it by speech at every step along the way.[18] As one theologian puts it, "Reality is a text to be interpreted, mediated by language, history, culture, and tradition."[19] As a part of this spoken reality, human beings are spoken as well. We too are words—words from God that inhabit other words.

If the world is God's speech, spoken into existence and sustained by his word, then we can see how progress in learning to speak the language of creation (and therefore to make culture) tracks with the three stages of man's vocational calling as God's image bearer. Each dimension of bearing God's image is particularly associated with a specific sensory organ.[20] Priests are associated with the ear, since they are charged with *hearing* God's direct speech and obeying. Kings are associated with the eye, since they are called to build upon what they've heard and *see* God's intent in new situations and circumstances.[21] Prophets are associated with the mouth, since they are called to consult with God in his council and then *speak* his word to the people.[22]

This progression—from ear to eye to mouth, and from hearing to seeing to speaking—clarifies the way that human beings come to name God's world. First, they hear what God has said verbally, including his commands and his description of what he's done.[23] Then they see what God is saying (nonverbally) elsewhere in his creation, reading his intent in things based on what they've understood of his character through his direct speech.[24] Such nonverbal reading leads to the recognition of God's intent in creation. Based upon this hearing of God's direct speech and the recognition of God's meaning in his nonverbal speech, man then must speak himself, adding his voice to God's and cultivating, subduing, and naming God's world. This last step is a kind of revelation—*God* revealing (more of) himself *through* the imagination and invention of his obedient, wise, and creative creatures.[25]

Enjoying the Gift of Creativity and Culture

If culture making describes our contribution to the growth and transformation of creation in fulfillment of God's mission, then we can now see why the making of culture and the enjoyment of culture are both good gifts from God that we ought to receive gladly and return to him in praise and adoration. To return to where this book began, culture making is one of the primary ways that God invites us to participate in his triune fullness. In cultivating creation, subduing the earth, and faithfully naming God's world (in all its varied forms), we are fulfilling the cultural mandate and participating in God's mission to fill the world with his glory.

When we write, perform, or listen to good music, we are being invited into the life of the triune God, who is the supreme harmony of all. When we write poetry or immerse ourselves in a novel or watch a good movie, our heart and mind can be enlarged so that we have greater capacity to worship God and love others. When we tend our gardens, change the oil, study for a math test, discover the characteristics of electrons, serve our customers, or build a new house, we are assisting in the enrichment of God's world, and we ought to enjoy these activities and their results with clear eyes and full hearts.

The Lord's Supper is a regular reminder that human culture can be a means of grace and a divine invitation. After all, we partake of bread and wine, not grain and grapes. In other words, God mediates grace to us through created goods that have been cultivated and transformed by human effort. Bread is grain, but transfigured. Wine is grapes, but glorified. Human creativity and labor mingle with the stuff of God's creation, and then God establishes the result as the church's sacramental meal. And this special sacrament testifies to the potential of all human activity to communicate the grace of God. Our cultural efforts are fully capable of enlarging our heart and mind to know God more fully.

But this process of heart expansion through human culture is not automatic. As we saw earlier, it requires receiving culture (or making culture) with a heart of gratitude that is governed by the Scriptures and dependent on God in prayer. It requires believing and knowing the truth, so that our efforts align with God's purposes, so that our creativity runs in biblical ruts, so that we cut with the grain of God's world and not against it.

Culture, like creation, has the capacity to draw us out of ourselves, to lead us into the blessed self-forgetfulness that is the first step toward true enjoyment of God. As Lewis once said, "To love and admire anything outside yourself is to take *one step away* from utter spiritual *ruin*."[26] *Losing oneself in a good book or a sweet song or an engaging hobby is a wonderful way of finding oneself.*

What about Evil?

This raises again the question of evil and sin in culture. Everything created by God may be good, but now it is tainted by sin and rebellion. Given the pervasive presence of evil and sin in culture and culture making, how can we enjoy it and not be tainted? Won't the worldliness and wickedness of rebellious culture rub off on us?

Limitations of space prevent a full treatment of this question. But a few observations will at least point the way forward. First, the presence of evil in culture doesn't inherently prevent us from enjoying culture, any more than the presence of evil in creation prevents us from enjoying creation.[27] Creation is good and cursed (Gen. 3:17–19), and it groans in subjection to futility (Rom. 8:19–22). Nevertheless, the curse on creation doesn't completely overthrow God's goodness in it.

Second, evil, pain, and suffering often instruct us by way of contrast. The futile subjection of creation is not an end in itself. It is meant to point us forward to a world made whole. The groaning of creation anticipates the liberation to come. The pain of childbirth directs our gaze to the joy of holding a newborn baby. So, then, the presence of evil within human culture can awaken us to our desire for a renewed and transformed world.

Third, God is able to communicate truth about himself through evil things in the world. The Devil is a thief who comes to steal, kill, and destroy (John 10:10). At the same time, Christ promises to return like a thief in the night (Matt. 24:43). The Devil prowls like a roaring lion seeking someone to devour (1 Pet. 5:8). At the same time, Christ is the Lion of

Judah (Rev. 5:5), who conquers all of his enemies. Thus, we see that both moral evil (thievery) and natural evil (predation) can point us to God.[28]

Fourth, we can have complex emotional reactions to both creation and culture. It is possible to be amazed at the hunting prowess of a wolf pack while simultaneously lamenting the reality of violence in God's good world and longing for the day when wolves lie down with lambs. Likewise, we can admire and be inspired by the courage and discipline of soldiers (whether in reality or in a story), and still lament that we live in a world where it's necessary for rough men to stand ready to do violence to those who would do us harm.

Fifth, there is a crucial difference between recognizing evil and delighting in evil. It's one thing to enjoy a story in which evil has its moment in the sun before being crushed. It's another to enjoy the specific moment when evil is triumphant. The former is noble and worthy, the latter is base and wicked. The crucial difference lies in the framing of evil, in seeing the outrage and absurdity of evil within a larger narrative that puts evil in its place. In other words, we should delight in stories that faithfully reflect God's treatment of evil in the grand story that he is telling.

Sixth, the presence of sin and wickedness in stories, movies, television, and music creates the opportunity to grow in biblical obedience by abhorring what is evil and clinging to what is good (Rom. 12:9).[29] We need as much practice and help in learning to hate what God hates as we do in learning to love what God loves. Culture and the arts can assist us by unveiling the true face of evil and thus awakening holy and righteous responses in our hearts. The sense of outrage we feel at the evil in a book or on a screen can help to form and shape us into the kind of people that God wants us to be.[30]

Seventh, the evil in our flesh means that the evil of the world can find an eager reception in our hearts, especially when stoked by the evil of the Devil. These three conspire together against God and against our joy, and therefore we must recognize the dangers of immersing ourselves in rebellious culture.[31] Culture engagement (and enjoyment) can easily become a cover-up for indulging sinful desires, an excuse to watch trashy movies. We must never forget that worldliness is easy, that plundering the Egyptians is hard, and that many an Israelite has convinced himself that he is absconding with the world's wealth when he's merely in the process of going native. As one pastor put it, what many call "plundering the Egyptians" is nothing more than dumpster diving in Egypt.[32]

Evaluating Our Culture Making and Culture Enjoyment

How then can we tell the difference? Here is a short (and nonexhaustive) list of questions that may help.

Does our cultural enjoyment lead us to worship God? After we've read what we've read or watched what we've watched, is our first impulse to want to thank God for it?[33] Or do we find ourselves sheepishly and fearfully hiding behind a tree, hoping that the Glory Cloud doesn't pass by on his evening stroll?

Where does our enjoyment of culture push us? When we're done, are our hearts enlarged and expanded so that we're eager to run back into the world in the cause of love? Or are our hearts shriveled up like prunes left out in the Arizona sun?

Does our cultural enjoyment harden us like a rock? If someone pricked us, would we bleed pebbles? Or has our cultural enjoyment of creation made us more tender of heart?

If you were to conform your actions and attitudes to those of your favorite characters, would your life be better or worse than it is now? I've met many college students who seem to think that the world is a sitcom starring them, and that it is in fact possible to be sarcastic, rude, and annoying to everyone around and still have friends for eight seasons. If you're in a one-on-one conversation, yet you find yourself saying things in order to get a laugh from the viewers at home (or the viewers in your own head), then it may be time to take a hiatus from some of your favorite shows.

Do the stories you like to write/read/watch/tell reflect the stories that God likes to tell? This doesn't preclude those that contain great evil; after all, God's story has been known to have a villain or two (or seven billion). The presence of evil isn't the issue, but the depiction of evil is. Are things that God hates portrayed as good and worthy? Is the evil of evil minimized or clarified? Do brutish men get overthrown or promoted? Are dragons slain or triumphant? This doesn't mean that you must avoid all stories that flow from the minds of rebels; it does mean that you recognize and resist what those stories are trying to do to you. It also means that you should know your own weaknesses and cut off your hand if it causes you to sin.

In sum, culture, both the making of it and the enjoyment of it, is a tremendous gift from God, one that we ought to receive with wisdom and gladness. Like all of God's gifts, it has the capacity to enlarge and expand our soul that we might know him better, love him more, and become more fully conformed to the image of his Son. Thus, we should be on the lookout for the true, the good, and the beautiful wherever we can find it. As Paul says, "Finally, brothers, whatever is true, whatever is honorable, whatever is just, whatever is pure, whatever is lovely, whatever is commendable, if there is any excellence, if there is anything worthy of praise, think about these things" (Phil. 4:8). In order to do this rightly, we must pray, as Paul did, that our love may abound in knowledge and all discernment so that we can recognize and approve what is good, better, and best and in so doing be pure and blameless until Christ returns, filled with the righteous fruit that comes from Christ, all to the glory and praise of God (Phil. 1:9–11).

For my own part, I've seen the glory of manhood in King Lune of Archenland and in *Cinderella Man's* Jimmy Braddock. I've seen the simple face of evil in *Perelandra's* Un-man, and the torture of hypocrisy and hidden sin in *The Scarlet Letter*. I've identified with Hamlet's incomprehensibility, marveled at evil in *Hotel Rwanda*, and laughed at (and with) Buddy the Elf. I've been awakened afresh to the world through Mozart's concertos, through Josh Garrel's soulfulness, and through Andrew Peterson's storytelling in song. I've danced with my wife to Garth Brooks, Gavin DeGraw, and Ella Fitzgerald and with my sons to hip-hop, bluegrass, and the fight songs of university marching bands. I've composed love poems, made up silly songs, cultivated a garden, built a fireplace, and written a book. In all this—in both my culture making and culture enjoyment—I've seen the wisdom in Tolkien's wonderful statement about the wonder of subcreation:

> The Christian has still to work, with mind as well as body, to suffer,
> hope, and die; but he may now perceive that all his bents and facul-

ties have a purpose which can be redeemed. So great is the bounty with which he has been treated that he may now, perhaps, fairly dare to guess that in Fantasy [and all of our culture making and faithful naming] he may actually assist in the effoliation and multiple enrichment of creation.[34]

8

Desiring Not-God

For Christ plays in ten thousand places,
Lovely in limbs, and lovely in eyes not his
To the Father through the features of men's faces.

Gerard Manley Hopkins

We may, by fixing our attention almost fiercely on the facts actually before us, force them to turn into adventures; force them to give up their meaning and fulfill their mysterious purpose. . . . The world will never starve for want of wonders; but only for want of wonder.

G. K. Chesterton

The real labor is to remember, to attend. In fact, to come awake. Still more, to remain awake.

C. S. Lewis

Human beings are imitative creatures. We can't help it. Before we become self-aware, we are aware of others. Children imitate parents and siblings. Young athletes imitate sports stars. Young musicians imitate rock stars. Readers imitate their favorite characters. Preachers imitate their sermonic heroes. Imitation is woven into the fabric of human existence, and we ought not resist it. "Be imitators of me, as I am of Christ" (1 Cor. 11:1). "What you have learned and received and heard and *seen* in me—practice these things, and the God of peace will be with you" (Phil. 4:9).

Perhaps, then, the most concrete way to get practical with what I've been saying is simply to describe some moments from my own life, attempts at integrated rhythms of godwardness and reception of God's gifts for his sake. These illustrations are just that—illustrations. They are limited by my experiences, locations, relationships, abiding sinfulness, maturity, and so forth. For most of these snapshots I don't provide full explanations of their meaning. My hope is that you will be able to read between the lines and see how the scenarios illuminate the Christian life. If nothing else, hopefully they can put some meat on the bones of everything we've considered thus far.

* * * *

Seven-thirty a.m. My house. Room time for the boys (the time after breakfast when they play in their room while Dad gets his act together for the day).

From the room: "Dad. Dad. Dad. Daddy. Daddy."

Pause.

"Dad. Dad. Daddy. DaDa. Daddy. Daddy. Dad. Daaaaa-ddddyyyyy. Daddy. Dad."

Pause.

"Dad. Daddy. Daddy, come here. Dad, come here. Daddy. Dad. Daddy. Dad."

I relent and make my way to the room. If Jesus had visited my house, it would have been called the "Parable of the Persistent Three-Year-Old" (Luke 18:1–8).

* * * *

My one-year-old walks up to me with arms outstretched. I can see it in his eyes. He is searching for something: approval, affirmation, acceptance. The kind that only a father can give. He is hungry for a father's love, for the Father's love.

Either the laughter in my eyes, the smile on my face, and the strength and tenderness of my arms will tell the truth about God, or their absence will blaspheme the Father of lights.

My son is reaching for me, and looking for God.

My son, the theologian.

. . . . .

We are, all of us, prone to wander. In my case, I'm prone to wander into anxiety, into doubt, into depression. I've had my share of dark nights of the soul, some long, some short. I still tremble at the memory of some of the panic attacks, the disorientation flowing from an incessant doubt that refused to give me a moment's rest. I remember the surreal feeling of experiencing what one pastor calls "a kind of self-extinction," mentally spinning into a deranging inability to know who I was anymore. I remember the loneliness and the fear, the nights spent staring at the ceiling, frantic thoughts looking for any way out, and the terrifying sense of despair that would wash over me in moments of hopelessness and fatalism about the future.

But I have other memories of those times. Faithful friends and family who listened to my questions, some laboring (and even researching and writing) in order to attempt specific answers, others praying and encouraging and (in some cases) rebuking sins that would show their ugly heads. Wise, older men, fathers in the faith, who listened and counseled from mature experience about how to keep faith when the foundations are shaking.

And, in the later seasons of doubt, the unshakeable hope and stable tenderness of my remarkable wife. Her words, her hope, her touch anchored me in ways that defy my explanations. I felt the comfort of God in my wife's faithful presence. Her faith picked up the weak and shivering remnants of my own and carried them when all I could do was weep.

I don't have to wonder what God would have said to me and done for me had he been physically present in the midst of those dark times. I know, because he was present in her presence.

. . . . .

Joy is music. It starts simple and grows in complexity. My son knows the melody line of joy and delight. He calls it "fun." He's learned it through playgrounds, petting zoos, tickle fights, and hide-and-seek. He bears witness to this melody every time he says, "Do it again," through belly-tightening laughter.

As a father, one of my chief goals and responsibilities is to play that melody line again and again and again. I want his heart to be tuned to the sweetness of fatherly delight and pleasure, to have the purity and wonder of simple and deep delight echo in his soul and call him outside of himself.

There are other joys, complex pleasures that defy simple explanations. There is the slow and tender joy of marital intimacy. There's the sweet, breathtaking delight at a beautiful sunset over a calm ocean. There's the thrilling satisfaction of intellectual discovery and growth in wisdom. And then there's the strange joy of absence, sorrow, and longing. As Lewis says, "The best havings are wantings."

Yes, there are layers to joy, depths that my son simply can't fathom yet. So my job is to prepare him for the mature joys, to get him ready to hear and play harmonies. His knowledge of God and his experience of joy in God will grow by addition. The melody line will always be there (simple laughter never ceases to amaze), but it will be layered and enhanced and enriched by his growth in Christlike maturity.

And we are all like my son, practical infants when it comes to solid joys and lasting pleasures. We can't imagine what God has in store for us. Our minds are not big enough yet. Our hearts are not large enough yet. Eye has not seen, ear has not heard. And the only way to prepare for the coming glories is to press into what God has given us now. If we're to eventually be entrusted with the laughter of heaven, we must faithfully enjoy the music of God that we hear now.

· · · ·

I love to see those I love happy. I love it even more if I am a contributor to their happiness. When my son is awestruck by the ocean or struck with the giggles by a funny moment in a cartoon, joy floods my heart. My soul swells with his laughter. When I've surprised my wife with a clean house or a just-because-I-love-you gift, and I see the unexpected happiness in her eyes, I want to freeze time and savor the moment, because in that moment I have access to the inner meaning of things. I'm not trying to be esoteric or weird. The inner meaning of things actually lies on the surface. Sin has broken it up, covered it over, and distorted it beyond recognition. But it's still there, waiting to be found by the regenerate heart.

When you encounter it, you recognize it as the most beautiful and natural thing in the world. Reality clicks. Something snaps in your soul, and everything falls into place. The inner meaning of things is the sense of coherence and unity, the brilliance of the harmony that God has embedded in creation. The ancients called it "the music of the spheres." Tolkien dramatized it as the music of the Ainur, potent symphonic themes that effected the creation and order of the cosmos. In Christian terms, it is the creational instantiation of the triune fullness. It is the glory of the living God *ad extra*, outside of himself. "The fullness of the whole earth *is* his glory."

* * * *

I have a memory. An early morning in 1993. An eleven-year-old me rolls over in bed as the sun peaks through the blinds. Bleh. School day.

I feel a hand on my back. It rubs for a moment and then gently scratches. I lift my shoulders, prodding the fingers for a little more. It's a familiar routine, and the fingers don't fail.

The back rub turns to a pat. "Time to get up, buddy."

I roll over. My dad sits on the edge of my bed, dressed in a button-down shirt and dark pants. He's been up for a while. He's showered and shaved and ready for work. I can smell his aftershave.

I stumble bleary-eyed into the kitchen. The cereal, milk, and bowl are on the counter. My lunch is packed. Turkey and mustard on daily bread. Grapes and Ranch Doritos. My dad knows what I like.

He picks up his briefcase, kisses me on the forehead, and heads out the door.

A lesson in eschatology. There is something worth getting out of bed for. There is hope for the future.

* * * *

Fast-forward fifteen years. Home for Christmas. I've always loved the holidays.

My dad slowly walks out of his room, shuffling his feet. His hair is disheveled, his beard unshaven. He's wearing an old T-shirt and pajama bottoms.

It's 1:30 in the afternoon.

He pauses and looks around with apprehension and a tinge of panic in his eyes. The look on his face unnerves me for a moment.

I hate dementia.

"Here, Dad. Come sit here on the couch. I'll get you something to drink."

"Even to your old age I am he, and to gray hairs I will carry you. I have made, and I will bear; I will carry and will save" (Isa. 46:4).

Oh, Lord, please do.

* * * *

One more jump. This time two years forward. Christmastime again.

The steadfast love of the Lord endures forever.

He sits (if you can call it that) in a special chair. It's been months since he's walked. He weighs about one hundred pounds. Skin and bones, but his skin still looks good.

The steadfast love of the Lord endures forever.

My mom sits next to him, holding his ever-shaking hands. Damn Parkinson's. He breathes in a low wheeze. It sounds awful, but the nurses say it's normal.

The steadfast love of the Lord endures forever.

Those hands. They held me when I was young. They rubbed my back during church services. They taught me how to throw and hit. "Keep your eye on the ball," he'd say. "Step toward the pitcher and keep your head down."

The steadfast love of the Lord endures forever.

I watch my mom as she searches his face, lovingly looking for recognition, for something beyond the vacant stares. She's walked with him through every bit of the slow death—through diagnoses and experimental treatments and cautious optimism and crushing loss at a sudden turn for the worse. This is not how she envisioned her golden years.

The steadfast love of the Lord endures forever.

"Billy. Billy. Hey, Sweetie."

She catches his eye. A flash of something, and a smile plays at his lips.

The steadfast love of the Lord endures forever.

"Hey there," he says, and a chuckle rises up from his throat. We all smile and laugh with him, his eyes darting from person to person.

She leans in to give him a kiss, and he puckers. Not everything in the old mind is lost. She leans back; he stays puckered. We laugh as she kisses him again, still holding his trembling hand.

Covenants run deep. Till death do us part. "This mystery is profound," said the apostle (Eph. 5:32).

The steadfast love of the Lord endures forever.

● ● ● ●

Before our oldest son was born, my wife and I struggled for a few years with infertility. The doctors weren't sure that we'd be able to have children. This was especially hard on my wife, and there were many tears shed and prayers prayed. When the Lord answered our prayer for a son, we took seriously the responsibility of naming him. As we tossed around and debated various names, I finally went into my office and sat down and wrote a poem in order to choose his name. I did the same for our second son.

Our oldest's name is Samuel Jonathan. Samuel means "God has heard," and Jonathan means "the Lord has given." Our second son is named Peter William, after our fathers, who were both enduring serious health issues when we got pregnant. I'm including the poems I wrote, because it provides a window into my feeble attempt to read my Bible and the world and my own story and to capture all of it in a poetic snapshot.

Samuel Jonathan

For three long painful years we sat
In dry and barren darkness that

The Things of Earth

Like Hannah, left us vexed in soul
By circumstance beyond control
Of us or any mortal man.
We'd cry, "A child is better than
All other earthly gifts that God
Could ever give. This painful rod
Of childlessness makes sick our hearts
With grief that by its fits and starts
Did bring us to our knees in prayer.
O LORD who made the earth and air,
Why have you closed this mother's womb?
For in our heart and home there's room
For ten children. And yet right now
We ask for only one and bow
The knee in humble hope and trust
That you will never forget us.
And lest our desire grows too strong
And in sorrow we charge with wrong
The God who holds us day by day
In everlasting arms, we say:
The greatest gift that you could give
Is naught compared to Christ who lives
To intercede for sinners poor
And needy. In him we find sure
joy, the likes of which any child
Is but a faint echo." Beguiled
And wearied by this burden, we
Let loose our strong and silent plea
And, like sweet incense, it arose
To the Father of Lights who knows
Exactly what his children need.
And from his throne with swiftest speed
Goes forth a sure and sovereign word,
"Make no mistake, your God has heard.
And so, rejoice, O barren one,
For I will give to you a son.

Upon his life you'll have no claim,
But to you it will fall to name
This little boy, so choose thee well,
A name to shake the gates of hell,
A name that calls to mind the One
Who heard your cries and gave His Son
To die upon that judgment tree
To give you life and make you free,
Not only from your barrenness,
But from your sin, so you could bless
His holy name for all your days,
And render him all thanks and praise
For giving you ev'ry good thing
That makes you glad and makes you sing,
And even those that made you weep
And plead with God that he would keep
And hold you up in darkest night,
Yes, even those in Him are light."
Is there a name that says all this,
A name that calls to mind the bliss
And joy that fills our hearts these days
Without neglecting all the ways
That we have grieved for three long years,
That will remind of all the tears
And prayers we offered to the Lord?
Is there a name to strike this chord?

So, my son, that's how we thought
About the name that is your lot.
We chose it to remind of both
The sorrow and the blood-sealed oath
Of God to ne'er forsake his own
In painful trials and griefs unknown.
Your name displays God's faithfulness,
For we asked for you, and he said, "Yes."
Your name is Samuel Jonathan,
For God has heard and God has giv'n.

The Things of Earth

Peter William

The saying goes, "My, how things change!"
So in our case, it's not too strange
That two years have brought shifts indeed
As time has run on swiftest steed
And changed a woman's barren tears
That flowed through the infertile years
From weeping to parental joy:
Into a laughing toddler boy
an infant son transformed. And more,
from basement to a home adored
for size and shape and rays of sun
that stream through windows on such fun
as Sam can have with Mom and Dad.
And into hearts so full and glad
A question comes, no trace of fret,
"Can it get still better yet?"

But not all change is good, we find,
As cancer hits us from behind,
A fright'ning, fearsome stumbling block
that beats upon the family rock,
upon the one who's always there
to guard and keep those in his care,
The one who always has a plan,
A safe and strong and godly man.
But with humor and with grace,
Papa shows us how to face
The broken world in which we live,
And receive what God may give
With patient joy and gratitude:
Our Father's wise, and he is good.

More sorrow yet, and deeper still
As cruel disease stalks Daddy Bill,
Assaulting mind with slowest death

Whose sons and wife with tearful breath
have prayed a thousand earnest prayers.
A tired smile is all he wears
As words flow jumbled from his lips
Instead of sly, quick-witted quips
That used to grace his clever tongue
When mind and heart were both still young,
Back when he'd rise before his brood
And lovingly prepare them food,
And gently rouse them with a rub,
"Time to wake up. It's morning, bub."
And without words, he seemed to say,
"Life's worth living. Let's face the day."
And now the arms that held a mitt
And taught me how to throw and hit
Lie shaking, trembling and frail,
But held by arms that cannot fail,
Arms that from the dust formed man
And guide us by a perfect plan,
Until to dust returning, we
Await the Hope we don't yet see,
The Hope that bruised and dying bled,
The Hope that God raised from the dead.

Into all this change there comes
A child, with perfect hands and thumbs
And feet and cheeks and ears and toes,
With reddish skin and snuggly nose.
Into the sorrow and the joy
We welcome a new baby boy.
And once again, to us it falls
To name him with a name that calls
To mind the God who bears us up,
Who sent his Son to drink the cup
Of foaming wine on our behalf,
And comforts us with rod and staff
Whene'er we walk through valleys grim

And dark with death. We lean on Him
When earth gives way, and waters foam,
When shadow falls on hearth and home,
When nations rage and kingdoms mock,
Then we stand on God, the Rock.
And in our Father's Will we rest
And from his hand receive the best.
To capture this, what name to choose?
Of change, and life that we must lose
If we're to gain a better one
Whene'er the Land Beyond the Sun
Descends to earth with festal shout
And Death is finally cast out?
And of course, our fathers too,
Who've given us a hope that's true,
A hope that laughs at times to come,
That knows where joy and mirth is from,
A hope that works in silent womb,
The hope that lives beyond the tomb.

So, on this Rock, we place your name,
Renouncing every earthly claim,
And to this Will, entrust your care,
Our God will guard, no matter where.
Your name is Peter, and William too.
For God is your Rock, and will always keep you.

* * * *

I love to teach. I hate administrative tasks. And today is an administrative day. The to-do list is filled with e-mails that need to be written, proposals that need to be edited, phone calls that need to be made. Maybe I can call in sick.

The laundry is dirty. Again. I have no shirts, and my only clean socks have holes. The pile of soiled garments near the closet mocks me.

It's 6 a.m. I wake with my boys, who I'm convinced are part rooster. I push through the kitchen door and see the sink, still full of dishes.

I knew I'd regret putting them off. Now I'll have to scrub. Melted and dried cheese is such a pain.

We return from our summer vacation. After unpacking the ice chest, I head to the garage to put it away. I'm stopped short by the flora in my backyard. It looks like a jungle in Sumatra. The Virginia creeper has claimed two of the patio chairs. The dandelions have annexed part of the green grass. Tall weeds whose name I've never bothered to learn tickle my waist as I pass. I can't even see the rocky flowerbeds that I know lie beneath them. My Saturday just got ruined.

Autumn comes. The three large trees that surround our house in summer and keep our cooling bill down dump their brightly colored shade on my lawn. The weather prophet promises showers tonight. I hope he's wrong. I hate digging wet leaves from my rain gutters.

Minnesota in February. The kind of land that only the White Witch could love. Always winter, never Christmas. And now I'm paying for being away from home for the holidays. The New Year's blizzard has frozen on the edge of my roof, and the ice dams are six inches thick. If I don't deal with them now, there will be water running down my walls this spring. I'll get the ladder and the panty hose filled with rock salt.

Seriously? You filled your diaper again? I just changed it ten minutes ago. What did you eat today?

Vanity of vanities, says the Preacher . . .
   All is vanity. . . .
All things are full of weariness;
   a man cannot utter it;
the eye is not satisfied with seeing,
   nor the ear filled with hearing.
What has been is what will be,
   and what has been done is what will be done,
   and there is nothing new under the sun. (Eccles. 1:2, 8–9)

* * * *

Cursed is the ground because of you;
   in pain you shall eat of it all the days of your life. (Gen. 3:17)

• • • •

The little boy jumps around in his black and red outfit.

"I'm Spider-Man," he says. He's never even seen Spider-Man. He just likes costumes from his grandmother.

"And what does Spider-Man do?"

"He flies around. And kills dragons."

Yes. Yes, he does. It's not every day that you get to see the future church militant.

• • • •

I have a vision. Two little men with pointy ears and hairy feet dance on a table with large pints of ale in their hands. They're singing a song about the Green Dragon, and everyone is laughing at them. Or laughing with them. In this situation, I'm not sure there's a difference.

Another vision. A wedding out of an old book, written for women, that was turned into a movie that I was obligated to see. I mean, that I had the privilege of seeing on a date with my wife.

Anyway, the wedding. The place is bright, even at night, and the people dance together. It gets a bit rowdy, and everyone is displaying a remarkable lack of self-consciousness. And there's the weird laughter thing again. Even the laughing *at* is really a laughing *with*.

It's the sort of party that you wish you were invited to. You could make a total fool of yourself, and no one would hold it against you. It's the kind of place where you would be free of the crushing obligations you place on yourself on behalf of others. The obligations that paralyze you with fear that someone is watching and waiting for you to trip, or slip, or say something odd.

The end of history is a Wedding Feast. Heaven will be this kind of party. I hope they invite the hobbits.

• • • •

The Texas Hill Country in July. Ultimate Frisbee.

This is a great afternoon. After chasing the disc for a few hours, I jog to the tree where the cooler has been brought. The throat is parched, and the inside of the mouth has that gross sticky feeling. I place my cup beneath the spout and push the button.

I notice the grassless ground beneath the big oak. The thought flashes through my mind: "To shovel that dirt into my mouth with a potsherd right now would be insane."

And, according to Jeremiah 2:12, a parable of great evil.

* * * *

I admit it. I'm needy. I'm practically made of need. If need were money, I'd be the Bill Gates of need. Especially this week.

You know how it happens. You say yes to one too many things (or five too many). I teach six times this week: the theology of the first three chapters of Genesis. Rhetoric. Popes and kings of the high Middle Ages. What does it mean to be a creature? Attributes of spiritual leadership. Anselm's ontological argument for God's existence.

Then I'm preaching four times over the weekend. Bethlehem College is holding its Preview Days. And Desiring God has its national conference (I'm hosting one of the speakers).

Oh, did I mention that my tire is flat? Looks like a nail in it. And that I have two children under four? And I think I'm losing my voice (all that teaching, you know).

Yes, I have lots of needs, and this week I feel them acutely.

"My God will supply every need of yours according to his riches in glory in Christ Jesus" (Phil. 4:19).

How will he do it?

Hey, everybody, could you pray for me this week? It's gonna be crazy.

A college student will help me to change my tire (by which I mean, he'll change the tire while I look on helplessly). Another will give me some Hall's cough drops with triple soothing action. I'll eat them like candy. My wife will transform into Super-Mom and hold down the home front while keeping me fed. A colleague will cover my responsibilities at the conference so I can pray and prepare for the sermon. Lots of people will pray.

And I'll move from class to class, from task to task, asking for God's help and trusting his promises as I labor with all my might.

It's Sunday night. Classes: taught. Preview Days: done. Sermon: preached. Sons: alive. Wife: sane (barely). My soul: full.

Needs met by the riches of his glory in Christ Jesus: My family. His church. And cough drops.

• • • •

West Texas. The place where God ran out of ideas.

At least that's what they say. (Actually that's what I say as a joke whenever I introduce myself to new people).

But God did have one big idea when he made West Texas. Sky. Lots and lots of sky. Big sky. Blue sky. Red and orange sky (with some purple thrown in for good measure). And we all know that the sky is a preacher, a prophet of God's glory and handiwork.

I remember West Texas thunderstorms buttressing my battered faith during a dark night of the soul. In the midst of my doubts and wrestling, I couldn't deny the beauty I saw when the dark clouds rolled along the horizon, dumping brief floods on thirsty ground. I could sometimes see the setting sun, blazing through the edges of the storm clouds like it was going to light them on fire.

The wind always blows in West Texas, but it blows differently when the storms are coming in. There's something in the air, maybe a smell, maybe atmospheric pressure (whatever that is), maybe a promise or a prophecy. Maybe a little bit of all of them.

You can scan the horizon and see the storm getting darker where the rain is thickest. You can see the lightning flash from the dark billows, a tongue of fire shooting from God's fingertips.

He rides on one of them, you know. The clouds, I mean. If you could get close enough to one, really get up in it, would you see the wheels of his chariot? Like Ezekiel, would you see the cherubim, the palace guards of Yahweh's glory cloud, shining like coals of fire and darting to and fro like lightning? Would you hear in the flapping of their wings the roaring of the ocean in a tempest, the tumult of a battalion on the march?

If you could see above the clouds to the throne of the eternal one, high and lifted up, would you see the bright seraphim, those ancient flaming serpents with six wings? Would you hear them chanting their thrice-holy song while the train of his glory robe fills the temple and covers the world?

With the right eyes, you can see a lot in a West Texas thunderstorm.

* * * *

Romans 1, on the other side of the new birth:

For the pleasure of God is revealed from heaven upon all godliness and righteousness of men, who by their righteousness celebrate the truth. For what can be known about God is plain to them, because God has shown it to them. For his invisible attributes, namely, his eternal power and divine nature, have been clearly perceived, ever since the creation of the world, in the things that have been made. For because they know God, they honor him as God and give thanks to him, and they become fruitful in their thinking, and their humble hearts are enlightened. Having become fools for Christ, they became wise, and received the glory of the immortal God and saw his glory in mortal man, birds, animals, and creeping things. Therefore, God restored them in the desires of their hearts for purity, to the honoring of their bodies among themselves, because they gladly received the truth about God instead of lies and worshiped and served the Creator, who is blessed forever, rather than the creature. Amen. For this reason, God renews their desires and delights and passions. For the women glory in the masculinity of their husbands, and the men likewise revel in the femininity of their wives, and are consumed with passion for them, men honoring the marriage bed and receiving in themselves the due reward for their obedience. And since they saw fit to acknowledge God, God has reoriented their renewed minds to do what ought to be done. They are filled with all manner of righteousness, goodness, contentment, benevolence. They are full of gratitude for others' gifts, brotherly love, peace, truth telling, magnanimity. They are edifiers, encouragers, lovers of God, courteous, meek, humble, inventors of good, obedient to parents, wise, faithful, compassionate, merciful. Because they know God's decree that those who practice such things will receive eternal life, they not only do them but give approval to those who practice them.

●   ●   ●   ●

He's a squirmy one, he is. If I don't watch him, he'll wriggle off the bed. But he doesn't want to. He's enjoying the tickle fight too much. I can't blame him. Those giggles make this father's heart want to leap out of my chest. I wonder how long this laugh will last.

Reflect on the tickle fight with me. See the layers of reality at work.

On the surface: an adult male and a one-year-old of the species, smiles, laughter, darting fingers, kicking legs, squeals, deep breaths, rapid kisses on the neck, raspberries on the belly, and did I mention the laughter?

Beneath the surface: emotional bonding, fatherly affection, wide-eyed childhood delight. A contribution to the child's sense of safety and security in the world. Perhaps he'll be well-adjusted (or, at least, better adjusted). This will no doubt help him on his SATs.

Beneath and in and through it all, Trinitarian fullness is being extended. The joy that made the mountains is concentrated in my bedroom. Fatherly delight is at the heart of reality. "This is my beloved Son, with whom I am well pleased." It plays on a perichoretic tape in the back of my mind. Thus sayeth the Lord to his Son. Thus sayeth the Lord to all of his sons that are in the Son.

This is the pitch of fatherhood. This is the melody line of motherhood. This ought to be the dominant note in the familial symphony. Delight, pleasure, joy. This tickle fight is high theology. This scene is a picture, a parable of a glory that existed before the world did. It's a display and an invitation. Father and son are being beckoned into the divine life and joy.

Only I will remember it distinctly. The scene will pass through my son's mind and out of his memory. And yet, in a sense, it's the most spiritual thing I can do for him. My delight and pleasure in him can leave a mark on him that will outlive the sun.

"Father," I pray, taking a breath in the war of laughter to go directly to God, "make it so."

The lesson for fathers (and mothers): be the smile of God to your children.

●   ●   ●   ●

The goal of these musings is illustrative, not exhaustive. These are examples to inspire, not slavishly copy. Make them your own. Consider yourself loosed and don't be restrictive in your applications. This type of God-besotted, Christ-exalting, Scripture-saturated life is as wide as the world. The earth really is the Lord's, including all the fullness.

Let me close this chapter with a few reflections on living out this type of paradigm.

First, don't feel that you need to add a Bible verse to every one of your pleasures. You shouldn't feel guilty if you can't readily identify the specific attribute of God that is communicated in your enjoyment of something. Sometimes a pleasure is just a pleasure. Period. Full stop. God is honored in your enjoyment of it, your gratitude for it, and its fruitfulness in your life for the sake of the kingdom. So just receive the gift as one of the many pleasures at his right hand.

Second, recognize the layering of reality. God is a father, and God is a rock, which means that somehow fathers are like rocks (and shepherds and fortresses and kings). Dive into God's metaphors. Think about the relevant similarities and differences in the analogies and comparisons in the Bible and then feel free to make applications. For example, the relationship between Father and Son in the Godhead is pictured in human fathers and sons. But it's also pictured in fathers and daughters, and mothers and sons, and mothers and daughters, all while allowing for the distinctive glory in those relationships.

Or again, think of the way that Paul reasons in Ephesians 5:25 and 1 Corinthians 11:3:

> Husbands, love your wives as Christ loved the church and gave himself up for her. (Eph. 5:25)

> But I want you to understand that the head of every man is Christ, the head of a wife is her husband, and the head of Christ is God. (1 Cor. 11:3)

Husband and wife picture Christ and the church, which is downstream from God the Father and Christ. Extending this outward, I think we can see something profound about Trinitarian life in every relationship that involves headship and authority. This includes grandparents and grandchildren, employer and employees, a king and his subjects, a coach and his team, and so on. The same dynamic of head and body, initiative and response, what C. S. Lewis calls "The Dance," is played out in dozens of unique relationships.

Third, the best safeguard for this type of analogical and metaphorical reasoning and feeling and worshiping is a thorough knowledge of the Scriptures. Read your Bible. Train your mind to run in biblical ruts. Learn the patterns and rhythms of Scripture. Chaos and order. Exile and return. Death and resurrection. Let your imagination be shaped, molded, corralled, and harnessed by the living Word of the living God.

Memorize whole passages (singing helps). Be familiar with the whole counsel of God. Know your way around the various books so that even if you can't recite a particular passage word-perfect, you at least know where it is in general and can find it with relative quickness. Regular, prayerful meditation on the Scriptures keeps our analogical thinking from jumping the rails.

Fourth, as you think about expanding your soul through robustly engaging with and gratefully receiving God's gifts, be sure to take the long view. In emphasizing that we should dive into creation and then go godward in worship so that our souls are increasingly enlarged, I don't mean to suggest that this process is a straight line, onward and upward. Progressive sanctification is a lifelong process, and a bumpy one at that. There are times when our joy in God and his gifts takes off like a bottle rocket; other times, we experience the hardship of the lean years.

> Even youths shall faint and be weary,
>   and young men shall fall exhausted;
> but they who wait for the LORD shall renew their strength;
>   they shall mount up with wings like eagles;
> they shall run and not be weary;
>   they shall walk and not faint. (Isa. 40:30–31)

Sometimes we soar, flying through holy skies with grace beneath our wings. Sometimes we run, arms pumping as we make good time on the Spirit's road. Sometimes we walk, faithfully plodding on our journey to a far country. And sometimes we may simply face in the right direction, sitting on the path, weighed down by burdens and cares, perhaps working up enough strength to crawl for a minute or two before collapsing. The fundamental thing is to be always moving toward the heavenly city, irrespective of speed. As someone once said, God is after a long obedience, and our direction is more important than our pace.

Finally, keep the gospel central. When seeking to be the kind of character that God wants you to be in the story, remember that your main goal is to image God in Christ to those around you. Your aim is to be a walking gospel proclamation. You want to proclaim Christ crucified with your words and in your words. You want to portray him in your actions, attitudes, and demeanor, displaying the appropriate emotional and spiritual response in a given situation.

I've personally found that viewing all of reality as communication from God has a tremendous effect on my pursuit of holiness. Because if everything is speaking about God, then *I* am speaking about God in everything I say and do. And I will be either telling the truth about God or lying about him. I will be either an extension of God's love for people or a barrier to their experience of that love.[1] It forces me to ask, What would God say if he entered the room right now? What does he want said, and how can I say it in my words, demeanor, and actions? I can't tell you how many times that sort of question has prevented me from saying or doing something sinful or foolish or has encouraged me to enter a room with a deliberate and Spirit-empowered intention to communicate God's love or his faithfulness or his gladness or his displeasure or his playfulness.

In all of your life, you want to display the worth and value of Jesus and the vitality of the divine life. So ask yourself questions such as:

- Am I a model worth emulating? Are my patterns of thinking and feeling worth passing on? Is what I say worth repeating? Are my emotional responses appropriate and fitting?
- Do I weep when it's time to weep? Do I rejoice when it's time to rejoice?
- When courage is required, am I as bold as a lion?
- When it's time to give advice, am I ready with wise counsel? When it's time to receive orders, am I ready to take them with a glad salute?

- Do I model leadership and initiative when appropriate? Do I model submission and obedience when appropriate?
- Do I take responsibility for my actions? Do I model how to humbly receive instruction and correction and rebuke from others?
- Do I model wisdom and violence in the war against sin?
- Am I an example of faithful suffering?
- Do I give thanks always and for everything?

In seeking to live this way, we must remember the grace of God. It is grace that pardons us, grace that heals us, grace that strengthens us, and grace that empowers us to live the Christian life. And when we receive and proclaim and portray Christ in this way, we become the extension of God's triune fullness in the world. Such a life is what creaturely participation in God's life looks like on the ground. That's the ballgame. That's the whole enchilada. That is the great calling to which we've been called.

9

Sacrifice, Self-Denial, and Generosity

God has a way of giving by the cartloads to those who give away by shovelfuls.

Charles Spurgeon

Earn as much as you can. Save as much as you can. Invest as much as you can. Give as much as you can.

John Wesley

The New Testament has lots to say about self-denial, but not about self-denial as an end in itself.

C. S. Lewis

God is the source of all our blessings—he is the ocean of blessings. Creatures are but the hands which distribute his charity through a needy world.

Samuel Davies

We come now to a few of the central challenges to the vision of the Christian life presented in this book. Does an emphasis on receiving and enjoying all God's gifts to us undermine the biblical call to voluntarily give up good things in the cause of love? Does it undermine missionary endeavors, especially to the unreached and unengaged? And what about self-denial? Will people who aspire to honor the giver by enjoying his gifts really sell everything they have in order to faithfully follow Jesus? Or are we essentially inverting Jesus's words in Acts 20:35, turning "It's more blessed to give than to receive" into "It's more blessed to receive than to give"?

The answer is, "It depends." I'm not so naïve as to think that the exhortations in this book couldn't be abused. (If anyone figures out how to write a book that is immune to abuse, let me know.) It's entirely possible to twist what I'm commending into an excuse to receive good gifts and then sit on them, hoarding them for ourselves rather than wisely and generously stewarding what God has given. But it doesn't have to.

It's the burden of this chapter to show why celebrating God's gifts doesn't undermine missionary efforts, overthrow the biblical call of self-denial, or cut the root of radical generosity. In fact, before we're done, I hope to show that calling people to enjoy all that God freely gives can actually advance the mission of God among the nations and strengthen big-hearted, sacrificial, and open-handed generosity.

Enjoying God's Gifts for the Sake of the Nations

So how exactly does enjoying God in everything and everything in God further God's passion for the glory of the gospel of Christ among all the peoples of the world?

First, the call to enjoy God's gifts for his sake reminds us of one of the central aims of the Great Commission, namely, to teach the nations to obey all that Jesus commanded (Matt. 28:20). We are calling the nations to trust in Christ crucified and risen for sinners and then to love God and neighbor in the power of the Holy Spirit. But how will they love God if they don't know him deeply? And how will they know him deeply if they don't see him clearly and rightly in the things he has made? And how will they see him clearly and rightly in creation if the preachers who carry the gospel don't themselves see and savor God in all things?

I'm of the mind that one of our long-term goals with respect to the unreached peoples of the world is that they one day craft poems and hymns that rival Herbert, Watts, and Wesley, that they compose God-honoring symphonies that surpass Bach and Handel, that they author stories and epics that portray the beauty of Christ as did Milton and Lewis, that they write theology and philosophy that outshine Augustine, Calvin, and Edwards (partly because they stand on the shoulders of such giants). And the prerequisite to all such God-entranced cultural endeavors is the ability to see the truth, beauty, and goodness of God's world, indeed, to see *God* in God's world.

Don't misunderstand me; I'm not arguing that high culture making should be the first thing on our missionary agenda. Simple faith in Christ, obedience to God, and knowledge of the Scriptures should be the foundation that we seek to lay among the unreached. But we ought to remember that the purpose of a foundation is *to build a house on it*. And the house that we hope to build as God's fellow workers is one filled with heartfelt worship of the triune God through poetry, art, philosophy, music, and literature (as well as good food, clean diapers, laughter, medicine, and fruitful labor). Thus we must lay a gospel foundation that acknowledges the goodness of God in his gifts as those who have been enriched by the goodness of God in his gifts.

And to those who would scoff at the notion that the greatest theologians, philosophers, and culture makers in the history of the church might eventually hail from Somalia or China or Afghanistan, remember this one fact: a thousand years ago Vikings from Saxony, Norway, and Denmark were raping and pillaging their way across Europe. They worshiped the one-eyed, bloodthirsty god Odin and fought under the banner of the Black Raven. Before battle, they ate hallucinogenic mushrooms, painted themselves blue, and ran naked into the fray.

Five hundred years later, one of their heirs nailed a piece of paper to a door and ignited the Reformation. Five hundred more years, and their descendants settled the Midwest, invented hot-dish, and gave us Minnesota Nice. One of those descendants is the worship pastor at my church. From mushroom-crazed berserker to Christ-exalting worshiper. That's what the gospel does. That's what happens when the grace of God lands among rebels and turns them into friends of God.

That's why faithful gospel proclamation must include a robust theology of the goodness of God's gifts in creation. If God is calling the nations to know him as he has revealed himself in his Word and in the world, then a central element of discipling the nations must be teaching them to observe and delight in the beauty and glory of the triune God in nature, in food, in their families, in *everything*. Thus, like us, the nations and peoples of the world must learn to honor the giver by rightly enjoying his gifts.

Great-Souled Missionaries

This brings me to the second way that the enjoyment of God's gifts advances Christ-exalting missions and evangelism around the world. One of my deep desires for this book is that it will be used by God to create God-centered, creation-affirming missionaries. To cross the culture barrier into an unreached people group is to encounter idolatrous rebels who misuse God's world, worshiping and serving the creature rather than the creator. This is true whether it's worldly Westerners enthralled with technology, animistic tribes that bow before created spirits and stone statues, or ascetic Buddhists who seek to detach from the world in a misguided quest to extinguish suffering.

Wherever we take the gospel in this fallen world, we confront people who have rejected the creator God and therefore turned creation into a god, with all the resulting debased desires and people-harming conduct that flows from it. Therefore, a chief need of such people is a living, breathing example of rightly ordered desires, of the new way to be human, of an appropriate celebration of God's creation and gratitude for God's gifts and worship of God himself. Put another way: we cannot export what we don't have. Or, to riff on the apostle Paul, how will they imitate without a model?

We need missionaries with the heart of the apostle to the Gentiles, who gladly gave up good things for the sake of the gospel among the nations and then taught his churches that the earth is the Lord's and its fullness, that everything created by God is good and to be richly enjoyed, that we should think deeply about *whatever* is true, honorable, just, pure, lovely, commendable, and excellent. Paul is the perfect example of a radically self-denying and gloriously creation-affirming frontier missionary, and we should eagerly pray that his tribe would increase.

Thus, to commend the enjoyment of God in all that he's made is to hope and pray for blood-earnest, great-souled gospel witnesses who have had their minds and hearts and categories enlarged by the enjoyment of God and his gifts such that the greatness of the soul and the greatness of God remain, even when the goods and kindred that produced that greatness have been given up for the sake of Christ and his kingdom.

Biblical Self-Denial

This brings us to the question of self-denial. How does the call to enjoy God's gifts fit with Christ's call to deny ourselves and follow him? First, I should say that waiting to discuss it until now was intentional. Biblical self-denial can be rightly understood only against the backdrop of the goodness of what we're giving up. Biblical self-denial is always the giving up of a lesser, legitimate joy for the sake of a greater one. It's renouncing something good for the sake of something better. So then, what can we say about biblical self-denial?

First, as I'm using the term, biblical self-denial is the voluntary giving up of legitimate things for the sake of Christ and his kingdom. Thus, it is distinguished from the *involuntary* loss of good things (which I'll discuss in chapter 12). Moreover, self-denial is not identical to the mortification of sin. Self-denial is a part of sanctification, but it differs from giving up sinful practices. Giving up a luxury car for the sake of Christ is different from giving up a stolen car. Sin killing demands that we stop doing certain things because they are sinful, because the Bible forbids them. Biblical self-denial demands that we give up certain things because, though they are good, God has something more in store for us.

Second, biblical self-denial embraces what C. S. Lewis calls "the blessedly two-edged character of Christianity."[1] Christianity is a paradoxical religion in that it is both world-affirming and world-denying. It's world-affirming, Lewis says, because its adherents have always devoted themselves to affairs of this world: healing the sick, caring for the poor, celebrating marriage, producing works of art, literature, and philosophy. It's world-denying because its central image is an instrument of torture and death, because it calls for fasting as much as feasting, and because it calls its practitioners to lay up treasure in heaven and not on earth. The combination of these two elements sets Christianity apart from other major religions. Christians celebrate creation because it is made by God. But Christians also treat creation, in a sense, lightly because it's not God. Thus, Lewis writes, Christian self-denial differs from its pagan counterparts:

> Hence, in all true Christian asceticism, that respect for the thing rejected which, I think, we never find in pagan asceticism. Marriage is good, though not for me; wine is good, though I must not drink it; feasts are good, though today we fast.[2]

Christianity leaves us "free both to enjoy [our] breakfast and to mortify [our] inordinate appetites" (even our normal appetites, which may become inordinate).[3]

Third, biblical self-denial is one of the central ways that we establish the supremacy of God in our lives. It's exhibit A of the comparative approach that we explored in chapter 5. When we deny ourselves, we do so that we might follow Christ, and, as Lewis once pointed out, "nearly every description of what we shall ultimately find if we do so contains an appeal to desire."[4] In other words, we deny ourselves as thorough-going Christian Hedonists since, in the Bible, gaining Christ is universally shown to be "far better" than anything else in the world (Phil. 1:24).

Fourth, biblical self-denial is a kind of death. Jesus emphasizes the need for daily dying in what may be the most famous passage on self-denial in the Bible:

> He said to all, "If anyone would come after me, let him deny himself and take up his cross daily and follow me. For whoever would save his life will lose it, but whoever loses his life for my sake will save it. For what does it profit a man if he gains the whole world and loses or forfeits himself?" (Luke 9:23–25)

God has given us desires that they might be fulfilled, just as he's given us life that it might be lived. Thus, to renounce desires is to die, to journey with a cross on our back down the Calvary road. What's more, by tying self-denial to death and life, we are able to see it in rhythmic terms. There is a death and resurrection movement in all of our self-denial. We lose our life in order to save it. We forfeit the world that we might gain ourselves. We willingly suffer daily death that we might, like Christ, be triumphantly raised from the dead.

Fifth, biblical self-denial is always accompanied by "unblushing promises of reward."[5] Consider Jesus's words to his disciples in Mark 10. The rich young ruler had just refused to leave his wealth to follow Christ. Jesus then warns of the dangers of wealth and the difficulty of entering the kingdom with it (v. 23). After Jesus describes the impossibility of salvation apart from God, Peter says, "See, we have left everything and followed you" (v. 28). In other words, Peter drew attention to the self-denial of the disciples. Jesus's response is incredible:

> Truly, I say to you, there is no one who has left house or brothers or sisters or mother or father or children or lands, for my sake and for the gospel, who will not receive a hundredfold now in this time, houses and brothers and sisters and mothers and children and lands, with persecutions, and in the age to come eternal life. (Mark 10:29–30)

A few observations about Jesus's words. First, the self-denial is for Jesus's sake and the gospel. Second, those who deny themselves receive back things both "now in this time" and "in the age to come." Third, what they receive back in this time far surpasses what they gave up ("a hundredfold").[6] Fourth, the glory of what they receive back now is not untouched by pain and hardship but still carries persecutions with it.

From this, I conclude that when we leave good things for the sake of Christ, God gives us back good things, with interest. The form that the returned gift may take varies. You may give up your house for Christ, and he might return to you a better house (with "better" being defined by fruitfulness for you, your family, and the kingdom, not necessarily by size or expense). You may lose your family for the gospel, and God may restore familial fellowship through the church. The returned gift may simply be the manifest presence of God in your life in the midst of your losses.[7] But whatever form the replacement gift takes, Jesus is clear—we ought to expect a hundredfold value returned to us *in this life*, and we should expect the returned gift in the midst of suffering and persecutions.

What's more, the fact that Jesus speaks of the reward in earthly and earthy terms sets his call to self-denial apart from paganism. Socrates was willing to lose everything in this life for the sake of pursuing wisdom in an ethereal world of eternal ideas. He denied himself in this life and then took up his hemlock because he looked forward to leaving behind the prison house of his body and gaining the right to contemplate abstractions forever. Therefore, Socrates would have been entirely nonplussed by the promise of Jesus in this passage. Receiving a hundredfold of the earthly goods that he sought to renounce would not have sounded like good news. Yet Jesus offers us more of what we leave and lose if we will only lay it down for his sake.

Finally, biblical self-denial is glad-hearted, even in the midst of denying ourselves. It may be hard and painful (after all, it is a kind of dying), but it is endured and embraced with joy, because biblical self-denial flows from faith in the God who raises the dead. This means that biblical self-denial cannot be gloomy. When we subject ourselves to martyrdom, we do so without a martyr complex. Paul stresses the joyful quality of our self-denial in a brief but powerful passage in 2 Corinthians 12:

> Here for the third time I am ready to come to you. And I will not be a burden, for I seek not what is yours but you. For children are not obligated to save up for their parents, but parents for their children. I will most gladly spend and be spent for your souls. (vv. 14–15)

Self-denial appears at the end, in the spending and being spent. But Paul enables us to grasp self-denial by giving us a metaphor to explore. He helps us to understand ministry by showing us something profound about parenting. As Paul promises to return to the Corinthian church, he insists that he will not be a burden. By this, he means that he will not *take* anything from them. In other words, if Paul came to get something from them, he would be using them and would therefore be a burden. That's why Paul says he seeks the Corinthians themselves, not their stuff. In seeking them in this way, Paul is acting like a parent with his children. And parents do not burden or use their children. Instead, parents save up for their children. They come to spend and be spent for the souls of their children. The word for "save up" is the same word used in Matthew 6:19–20:

> Do not *lay up* for yourselves treasures on earth, where moth and rust destroy and where thieves break in and steal, but *lay up* for yourselves treasures in heaven, where neither moth nor rust destroys and where thieves do not break in and steal.

Drawing these passages together, we might say that there is a kind of saving up on earth that is also a laying up in heaven. When parents save up earthly goods in order to spend them for the eternal good of their children, they are simultaneously laying up treasures in heaven. They save up and spend for their children's souls and thereby store up again eternal treasure for themselves (and, God willing, for their children as well).

But not only do parents save and spend their earthly wealth for their children; they also spend themselves. And, perhaps most importantly, they do so "most gladly." Parents (and apostles) don't give grudgingly. Parental spending is a happy affair.

So also with us in all our voluntary sacrificing and self-denial. When a mother labors over a stove for her family, she is spending and being spent, and she must do so with a glad heart. When a father forgoes his own plans and hobbies in order to invest in his children, he must do so with a smile on his face and joy in his bones. When a waiter picks up an extra shift in order to help out a coworker, there ought not be any grumbling or complaining but a deep rejoicing in doing good to another. In short, there is a way of losing your life that looks like finding your life, because it is finding your life. There is a way of denying yourself that brings out your true self, your full self, your glad self. There is a way of embracing sacrifice and hardship and inconvenience (however great or small) that will be identified by some as a kind of enjoyment. You will look like you are having too much of a good time. You will spend yourself and be spent, and you will do so with a twinkle in your eye and laughter in your heart.

What then can we say about biblical self-denial in relation to the good gifts of God? Biblical self-denial celebrates the goodness of what's renounced. It accents the comparative worth and value of God over all his gifts. It is a kind of dying and therefore carries with it the promise of resurrection, since we are following the crucified and risen Lord. The reward for self-denial is given both now and in the age to come, and this enables us to gladly spend ourselves on behalf of others, since God "always gives back with his right hand what he has taken away with his left."[8]

What about Wealth?

But the Bible commends to us more than mere renunciation. The biblical call is also to give to others. In other words, the real question is whether stressing the enjoyment of gifts will sever the root of radical generosity. Does the call to enjoy gifts inevitably result in the sin of hoarding gifts, storing up treasure on earth, rather than treasure in heaven?

Before addressing the question of wealth, it's worth pausing for a public service announcement. Writing anything about the right use of wealth is a tricky business. Not only is the biblical teaching complex, but the range of applications makes it almost impossible to say anything helpful without being subject to serious misunderstanding. So let me stress that my goal for this chapter is relatively modest. I simply want to make progress. Maybe just a step or two forward in wrestling with what it means to honor God in the use of the resources he provides.

In order to do that well, let me draw attention to some of the inherent limitations of my treatment of wealth. Someone once said that the great challenge of communication is that you can't say everything all the time. All communication is selective, which means that it's subject to misinterpretation. "Why didn't you mention this crucial biblical truth?" "Because I had only five thousand words to work with. Because I didn't want to write a three-volume tome. Because I needed to take a nap."

The fact of selectivity is particularly difficult when it comes to addressing lifestyle decisions such as the proper use of money. Not everyone needs to hear the same encouragement or exhortation or warning. Not everyone has the same temptations, inclinations, and proclivities. Some lean left and need to be pushed right. Some lean right and need to be pushed left. But if you push to the right, you may cause those who lean to the right to fall over. And, as a general rule, I try to avoid pushing people over.

Some people lean on the ascetic side and are highly attuned to the danger of worldliness, consumerism, and materialism. They are sensitive to the threat of Mammon worship to the point that they must be reminded that God's gifts are good and ought to be received gladly. Others treat the danger of greed and idolatry lightly and are far too comfortable with the worldliness around them. Luxuries and comforts easily become necessities of life, and they need to be reminded that Jesus calls us to follow him on the road *to the cross*.

What's more, I'm limited by my own circumstances, tendencies, upbringing, and context. Rather than run from these limitations, I've decided to embrace them. My thoughts on wealth have been indelibly shaped by the fact that I'm a white, middle-class American who was born in Texas, went to public school and a state university, and now lives in Minneapolis. And while I firmly believe that the Bible addresses all times and places with an authoritative word from God, it doesn't address all times and places *in the same way*. So I'd just ask you to read charitably, think carefully about what I say, test it all by the Scriptures, and cut me some slack.

Three Basic Affirmations

I want to begin by making three basic affirmations about wealth in the Bible: wealth is more than money; wealth is good; wealth is dangerous.

1) Wealth Is More Than Money

The Bible defines wealth broadly. While we normally think of wealth in terms of money, money is not really wealth. Money is a measure of wealth. The little pieces of paper in my pocket (or the numbers in my bank account with the $ in front of them) are ways that we gauge how much wealth we have. Put me on a desert island with a mountain of greenbacks and I'm as poor as any medieval peasant. Real wealth includes all the things that the money can buy.

Without attempting to be exhaustive, this includes iPhones, houses, minivans, blue jeans, college education, Chinese food, Calvin's *Institutes*, computers, waiter service at Outback (and the cooks and busboys), central air-conditioning, photos of the kids, a trip to Disney World, the Internet, CAT scans, and comfortable tennis shoes. In other words, it includes both goods and services.

It also includes a number of things that we are even more prone to take for granted such as roads, bridges, other infrastructure, a functioning legal system, access to qualified doctors and nurses who know how to bring down the fever, the machines and processes that somehow turn oats and honey into Cheerios and then get boxes of it to the grocery store where I can pick it up, and Amazon.com.

These are all things that money can buy, or things that money has bought that can facilitate the buying of other things. It involves both concrete things (like iPads), the invisible information that makes the things work (like the software), and the skills and expertise of the people who designed and made it (from Steve Jobs down to the guy who makes the metal backing). It also includes access to all sorts of intangible benefits that increase our knowledge and delight in this world such as our families, teachers, schools, friends, pastors, and mentors.

In short, wealth has to do with resources broadly speaking, and a narrow fixation on dollars and cents can obscure and distort more than it can help illuminate.

2) Wealth Is Good

In the Bible, wealth is a sign of blessing. Prosperity and abundance are gifts from God:

> You shall remember the LORD your God, for it is he who gives you power to get wealth, that he may confirm his covenant that he swore to your fathers, as it is this day. (Deut. 8:18)

> Blessed is the man who fears the LORD,
>   who greatly delights in his commandments! . . .
> Wealth and riches are in his house,
>   and his righteousness endures forever. (Ps. 112:1, 3)

> The crown of the wise is their wealth. (Prov. 14:24)

> Everyone also to whom God has given wealth and possessions and power to enjoy them, and to accept his lot and rejoice in his toil—this is the gift of God. (Eccles. 5:19)

> And the LORD will make you abound in prosperity, in the fruit of your womb and in the fruit of your livestock and in the fruit of your ground, within the land that the LORD swore to your fathers to give you. The LORD will open to you his good treasury, the heavens, to give the rain to your land in its season and to bless all the work of your hands. And you shall lend to many nations, but you shall not borrow. (Deut. 28:11–12)

> As for the rich in this present age, charge them not to be haughty, nor to set their hopes on the uncertainty of riches, but on God, who richly provides us with everything to enjoy. (1 Tim. 6:17)

The fact that I'm typing this book on a computer is a good thing. The fact that I can take my wife to the doctor when she gets sick, and they can give her medication to help make her feel better, is a good thing. The fact that on my way home from work I can pick up a hot pizza for dinner is a good thing. And all these are examples of wealth.

The Bible does warn us of the dangers of wealth (see the next point), but the fact that it's dangerous doesn't mean that it's not good. We are not spreading a curse to poor villages in Africa when we dig a well so they can have potable water. We are not afflicting them with a disease when we teach people better methods of farming or build a factory so that they can have steady employment. When we spread the wealth in this way, we are spreading a good thing.

3) Wealth Is Dangerous

Wealth is a good gift, and like all of good gifts it is profoundly dangerous:

> But godliness with contentment is great gain, for we brought nothing into the world, and we cannot take anything out of the world. But if we have food and clothing, with these we will be content. But those who desire to be rich fall into temptation, into a snare, into many senseless and harmful desires that plunge people into ruin and

187

destruction. For the love of money is a root of all kinds of evils. It is through this craving that some have wandered away from the faith and pierced themselves with many pangs. (1 Tim. 6:6–10)

Jesus looked around and said to his disciples, "How difficult it will be for those who have wealth to enter the kingdom of God!" (Mark 10:23)

No one can serve two masters, for either he will hate the one and love the other, or he will be devoted to the one and despise the other. You cannot serve God and money. (Matt. 6:24)

Keep your life free from love of money, and be content with what you have, for he has said, "I will never leave you nor forsake you." (Heb. 13:5)

Desiring to be rich, loving money, craving wealth, serving Mammon—all these undermine our faith and imperil our soul. As good as wealth is, it can keep us from entering the kingdom. It can easily become a rival to God, the kind that makes us despise him. And Paul tells us that if you see an evil walking around in the world, there's a good bet that the love of money is lurking somewhere underneath it.

Wealth Is for Receiving and Giving

Given the goodness *and* danger of wealth, God calls us to two fundamental activities in relation to it. The first is gratitude for God's provision. The second is generosity with God's provision. Or, to use the categories that we developed in chapter 4, wealth is given for our needs and enjoyment, and wealth is given as provision for mission.

Before looking at generosity and mission, let me quote Richard Baxter on the proper response to God's provision of earthly goods:

We need to guard our lives against the love of riches and worldly cares. All love for earthly goods, however, is not a sin. Their sweetness is a drop of his love and they have his goodness imprinted on them. They kindle our love for him as love tokens from our dearest friend. Loving them is a duty, not a sin.[9]

It's a duty to love the earthly goods God provides. Indeed, it's a sin to fail to receive them gladly:

> Because you did not serve the LORD your God with joyfulness and gladness of heart, because of the abundance of all things, therefore you shall serve your enemies whom the LORD will send against you, in hunger and thirst, in nakedness, and lacking everything. And he will put a yoke of iron on your neck until he has destroyed you. (Deut. 28:47–48)

Our service to the Lord must be filled with joy and gladness *because of the abundance of all things*. Not joyfulness in the abstract, but joyfulness because God lavishes us with blessing like the sky lavishes snow in a Minnesota winter. Otherwise, God promises judgment against our ungrateful and joyless service.

However, it's not enough to merely receive abundance from God gladly. Receiving and enjoying earthly goods quickly becomes soul endangering if it's not coupled with the second necessary response. This is what separates the exhortations in this book to gladly receive God's provision from the damnable error of the health, wealth, and prosperity gospel.[10]

Here is the second necessary response. Having gratefully received provision for our needs from God's hand, we are called to use what we've been given to bless others—to meet their physical needs, their emotional needs, and, most importantly, their spiritual need for the gospel. Or, again, we are to use what we have gladly received from God in order to fulfill the mission God has given us:

> Sell your possessions, and give to the needy. Provide yourselves with moneybags that do not grow old, with a treasure in the heavens that does not fail, where no thief approaches and no moth destroys. For where your treasure is, there will your heart be also. (Luke 12:33–34)

Identify needs. Sell your possessions and meet those needs. In so doing, you will be laying up treasure in the heavens that never wears out. It's these actions that testify that your highest treasure is not in God's gifts but in God himself, and that when you do delight in earthly goods, your delight is also a delight in God.

Paul's Surprising Word to the Wealthy

These two responses to wealth aren't simply the result of creative proof-texting. They show up together in a crucial passage in 1 Timothy. As we saw earlier, in Paul's letter to his protégé he firmly warned of the dangers of loving money, of desiring to be rich, of craving wealth (1 Tim. 6:5–10). Such desires are a deadly temptation, a harmful and destructive trap, the source of all kinds of evil, including apostasy. A few sentences later, he returns with a particular charge to those who have great wealth:

> As for the rich in this present age, charge them not to be haughty, nor to set their hopes on the uncertainty of riches, but on God, who richly provides us with everything to enjoy. They are to do good, to be rich in good works, to be generous and ready to share, thus storing up treasure for themselves as a good foundation for the future, so that they may take hold of that which is truly life. (1 Tim. 6:17–19)

There are three exhortations in verse 17: (1) Don't be puffed up. (2) Don't set your hope on wealth, which can perish at any moment. (3) Set your hope on God, for he is steadfast and stable. So far, this exhortation makes a lot of sense. But then Paul surprises us by reminding the wealthy that God richly provides us with everything to enjoy. We must not miss this. Paul wants the *rich* to know that God *richly* provides their wealth for their joy. As we've seen, gifts are given to us for our enjoyment. They are not given to us so that we could set our hopes on them. But there must be a difference between setting one's hope on something and simply enjoying it. Paul, as we saw in chapter 5, distinguishes between setting our minds (*phroneo*; Col. 3:1–4; Phil. 3:19) on something and considering (*logizomai*; Phil. 4:8) something. Likewise here in 1 Timothy, we are called to set our foundational hope on God and then deeply enjoy what he richly provides.

But in reminding the wealthy of God's purposes in his gifts, Paul does not lose sight of the second response we must make: our joy in God's gifts must flow forth in doing good. The rich in this present age must be rich in good works. Enjoying must not be hoarding; instead, we must be generous and eager to share what we have. But even generosity rebounds for our good, because in richly sharing what we've richly been given, we are also storing up treasure for the future. This heavenly treasure is stable and certain, unlike the uncertain riches of this age, and on that foundation we will lay hold of true and eternal life.

In chapter 4 we saw that Genesis 1–3 teaches us that gifts are given to us for our enjoyment, and they are given as provision for mission. Paul confirms that these purposes abide even in this fallen and sinful world. God provides everything for our enjoyment. And he provides everything for the sake of his mission in the world. Gifts are meant to be fruitful in our own lives as well as fruitful for God's kingdom. Everything is for our joy, and our joy is increased when God's provision multiplies in good works, lavish giving, a wealth of generosity, and eager and open-handed sharing.[11]

How Much Should We Give?

How much of our wealth should we then give? In the Scriptures the amount varies. The Old Testament required a tithe of the fruit of the land (Deut. 14:22–27). Jesus called the rich young ruler to sell everything to follow him (Luke 18:22). When Zacchaeus was saved, he gave half his goods to the poor (Luke 19:8). Barnabas sold a field and put the money at the feet of the apostles (Acts 4:37). The poor widow put two pennies in the offering box and was commended by Jesus (Luke 21:1–3). The amounts may vary, but the basic call is the same—use wealth to meet the needs of others.

In his exhortation to the Ephesians, Paul underscores the progression from receiving wealth to giving wealth to meet needs:

> Let the thief no longer steal, but rather let him labor, doing honest work with his own hands, so that he may have something to share with anyone in need. (Eph. 4:28)

Notice in that verse the three possible orientations to wealth. First, we can be thieves, gaining wealth through sinful means. Second, we can forsake theft, doing honest work with our hands so we gain wealth

The Things of Earth

honorably. Finally, we can receive wealth from honest work so that we can share with others, being generous with what God has provided through our labor. Steal, work to have, work to have to give—these are the three options, and only the last one reflects the nature of the giver of all good things.

Finally, the most well-known passage on giving in the Bible implies this progression of receiving and giving:

> You yourselves know that these hands ministered to my necessities and to those who were with me. In all things I have shown you that by working hard in this way we must help the weak and remember the words of the Lord Jesus, how he himself said, "It is more blessed to give than to receive." (Acts 20:34–35)

As in his exhortation to the Ephesians, Paul labors to have in order to meet his needs and then generously gives to alleviate the suffering of the poor and weak, motivating himself with the words of Jesus. But notice the implication of Jesus's words. To say that it is more blessed to give than to receive is to say that it is more blessed to receive *in order to* give. There's no shortcut here; we cannot give what we don't have, and we can't have it if we don't receive it (1 Cor. 4:7). So before we can be generous givers, we must first be grateful receivers (and, according to Paul, hard workers). Open-handed generosity flows from glad-hearted reception.

That is precisely what we see in the book of Acts:

> And day by day, attending the temple together and breaking bread in their homes, they received their food with glad and generous hearts, praising God and having favor with all the people. And the Lord added to their number day by day those who were being saved. (Acts 2:46–47)

Receiving gladly and giving generously go hand in hand. The early church joyfully received the wealth that God supplied and then used that wealth to meet the needs of their fellow Christians (Acts 2:45). The wealth that God supplied was not a barrier to their generosity but the means of it.

And this receiving-leads-to-greater-giving dynamic is exactly what I've discovered in my life. My experience is that grateful and glad-hearted reception of gifts doesn't undermine generosity; it increases it. It's possible to receive a gift and hoard it, but when a gift is received as it is meant to be—gratefully, cheerfully, happily—it has the effect of enlarging the soul and overflowing outward in lavish giving. Having experienced the joy of receiving, we seek to spread this experience to others—to give concrete gifts that meet real needs, to give thoughtful gifts that satisfy long-held desires, to give surprising gifts that awaken unanticipated delight. Before you can be a lavish giver, you must first be an eager and grateful receiver.[12]

Motivation for Giving

This brings us to the question of motivation to give. For Paul, the motivation for giving is as important as the act of giving. In his extended reflections on Corinthian giving for the relief of the saints in Jerusalem, in 2 Corinthians 8–9, he returns again and again to the issue of motivation. (Given the length of the passage, you can read along in your own Bible. Go ahead and get it; I'll wait.)

(No, seriously, get your Bible. That way you can follow along with the comments.)

First, Paul repeatedly refers to generous giving as an expression of the grace of God and as an act of grace (8:1, 6, 7, 19; 9:14). In order for grace to be grace, it must be given freely, voluntarily, without constraint.

Second, Paul knows that he is dealing with churches that have already expressed a willingness to give. Titus had initiated the plan for a gift for the relief of the saints in Jerusalem a year prior (8:6, 10).

Third, he seeks to strike the balance between stirring up the generosity of the Corinthians while doing everything he can to avoid any hint of compulsion or coercion. He wants to exert persuasive pressure, but he wants to do so without taking the Corinthians on a guilt trip. He holds up the example of the Macedonians, who gladly gave beyond their means in the midst of their own affliction and poverty (8:1–4). But he then immediately says, "I say this not as a command" (8:8). He points to Jesus as the model, who "though he was rich, yet for your sake he became poor, so that you by his poverty might become rich" (8:9), and then immediately highlights the fact that they not only began to do the work, but more importantly began to *desire* to do it (8:10). He sends Titus and others ahead of him in order to ensure that the promised gift is ready as "a *willing* gift, not as an exaction" (9:5).

And, of course, one of the most well-known passages on giving: "Each one must give as he has decided in his heart, not reluctantly or under compulsion, for God loves a cheerful giver" (9:7). We ought not give reluctantly. We ought not give under compulsion. We ought to give *cheerfully, gladly, willingly*. There is a qualitative element to our giving that must be present. The absence of this quality ruins the gift.

Guilt or Gratitude?

It's worth dwelling on the issue of motivation a little more. Guilt is a terrible motivator. When we give out of guilt, we only give enough to make the guilt bearable. And such guilt does little to help those in need. Simply feeling guilty because we live in the West does not help the poor gain adequate food or access to the gospel. What might help relieve suffering around the world is glad reception of what we've been given and deep gratitude for God's kindness that explode out of our lives in a wealth of generosity.[13]

This is the picture Paul paints in 2 Corinthians 8–9. Grace lands in the poverty and affliction of Macedonia and unleashes a torrent of glad-hearted generosity (8:1–4). Grace lands, and they give until it hurts. Or, again, in the amazing promise of 9:8: "And God is able to make all grace abound to you, so that having all sufficiency in all things at all times, you may abound in every good work." Grace abounds, we have all we need, and, therefore, we can abound in every good work. God gives us grace and gifts and wealth that our needs might be met, our desires might be satisfied, and his global mission might be accomplished.[14]

God supplies seed to the sower so that it will be sown bountifully. When God identifies bountiful sowers, he multiplies seed and provides bread for food. In other words, he meets our needs and gives extra so that we can distribute it freely and increase the harvest of our righteousness (9:9–10).[15]

Paul supports this notion of wealth and generosity by quoting Psalm 112:

> Praise the LORD!
> Blessed is the man who fears the LORD,
>> who greatly delights in his commandments!
> His offspring will be mighty in the land;
>> the generation of the upright will be blessed.
> Wealth and riches are in his house,
>> and his righteousness endures forever.
> Light dawns in the darkness for the upright;
>> he is gracious, merciful, and righteous.
> It is well with the man who deals generously and lends;
>> who conducts his affairs with justice.
> For the righteous will never be moved;
>> he will be remembered forever.
> He is not afraid of bad news;
>> his heart is firm, trusting in the LORD.
> His heart is steady; he will not be afraid,
>> until he looks in triumph on his adversaries.
> He has distributed freely; he has given to the poor;
>> his righteousness endures forever;
>> his horn is exalted in honor. (vv. 1–9)

This man is blessed because he fears the Lord and delights in his law. Twice, the text mentions that his righteousness will endure forever: first when God fills his house with wealth and riches (v. 3) and then again when the wealthy man freely and lavishly gives that wealth to the poor (v. 9).

Finally, notice the progression in 2 Corinthians 9:11–12:

> You will be enriched in every way to be generous in every way, which through us will produce thanksgiving to God. For the ministry of this service is not only supplying the needs of the saints but is also overflowing in many thanksgivings to God.

As we saw earlier, the Corinthians are enriched in every way so that they will be generous in every way so that gratitude will abound in those who receive the gift. Note this: the result of the generosity is not merely meeting the needs of people but is also overflowing gratitude to God. That's the aim of our generosity, because it's also the aim of God's generosity. This means that the first step in cultivating a generous and giving heart and life is to cultivate profound gratitude to God for what he has provided. As one author puts it, grace begets giving, which begets gratitude, which begets more gratitude.[16]

Therefore, Paul's lesson in 2 Corinthians is clear. Put to death soul-shrinking, false guilt. Guilty receiving produces grudging giving. Instead, receive God's provision gladly and then, with needs met and gratitude abounding, give according to your means (and beyond them!). Freely receive and so freely give.

10

When Wartime Goes Wrong

Put your kids to bed, secure, well-fed, and warm, thank God for it from the low bottom of your heart, and plot how to extend that wonderful grace to others.

Douglas Wilson

Would you know who is the greatest saint in the world: It is not he who prays most or fasts most, it is not he who gives most alms or is most eminent for temperance, chastity or justice; but it is he who is always thankful to God, who wills everything that God wills, who receives everything as an instance of God's goodness and has a heart always ready to praise God for it.

William Law

We've seen that wealth is good and dangerous, that glad-hearted reception should lead to open-handed giving, and that our motivation to give is as important as our act of giving. This chapter will address one helpful and increasingly prominent way of describing the Christian's relationship to wealth, namely, the wartime lifestyle. The call for such a lifestyle is rooted in biblical passages that describe the Christian life in terms of a struggle and fight. Paul *struggles* with all of Christ's energy on behalf of the Colossians (Col. 1:29), just as Epaphras struggles on their behalf in prayer (Col. 4:12). Paul describes his own sanctification as a boxing match and a race (1 Cor. 9:26–27) and therefore disciplines his body so as to win the prize. He tells the Corinthians that we wage war, but not according to the flesh. We have divine power to demolish strongholds and bring thoughts captive to obey Christ (2 Cor. 10:3–5).

In his exhortation about ministry, Paul tells Timothy to "wage the good warfare" (1 Tim. 1:18) and that no soldier gets entangled in civilian pursuits (2 Tim. 2:4). And then, of course, Ephesians 6:12–18 unpacks the Christian life in terms of a war not "against flesh and blood, but against the rulers, against the authorities, against the cosmic powers over this present darkness, against the spiritual forces of evil in the heavenly places." Thus, John Piper rightly concludes that according to the Bible, "life is war."[1]

He then goes on to describe the type of lifestyle that results from a deep recognition that we are in a war:

> In wartime, the newspapers carry headlines about how the troops are doing. In wartime, families talk about the sons and daughters on the front lines and write to them and pray for them with heart-wrenching concern for their safety. In wartime, we are on alert. We are armed. We are vigilant. In wartime, we spend money differently—there is austerity, not for its own sake but because there are more strategic ways to spend money than on new tires at home. The war effort touches everybody. We all cut back. The luxury liner becomes a troop carrier.[2]

Later, he writes:

> Jesus presses us toward a wartime lifestyle that does not value simplicity for simplicity's sake but values wartime austerity for what it can produce for the cause of world evangelization. He said, "Sell your possessions, and give to the needy. Provide yourselves with money-bags that do not grow old, with a treasure in the heavens that does not fail" (Luke 12:33). "Make friends for yourselves by means of unrighteous wealth, so that when it fails they may receive you into the eternal dwellings" (Luke 16:9). "Do not seek what you are to eat and what you are to drink, nor be worried. For all the nations of the world seek after these things, and your Father knows that you need them. Instead, seek his kingdom, and these things will be added to you" (Luke 12:29–31).
>
> The point is that an $80,000 or a $180,000 salary does not have to be accompanied by an $80,000 or $180,000 lifestyle. God is calling us

to be conduits of his grace, not cul-de-sacs. Our great danger today is thinking that the conduit should be lined with gold. It shouldn't. Copper will do. No matter how grateful we are, gold will not make the world think that our God is good; it will make people think that our god is gold. That is no honor to the supremacy of his worth.[3]

In advocating this type of wartime lifestyle, Piper acknowledges the need for pastors to take the lead in helping people to make wise, kingdom-advancing decisions with their money:

What should a pastor say to his people concerning the purchase and ownership of two homes in a world where twenty-four thousand people starve to death every day and mission agencies cannot penetrate unreached peoples for lack of funds? . . .

Then you will ask, "Is it wrong to own a second home that sits empty part of the year?" And you will answer, "Maybe and maybe not." You will not make it easy by creating a law. Laws can be obeyed under constraint with no change of heart. Prophets want new hearts for God, not just new real-estate arrangements. You will empathize with their uncertainty and share your own struggle to discover the way of love. You will not presume to have a simple answer to every lifestyle question. You will acknowledge that your own lifestyle, if it's in America, is lavishly comfortable in comparison with most people in the world.

But you will help them decide. You will say, "Does your house signify or encourage life at a level of luxury enjoyed in heedless unconcern for the needs of others? Or is it a simple, oft-used retreat for needed rest and prayer and meditation that sends people back to the city with a passion to deny themselves for the evangelization of the unreached and the pursuit of justice for the suffering oppressed?" You will leave the arrow lodged in their conscience and challenge them to seek to live a lifestyle in sync with the gospel.[4]

So, then, wealth is a broad term encompassing all the resources God supplies. Wealth is both good and dangerous, and given that life is war, we ought to live a wartime lifestyle, strategically using our resources for the glory of God and the good of people.

The Challenge

With those as some fundamental biblical assumptions, let me now introduce a challenge that I've run into in seeking to live this type of lifestyle. Put simply, it is this: there is a way of embracing a wartime lifestyle that undermines big-hearted, open-handed, radical generosity and harms deep, life-giving, Christ-honoring relationships. Note this: wartime is a useful model for understanding the Christian's relationship to wealth and lifestyle. I'm not challenging the metaphor itself. But I am seeking to bring other biblical and experiential realities to bear on our understanding of wartime so that we avoid a truncated, narrow understanding of how to use wealth for the advancement of the kingdom.

My main reason for addressing the issue at all is that it's an important part of my own story. For years I cultivated an understanding of wealth and wartime that not only damaged some important relationships in my life but actually undermined the very goal of a strategic use of resources, namely, radical generosity in the cause of love. So the rest of this chapter is essentially a recounting of some key moments in my own struggle to come to grips with money, interspersed with biblical reflections where appropriate. Most of the stories are drawn from my own life, though some are made up and others are actual anecdotes in which the names have been changed to protect the guilty.

One last caveat: I'm fully aware that my struggles are not everyone's struggles. My temptations and sinful tendencies are not universal, which means that more needs to be said than what I can say here. This is the great challenge of a chapter like this. So if you think that I've left out something crucial about our use of money, you're probably right. My hope is simply that these reflections can be a corrective to others who are like me and perhaps encourage patience in those who aren't.

The Beginning

I was born in the wealthiest nation in the history of the world, to a middle-class family in West Texas. I attended a quality, nonreligious, private elementary school, and then made my way through a great public school system with dedicated teachers who taught me to read, write, and 'rithmetic. I had loving parents who brought me to church, coached my baseball team, encouraged excellence in whatever I pursued, and made my early years largely delightful. I worked hard, made good grades, played sports, had good friends, and mostly stayed out of trouble. I was given a car when I turned sixteen (a Toyota that was older than I was), and then, as a reward for all my hard work, I was given a new truck when I graduated with honors from high school and received academic scholarships to attend Texas A&M University. I've always had food on my plate and a roof over my head, and I've been showered with blessings, opportunities, and gifts at every turn.

I also live in a world in which other children are orphaned, abused, starved, and thrown into unfathomably awful situations. There are people with no access to the gospel of Jesus Christ, or to quality education, potable water, indoor plumbing, healthy meals, and a thousand other blessings that I take for granted. Given that disparity in the world, what should my *first* response be to all that I have received?

Gratitude. Unbridled gratitude. Abounding and overflowing thanksgiving. Not guilt. Not shame. Not self-reproach for being born in America or having the opportunities that I've had. And the reason for the gratitude is at least threefold.

First, Paul tells us to give thanks always and for everything (Eph. 5:20). Were you born in Dallas? Be thankful. Were you born in Calcutta? Be thankful. Were you born rich? Be thankful. Were you born poor? Be thankful. Have your sufferings and challenges been relatively minor? Be thankful. Have they been heartbreaking and terrible? Be thankful.

I'm not saying it's easy or that we should be glib. But if the shipwrecked, beat-up-and-left-for-dead, falsely-imprisoned-and-tortured apostle Paul can be grateful for everything, then so can we.

Second, I did not choose the place of my birth, or my family, or the gazillion opportunities that God has given me. He determines the habitation and boundaries of all men on the earth (Acts 17:26), which means that to feel guilty about his decision isn't just silly; it's an offense against his inscrutable wisdom. Jesus did not die on the cross to deliver me from the sin of being born in America. Being Christians in the West doesn't give us license to live like the worldlings of the West; what we do with all of God's blessings and gifts matters immensely. But the Bible does banish false guilt over what God has graciously provided to us. We don't boast about the gifts ("What do you have that you have not received?"), but neither do we grovel and mope. We reach down deep and we marvel at his kindness to us and move forward in obedience to his Word.

Third, Paul tells us that there is a secret to facing plenty and abundance:

> I know how to be brought low, and I know how to abound. In any and every circumstance, I have learned the secret of facing plenty and hunger, abundance and need. I can do all things through him who strengthens me. (Phil. 4:12–13)

While we often recognize the need to learn how to face hunger and need, we aren't always aware that we need similar help to face wealth and abundance. It's not easy to face affluence every day without committing idolatry or succumbing to ingratitude. In fact, church history is filled with stories of sincere believers facing lowness, hunger, need, suffering, persecution, hardship, and death with Christ-honoring joy and faithfulness. But the stories of Christian fidelity in the midst of overwhelming abundance, provision, plenty, and wealth are fewer and farther between. This is why Jesus says that it is hard for the rich to enter the kingdom of heaven (Matt. 19:23). One of the chief challenges for Christians in the West is to learn to face our unprecedented abundance with the strength supplied by Christ and not by the wealth.

I mentioned earlier that my wife and I struggled with infertility early in our marriage, yet when God graciously gave us our first son, we discovered that we weren't nearly as ready to enjoy him. We struggled with guilt because through our struggle, we had met others in similar circumstances, and now we'd been given something that they had not. We wrestled with anxiety at the prospect that God would take our son, and this anxiety was rooted in a picture of God who didn't really want to give good gifts to his children. I remember having a conversation with my wife right after Sam was born in which one of us said something like, "I feel that I've been prepared to suffer well, but I haven't been trained to enjoy a precious gift from God in a way that honors him."

The point of this anecdote is not to equate children with wealth. The point is that receiving good things rightly is hard. It's difficult. It requires grace. And the Bible says that it's both possible and necessary that we learn to face abundance, to face plenty, to face life in an affluent society in a way that honors God *above* all wealth and honors God *in* all wealth. As Paul says, "I can do all things through him who strengthens me."

Wartime in College

When I was first introduced to the notion of a wartime lifestyle through Piper's ministry in college, it found a ready reception in my heart. I wanted to live for God's kingdom, and I wanted my use of God's provision to reflect that. So I lived on the cheap. Extra roommates to reduce rent. No fancy clothes or expensive furniture. Lots of ramen noodles and bread. My cost of living was all kinds of low.

But here's the thing. None of that was very hard. I didn't want to wear expensive clothes. I liked my roommates. And I think ramen noodles are actually pretty tasty. So living the wartime lifestyle wasn't really a sacrifice. Although the wartime metaphor did add biblical warrant to lifestyle choices I had already made, giving them a holy veneer and texture, my satisfaction in my strategic lifestyle was far out of proportion to the degree of sacrifice. Giving up things that you don't want anyway is easy, and it's a minefield of pride and smugness.

Don't get me wrong. I supported my local church and other ministries. I was generous with my time and talent. And I didn't have a lot of disposable income anyway. But I think something rotten was hatched in my soul in those years, a subtle attitude toward the lifestyle decisions of others that would grow and fester during my years of singleness.

Let me give an example. During those years, I rarely spent money on myself. I wore my clothes until they wore out. I ate inexpensive meals. I avoided extravagant spending on everything. Except books. I loved books, and I loved to buy books (I still do). And I justified my book budget in wartime terms. I figured that since I wasn't buying all of the "worldly" things that everyone else was buying, I was free to go crazy at Amazon.com. In other words, I exempted my own pet purchases from wartime simplicity on the grounds that they were spiritually strategic. I mean, come on. Are you going to tell me that Owen's *Mortification of Sin* isn't wartime? That my *fight* with sin isn't *wartime*?

And to be honest, I think that my reasoning in that case was absolutely right. Good theological books are (or can be) a strategic, wartime purchase for the purpose of feeding the soul and increasing holiness. The problem is that if others used their disposable income to buy nicer (or healthier) food or name-brand clothes or furniture from some place besides the side of the road, I subtly judged them because they weren't being strategic in their use of resources. In other words, having given up things I didn't want in the first place and exempting "spiritual" purchases that I did want, I was imposing my subjective application of wartime principles as a pattern for everyone else.

Paul appears to address precisely this sort of smug judgmentalism in a number of places:

> Who are you to pass judgment on the servant of another? It is before his own master that he stands or falls. And he will be upheld, for the Lord is able to make him stand. (Rom. 14:4)

> Why do you pass judgment on your brother? Or you, why do you despise your brother? For we will all stand before the judgment seat of God; for it is written,
>
> > "As I live, says the Lord, every knee shall bow to me,
> >   and every tongue shall confess to God."
>
> So then each of us will give an account of himself to God. (Rom. 14:10–12)

One eats, and one abstains. One shops at department stores, and one shops at thrift stores. One buys books, and one buys artwork. Let each be fully convinced in his own mind. Don't judge or despise your brother. To his own master he stands or falls. We will all stand before God's judgment.

So we must be mindful of how subjective our perceptions of what a faithful use of wealth can be. We must resist imposing our context-specific, personality-driven application of wartime on other people. This isn't to say that we should never raise questions about how money is used. It does mean that we shouldn't treat wartime as if it's a game of "How low can you go?" Because the answer to that is always "Lower."

Love and Marriage

When my wife and I were first married, we lived in a basement in Minneapolis. We had moved to Minnesota to participate in the apprenticeship program at Bethlehem Baptist Church. Like many newlyweds, our first arguments had to do with money. In particular, I couldn't understand why my wife felt the need to buy candles for our apartment. After all, this was the twenty-first century. We did, in fact, have lights in our home. And given how little money we had (I was in seminary and working part-time; she was working as an administrative assistant in an office), were candles really a strategic, wartime purchase? Or were they superfluous and unnecessary?

I remember being in a ministry seminar with our executive pastor Sam Crabtree. We were going around the room introducing ourselves. When it was my turn, I said, "My name is Joe Rigney. I'm from Texas. I've been married for about a month, and it's been really great. I still haven't quite figured why candles are so important, but we're working on it."

Pastor Sam looked back at me incredulously. "You don't know why candles are important?"

Somewhat taken aback, I said, "Uh, no." His next words hit me like a ton of bricks.

"Because *she* is."

Now to many people, the truth of that statement may seem obvious, but it wasn't to me. Even if I would have agreed in principle, it hadn't landed on me in the way that it needed to. So let me spell out what that humbling moment in the seminar accomplished in me.

As we've seen, wartime means strategic. But strategic for *what*? For the advancement of God's kingdom. For the expansion of the gospel. For spreading a passion for God's supremacy in all things for the joy of all peoples through Jesus Christ. Wartime means strategic.

This means money exists for people. Wealth exists to meet their needs. Spiritual needs. Physical needs. Emotional needs. And not just people in the abstract. Actual persons. Real persons. With names and faces and empty stomachs and thirsty souls and hearts that hunger for concrete expressions of the love of God.

That's what hadn't landed on me. For some reason, I had grown accustomed to viewing wartime in terms of what *I* was going without instead of what God had given the resources for. I had a truncated and narrow view of what strategic meant. But a healthy marriage is strategic. An honored and happy wife is strategic. A warm and welcoming home is strategic. Strong relationships with those close to you are strategic, and if purchasing some candles solidifies the relationship, then in my judgment it's a small price to pay.

A wartime lifestyle means that we divert resources from normal pursuits so that they can be used at the front. Most often we think of "the front" as frontier missionaries who are taking the gospel to unreached peoples in the hardest places. And we ought to think this way. We ought to give up our luxuries so that we can fund Paul-type missionaries who are planting churches in places without any gospel witness.

But we should also recognize that the front includes people and relationships that are closer to home. Family is part of the front. If we're parents, our children are part of the front. God has called us to raise them in the Lord, to communicate in word and deed and demeanor what it means that God is our Father through Christ. As we saw in the last chapter, parents are called to gladly spend and be spent for their children (2 Cor. 12:14–15).

Jesus says that even evil men know how to give good gifts to their children (Matt. 7:11). How much more should redeemed men give good gifts to their children? And "good gifts" doesn't mean expensive. "Good gifts" means creative and customized for our children. We teach our children the meaning of *lavish* by showering them with hugs and kisses and affection. We should lavish on them praise and delight and mac and cheese, and, every so often, cookies and ice cream. And when it's their birthday, we ought to give them thoughtful and personalized gifts, gifts that communicate that we're paying attention to them, that we're dialed into their desires and delights and interests. And we ought to buy and give such gifts *precisely because we want to be strategic in our use of our wealth.*

Hear me on this. I'm not calling for increased spending on toys. I'm not encouraging exorbitant presents. In fact, in many cases we can buy fewer things if we're buying better, more thoughtful gifts. What I'm attempting to get at is the *qualitative* dimension of buying presents for our children (or our spouses, our friends, or strangers). People know when we're giving something and feeling guilty about it. They know when there is a hitch in our gift, a reluctance in our spirit because we're not sure if this is a strategic, wartime use of our wealth. They can sense when we've forgotten that people are strategic, including the people who live under our own roof. In the long run, this sort of reluctant and guilt-ridden gift giving actually harms the relationship. On the flip side, generosity with our kids is one of the main ways that we can create kids who are generous themselves.

To come at the same issue from another direction, Proverbs warns us about the dangers of sitting at the table of the stingy (literally: "the man whose eye is evil"):

> Do not eat the bread of a man who is stingy;
> > do not desire his delicacies,
> for he is like one who is inwardly calculating.
> > "Eat and drink!" he says to you,
> > but his heart is not with you. (Prov. 23:6–7)

How much worse to actually be the stingy one, to inwardly calculate our giving with an evil eye, to direct our gaze more to what *we* are losing rather than to the joy of the people who receive our gifts. Such "giving" isn't even worthy of the name, since it offers gifts with no heart behind it. And it is particularly tragic when this kind of heartless generosity takes up residence in a Christian home under the banner of a wartime lifestyle.[5]

Biblical Obligations Work from the Inside Out

Highlighting the family as part of "the front" raises all sorts of questions about the varying responsibilities we have for our children, our church, missionaries, unreached peoples, and the local poor. So let me offer a few reflections on these responsibilities.

The Bible teaches us to think in terms of concentric circles of responsibility, with greater obligations as we get closer to the center. And though there are certainly exceptions to this, the general progression is from family to church to local poor and unbelievers to peoples around the world.

First, the priority of the family. Paul tells Timothy, "If anyone does not provide for his relatives, and especially for members of his household, he has denied the faith and is worse than an unbeliever" (1 Tim. 5:8). The implication is that the head of household has greater obligations to his family than to members of other families (though he also has some obligations there). Likewise, the prerequisite for leadership in the local church is that a man must "manage his own household well" (1 Tim. 3:4–5). This requirement is simply an application of Jesus's principle that we must be faithful in little before God will put us over much (Luke 16:10; 19:17).

Second, the priority of the church. Paul exhorts the Galatians, "So then, as we have opportunity, let us do good to everyone, *and especially to those who are of the household of faith*" (Gal. 6:10). Notice that we ought to do good to everyone, regardless of whether they are Christians. But there is a special obligation to the household of faith. I think this is why Jesus can say that the world will know that we are his disciples by the love we have for each other (John 13:35). The love, care, and provision of Christians for other Christians is a powerful apologetic and testimony to the reality of the gospel.

Third, the priority of local needs. The parable of the good Samaritan implies this sort of primacy. While there is a sense in which love for neighbor includes all people everywhere, Jesus's parable highlights the needs of those people who are right in front of your face. Jesus doesn't condemn the Levite who lives fifty miles away in Galilee for failure to help the wounded man; he condemns the Levite who walks by on the other side of the road. The Samaritan is commended precisely because he meets the needs of someone in his proximity, regardless of ethnicity and religious creed.

An additional support for the priority of the local may be found in Proverbs 17:24: "The discerning sets his face toward wisdom, but the eyes of the fool are on the ends of the earth." Obsessing about the horizon is often a way of avoiding clear and present obligations. As P. J. O'Rourke memorably put it, "Everybody wants to save the world, but nobody wants to help mom with the dishes."

Wisdom makes demands of us right where we are. Honor your parents—as in, the ones in the next room. Run from the adulteress—as in, the one beckoning from the recesses of the Internet. Avoid the close companionship of fools—as in, the guys at the gym who make lewd jokes and demean women. God plants us in a place and gives us responsibility. He commands us to be faithful at our post, to not shirk obligations while imagining our triumphs and feats of fidelity at another post somewhere over the rainbow.

Fourth, concentric circles doesn't imply that we can neglect the needs of those around the world who languish in poverty and face eternity without the hope of the gospel. The churches of Macedonia and Corinth gave money for the relief of the poor in Jerusalem (Rom. 15:26; 2 Corinthians 8–9). The saints in Jerusalem likewise longed and prayed for the Corinthians (2 Cor. 9:14). Paul expected the church of Rome to be deeply concerned about his planned mission to Spain (Rom. 15:24).

What's more, God calls some like Paul to shoulder a greater burden for the unreached peoples of the world. Paul was under obligation to preach the gospel far and wide, to Greeks and barbarians, to the wise and the foolish, to the Jews and the Gentiles (Rom. 1:14–15; 1 Cor. 9:19–23). His ambition was to preach Christ where Christ was not named (Rom. 15:20), and to that end he forwent a family and a stable church home and a local community of need in order to spread the gospel to the ends of the earth. And he enlisted the aid of Christians everywhere in accomplishing the vital task of completing the Great Commission.

This is the necessary counterpart to a focus on generosity at home. The biblical obligation to be generous with what God gives to us begins at home. We can't export what we don't have. But it *really* starts at home, and it *really* works its way out. If our generosity terminates with our family and friends, then we're not giving like Christians. We're no different from the evil men who give good gifts to *their* children. As Jesus said, "If you love those who love you, what reward do you have? Do not even the tax collectors do the same? And if you greet only your brothers, what more are you doing than others? Do not even the Gentiles do the same?" (Matt. 5:46–47).

Christian love and generosity overflow natural relationships. If our generosity and giving don't spill the banks of family and friends, then we're doing it wrong. Jesus said,

> When you give a dinner or a banquet, do not invite your friends or your brothers or your relatives or rich neighbors, lest they also invite you in return and you be repaid. But when you give a feast, invite the poor, the crippled, the lame, the blind, and you will be blessed, because they cannot repay you. For you will be repaid at the resurrection of the just. (Luke 14:12–14)

The point of this passage is not that we should always avoid having our friends to dinner. Jesus himself shared the Passover feast with his disciples. The point is that our table fellowship should extend beyond our family, friends, and patrons. We should share our food and festivity with outsiders, with those who are marginalized and ignored. We should throw wonderful banquets and parties and invite unlikely people to join our feasting.

So in emphasizing the importance of those close to you as part of the front, I don't want to in any way minimize the pressing needs around the world, both in terms of alleviating physical suffering and alleviating eternal suffering. But I think that working through these layered responsibilities prevents dislocations that undermine generosity at all levels. This sort of broad and directed wartime approach protects us from sacrificing our families on the altar of ministry.

In short, generosity should begin with glad and grateful reception of God's provision, extend to our immediate context (family, friends, and church), then overflow the banks to local spiritual and physical needs, and then flood the world with a wealth of gospel proclamation and deeds of love.

Thinking in Three Dimensions

Despite the rebuke in the seminar, my struggles with applying wartime didn't diminish. If anything, they increased. Thankfully, I had a patient wife who helped me to see where I was being shortsighted. For example, my conception of wartime centered particularly on the immediate cost of a purchase. I was myopic about price. When we were furnishing our apartment, we needed to buy a desk for me. I suggested that we get a cheap, particle-board desk, either on Craigslist or at the store. I thought we could spend under fifty dollars. My wife, on the other hand, suggested that we get a solid wood desk from World Market. It would cost around two hundred dollars. Needless to say, there was a heated disagreement.

But through it, my wife helped me to see how myopic I was being about the immediate price of the desk. "We could buy a cheap, ugly desk for fifty dollars, and we might need to buy another one in a year, and another one after that. Or we could get a nice, quality desk that we could own for years. See that bookshelf over there. I bought it in college, and I fully expect to give it to my grandchildren."

Essentially my wife pointed out that I wasn't thinking strategically *enough*. Short-term thinking is often not strategic. This isn't to say that you must always choose the quality desk over the cheap one. The point is to stress the great variety of factors to consider in our purchases and not to fixate on one dimension or another. What's more, we should be aware that different people can come to different, *godly* conclusions about how to spend money.

My definition of *strategic* was also truncated in that it lacked an appreciation for beauty and aesthetics. While I had certainly been the recipient of aesthetic, intangible blessings, I'd never thought of them as a strategic use of resources. But God made a beautiful world and calls us to imitate him, which means that time and money spent on making a home attractive and inviting to visitors is strategic. Beautification is strategic. Making the home into a refuge is strategic. Becoming a better cook and making good food for your family is strategic (especially if you make enough to share!).

The value of beauty remains even if we factor in its temporary nature.

In the morning, God clothes the flowers in Solomon-surpassing glory, and this glory dies by mid-afternoon. Such fleeting beauty still serves thousands of God-intended purposes—pleasing our eyes, reminding us of our own vaporousness, awakening us to the beauty of God, and many more. Likewise, our efforts at beauty—whether in art, music, home-making, or anything else—can serve similar purposes in nourishing our souls, in encouraging and blessing others, and in honoring the beautiful and beauty-making Creator.

The same goes for the value of vocation. Plumbers make the world a lovelier place, both in sight and smell. (If you doubt me, visit a country that lacks both plumbing and plumbers.) So do moms who change diapers. Good music excellently played beautifies the world, calling people out of the prison of themselves to something greater and grander. Literature, both writing and reading it, is strategic. How many people have been primed to receive the gospel because they read The Chronicles of Narnia as children? And how much medieval philosophy and classical poetry and fantastic fiction did C. S. Lewis have to read before he was equipped to write those precious books?

Another thing I learned about myself in those years was the role of appearances in my assessment of the wartime lifestyle. If something looked posh and expensive, I recoiled from it. If it looked dingy and used, then it was somehow more virtuous, regardless of the actual cost. Over time, I came to see that while appearances do matter, they are one factor among many and that there may be strategic reasons for choosing items that have the appearance of wealth.

Say a wealthy uncle gives you his old Lexus as a gift. Does a commitment to wartime demand that you sell it and buy a junky car, lest you communicate an ostentatious lifestyle? Or might you consider other factors: the safety and reliability of the car, honoring the one who gave it to you by accepting his gift, the added maintenance and time investment of the clunker. Again, the point is not to give a simple answer; it's to bring all the variables onto the table so that we can make a wise decision.

Along these lines, I noticed that the way I was approaching questions of wealth was affecting my relationships in deeper ways. I remember being mildly frustrated with my wife one time because she bought more expensive chips because she knew that I liked them. Here she was, showing me kindness in a simple and practical way, and all I could do was respond with ingratitude because I was fixated on the minuscule added cost.

Economics 101

During these years, I also began to grow in my understanding of basic economics. I don't mean high-level stuff with charts and graphs. I mean simple and obvious truths such as "There ain't no such thing as a free lunch." Someone will pay the cost. It may be hidden, but, rest assured, someone is paying.

To illustrate, imagine, if you will, a college student who sells his car to avoid the expense of insurance, fuel, and maintenance. With the extra money he supports a missionary among an unreached people. However, he now needs to hitch rides to school, work, and the grocery store, and his roommate is his usual chauffeur. The danger becomes obvious. The second student bears all the costs and maintenance of car ownership while the first student gets the benefits that the vehicle provides as well as the satisfaction of diverting his resources to the front. If he's not careful, he can begin to feel a subtle pride in his wartime lifestyle as compared to his roommate, who didn't sell his car.

Or take another economic principle that I learned during these years: the value of time. There are a lot of things that can be done more cheaply if you have the time and energy to make them happen. The problem is that time spent doing the cheap thing is time away from other pursuits, pursuits that might be more valuable than saving a couple of bucks. If we only think about dollars and cents and not about the value of our time, we can actually be less strategic in the use of all the resources God has given us to steward.

A final economic truth: God has not made a zero-sum world. There is not a fixed amount of wealth in the world so that if one person gets richer, another person necessarily gets poorer. Wealth can be created. Human beings can mix their creative labor with the vast potential of God's created order and develop and produce amazing things, increasing the total wealth and value in the world.[6]

Conclusion

To return to the original theme, the main point is to stress the complexity of living faithfully in a world of wealth. Is it possible to use what I've written here to hoard things for ourselves and justify our lack of concrete love for the unreached? Of course it is. Can we receive wealth wrongly and cultivate a sense of entitlement? Absolutely.

But our sinful tendencies in this respect are not addressed through low-grade guilt at the possession of wealth. We don't deal with our sin mainly by treating wealth like a hot potato. And the monastic and ascetic route has dangers of its own. Self-denial is dangerous. Renunciation is dangerous. Wartime is dangerous.

Instead we should seek to become big-hearted receivers of all that God gives and aim to be as generous as we can be as God gives us opportunity. We should embrace the reality that the front in the war begins with those closest to us and extends to those unreached peoples that we'll never meet, unless and until we meet them in heaven. We ought to seek to be open-handed receivers and then open-handed givers. We should seek to be as generous with others as God has been with us. In short, as I said before, freely receive, freely give.

11

Suffering, Death, and the Loss of Good Gifts

It hurts just as much as it's worth.

Julian Barnes

All pessimism has a secret optimism for its object. All surrender of life, all denial of pleasure, all darkness, all austerity, all desolation has for its real aim this separation of something so that it may be poignantly and perfectly enjoyed. I feel grateful for the slight sprain which has introduced this mysterious and fascinating division between one of my feet and the other. The way to love anything is to realise that it might be lost. In one of my feet I can feel how strong and splendid a foot is; in the other I can realise how very much otherwise it might have been. The moral of the thing is wholly exhilarating. This world and all our powers in it are far more awful and beautiful than even we know until some accident reminds us.

G. K. Chesterton

The enjoyment of God is the only happiness with which our souls can be satisfied. To go to heaven, fully to enjoy God, is infinitely better than the most pleasant accommodations here. Fathers and mothers, husbands, wives, or children, or the company of earthly friends, are but shadows; but God is the substance. These are but scattered beams, but God is the sun. These are but streams. But God is the ocean.

Jonathan Edwards

Gladly receiving good gifts for God's sake doesn't lead us to hoard and pile up treasure on earth. It makes us open-handed and big-hearted. It unleashes us to be as generous with others as God has been with us. It leads us to abundantly give our time, talent, and treasure to alleviate suffering, both near and far, both temporal and eternal. As John Piper says, "We Christians care about all suffering, especially eternal suffering."[1] So a focus on gladly receiving all that God supplies unleashes a radically generous people on the world who willingly give up good things in the cause of love.

But what about the involuntary loss of good things? What about when good and precious gifts that expand our capacities to know and enjoy God are ripped from our hearts? What does an integrated approach to the enjoyment of God and his gifts say when the gift is being torn from our hands? Won't this emphasis on receiving good things from God lead us astray if God should take our most precious earthly delights? Won't this lead us to cling to the gifts too tightly because we enjoy them so deeply? Aren't we setting ourselves up for idolatry by celebrating the goodness of gifts that we will one day lose?

In my mind, the entire thesis of this book is massively undermined if it can't biblically and faithfully address the heartbreaking loss of good things. The Bible is a book of suffering, from Genesis 3 to Revelation 20. Wives are lost. Husbands are lost. Children are lost. Wealth is lost. Houses are lost. Reputations are lost. Health is lost. Lives are lost. And this type of suffering and loss is promised to those who follow Jesus: "All who desire to live a godly life in Christ Jesus will be persecuted" (2 Tim. 3:12); "Through many tribulations we must enter the kingdom of God" (Acts 14:22). So a book about enjoying God's gifts simply must grapple with the inevitability of losing them.

Eating, Drinking, and Making Merry under the Sun

Ecclesiastes is a perplexing book, but my colleague Jason DeRouchie has helped me to see the hope that the preacher and sage of the book offers to us.[2] The book is an extended reflection on life "under the sun" (1:3, 9, 14), life in God's confusing, broken, and frustrating world. Everything under the sun is an enigma, an unsearchable mystery.[3] This world is broken and under God's curse yet still filled with gifts and pleasures for men to enjoy. However, because of the certainty of death, all these pleasures are fleeting and temporary, and we don't know when they will be snatched from us (or us from them). What's more, injustice abounds in this fallen world (4:1–2), but not always (2:26), and so we find ourselves vexed and confused by the incomprehensibility of the world and God's ways.

> We live in a crooked world that cannot with any level of human effort be made straight (1:15; 7:13). It is cursed, making the kindnesses of God sometimes difficult to visualize. "How is he working good in this?" Consider all the various things that mark our lives: unstable jobs, orphans, judicial corruption, blown tires, broken legs, sex-trafficking, leaky faucets, divine sovereignty vs. human responsibility, failed adoptions, monthly bills, envy, project deadlines, rainy vacations, broken marriages, chronic back pain, pride, pornography, slippery roads, severed relationships, selfishness, racism, bee stings, abortion, and the ever present death of loved ones (or ourselves). This is our world.
>
> We cry, "Why us? Why her? Why this hard? Why this way? Why this long?" Yet, like Job, we hear no answer. We gain no clarity—only more vexation. Our growth in wisdom only raises more questions, as our attempts to comprehend fully what God is doing or why he is doing it always reach dead ends, at least at some level.[4]

We are creatures, and we are under a curse, and thus we find ourselves incapable of grasping the workings of the world, unable to shepherd the wind. And thus we live in fear, frustration, and vexation, the kind that ruins our ability to enjoy what we do have. Again, DeRouchie helpfully summarizes the message of Ecclesiastes:

> Far too often the bright purposes and kindnesses of God are dimmed from vision behind cloudy skies, whether due to ignorance (3:11; 11:5), injustice and oppression (4:1), discontentment (4:8; 6:2), financial loss (5:13), unexpected trial (9:12; 11:2), persistent battle with sin (9:3), the sheer monotony of life's repetitions (1:4–11), the fleeting nature of wisdom, skill, and wealth (2:21; 5:16), or the fact that one's

life is simply forgotten after death (2:14–16). The curse has created a world where rebel and remnant alike experience both birth *and* death, love *and* hate, peace *and* war (3:2, 8). This is the nature of life "under the sun." How is one to respond under these all-pervasive enigmas?[5]

DeRouchie's answer, rooted in his careful reading of Ecclesiastes, is that though we may be unable to shepherd the wind, there is "one Shepherd" who can (12:11). It is he who grants wisdom to those who fear him and enables us to rest and hope in his wise and unsearchable providence. In so doing, we can recognize and embrace our creaturely limitations and replace our self-reliance and quest for total knowledge of the world with a deep and radical dependence upon God. Such dependence frees those who fear God "to be joyful and to do good as long as they live . . . everyone should eat and drink and take pleasure in all [their] toil—this is God's gift to man" (3:12–13).

> Why? It is because those who fear God today are enabled to enjoy this world as a gift of the Creator and therefore as a channel for worship (2:24–25; 6:1–2; 11:8; 12:1). It is also because those who walk in wisdom today, living in light of the future judgment, will escape the wrath that will one day fall on the wicked (3:17; 7:12, 18–19; 8:12–13; cf. 12:13–14). The fear of God leads to the approval of God, which frees you and me to delight in today as we hope for tomorrow. "Go, eat your bread with joy, and drink your wine with a merry heart, for God has already approved what you do" (9:7; cf. 2:26; 7:26). "Rejoice, O young man, in your youth, and let your heart cheer you in the days of your youth. Walk in the ways of your heart and the sight of your eyes. But know that for all these things God will bring you into judgment. . . . Remember also your Creator" (11:9; 12:1).[6]

So, yes, the earthly gifts of God are fleeting. Yes, they can (and will) be lost. But when we embrace our creatureliness and look to the one shepherd, the creator God who guides and governs this crooked world and who has bound himself to us for our good, we are freed to eat, drink, and be merry and to enjoy life with the people we love, all the days of our enigmatic lives, because this is our portion and God approves.

How Suffering Tests Our Integrated Enjoyment

It's one thing to see that the prospect of losing good gifts doesn't mean we shouldn't enjoy them. It's another to see how we should approach their loss in such a way that we honor God in both having them *and* losing them. To do so, we must begin by recognizing that involuntary suffering is a vital and unavoidable test of our integrated love and ordered desires. Suffering is the quintessential comparative test to ensure that our integration has not become idolatry (see chapter 5).

Of course, we ought to be regularly assessing our supreme love for God, even if it's only hypothetical. We do so by confessing with the psalmist, "Whom have I in heaven but you? And there is nothing on earth that I desire besides you. My flesh and my heart may fail [along with my family and my friends and my wealth and my good name], but God is the strength of my heart and my portion forever" (Ps. 73:25–26).

We underscore our ultimate devotion to God through the way we worship. We sing songs such as:

> Hallelujah! All I have is Christ.
> Hallelujah! Jesus is my life.[7]

And:

> Knowing you, Jesus
> Knowing you
> There is no greater thing.[8]

And:

> Let goods and kindred go
> This mortal life also
> The body they may kill
> God's truth abideth still
> His kingdom is forever.[9]

But the actual loss of good things puts these confessions to the test in a way that nothing else can. What will we do when our friends abandon us during our greatest need? Will our faith be undone? Or will we imitate the apostle Paul?

> At my first defense no one came to stand by me, but all deserted me. May it not be charged against them! But the Lord stood by me and strengthened me, so that through me the message might be fully proclaimed and all the Gentiles might hear it. So I was rescued from the lion's mouth. The Lord will rescue me from every evil deed and bring me safely into his heavenly kingdom. To him be the glory forever and ever. Amen. (2 Tim. 4:16–18)

Everyone deserted Paul. But he didn't lose hope. The Lord stood by him and strengthened him, and the Lord was better than any earthly friend.

What will we do if even our parents reject and forsake us, turning their backs on us in the hour of need? Will we say with the psalmist, "For my father and my mother have forsaken me, but the LORD will take me in" (Ps. 27:10)?

What will we do if the storm comes and blows the house down with our children inside it? Will we rage against heaven? Will we curse the God who formed and made us? Or will we say with Job, "The LORD gave, and the LORD has taken away; blessed be the name of the LORD" (Job 1:21)?[10]

In fact, the story of Job is introduced as a test of Job's affections for and allegiance to God. Job was a godly man, "blameless and upright, one who feared God and turned away from evil" (1:1). God had blessed him with ten children and wealth that surpassed all those in the east (vv. 2–3). Job was a faithful father who loved his children and prayed for their protection and offered sacrifices on their behalf.

When Satan appears before God, he accuses Job of idolatry. God has "blessed the work of his hands, and his possessions have increased in the land" (v. 10). But Job's piety is shallow, Satan says, and if God simply strikes all that Job has, "he will curse you to your face" (v. 11). In other words, Satan is challenging the integrity of Job's heart. He is claiming that Job's integration of gift and giver is, in fact, idolatry of the gifts over the giver. And so God puts Job to the test, taking his wealth and his children and his health and the happiness of his marriage. And though Job recognizes God's hand in all of it (1:21; 2:10), he does not sin or charge God with wrong (1:22).

So, then, suffering tests our supreme love for God more than anything else. Suffering brings the comparative approach to the giver and his gifts to the foreground and compels us to put our money and our family and our health and every other good thing where our mouth is.

Integration in Absence?

But the picture is more complicated than this. Suffering does underscore the supreme and ultimate and infinite value of God over against every good thing that he provides. But the presence of the comparative approach doesn't abolish integration of the gifts and the giver. Integration continues, *even in the absence of the gift*. To see how, we need to remind ourselves what integrated love for God and his gifts is doing to us and in us.

The heart of an integrated approach to God and his gifts is soul expansion. Love for God's gifts expands our mental capacity for understanding who God is. It expands our heart's capacity for delighting and rejoicing in who God is. It expands our soul's capacity to receive and embrace and treasure all that God is for us in Christ. Rhythms of direct and indirect godwardness send us into the gifts and then up to God, stretching and enlarging and widening our ability to see and savor Christ and the things of earth.

Put it this way: Paul tells us that the love of God in Christ Jesus is so broad and long and high and deep that it surpasses knowledge (Eph. 3:18–19). It's mind-blowing in its grandeur and glory, so much so that we don't have the strength to comprehend it. So Paul prays that God would grant us "to be strengthened with power through his Spirit in your inner being" (v. 16) so that we would have the strength to comprehend God's incomprehensible love. And one of the fundamental ways that God gives our hearts and minds a spiritual workout is communicating his goodness to us through created gifts.

The value of this mutually beneficial relationship is that our love for the gifts pushes our love for God to new heights, which means we can let the clutch out of our love for the gifts. If we're living and thinking and rejoicing in an integrated way, every time a pleasure in a gift shoots through the roof, it takes God with it, swelling our capacity to know him. To quote Edwards, "Spiritual appetites need no bounds."[11] And the whole point of this book is that all legitimate enjoyment, whether of God or anything else, is deeply and profoundly spiritual.

So, then, integrated heart expansion is the goal. But heart expansion and soul strengthening happens in more than one way. The heart can expand when the gift is present, *and it can expand when the gift is absent*, sometimes in ways that are only possible through the loss.

Experiencing Tremendous Loss

In chapter 8 I gave some snapshots of my life with my dad, who died of Alzheimer's and Parkinson's disease in 2013 at the age of sixty-eight. For the last year or so of his life, he no longer recognized me, nor did he make coherent sense when he spoke. For eight years I watched him die slowly, from a distance (he lived in Texas, I in Minnesota). When I returned home every few months, there was less and less of him there. It's horrific to watch someone you love die like that. And I've no doubt that it was far worse for my mom, who was there every step of the way as her husband and best friend slipped away.

It's silly to compare degrees of suffering. But I have a sense that as horrible as it is to lose a parent, or sibling, or spouse, or close friend, worse is the loss of a child. I have close friends who have lost children, and I have a good enough imagination to know the sorts of things that I would be feeling if something were to happen to one of my boys. A few years ago, some close friends lost their infant son after a six-month battle with a terminal disease. At one point during those heart-wrenching months, I remember seeing some pictures of my friend holding his little boy. As I watched him tenderly and tearfully touch his son's face, I begin to imagine the sorts of things that I would be feeling if I were in his place, facing the imminent loss of one of my boys. Out of that grief-filled imagining, I wrote my friend a letter, trying to encourage him as he and his wife faced an unfathomable loss:

> I take it as a given that Christ is supreme for you and your wife. I know that he's your treasure and your life. I know that faith in him runs deep in your bones, that your love for him is at the core of who you are. And I can imagine that at times like this your love for God and trust in his sovereignty produces questions like, "If God is taking our son to himself, is it okay for me to want to keep our little one in

my arms for as long as possible? Am I resisting God in some way if my desire for my son is so real and so intense and so undeniable, and yet it is so clear that God is taking my baby from me?"

So I just wanted to affirm that, given the deep reality of your supreme and full love for God, your love for your dying son cannot be too intense. It is impossible for you to feel too deeply for him, for you to want to hold him too much, for you to long for his health and happiness with too much fervor.

Let me say it again: You cannot love your son too much. This is because, as you've said to me over and over again, he is a gift to you. God has given him to *you*, as a gift, and you are receiving him as a gift. Your son is a work of God, an expression of God's glory and grace and love, and one that is customized for you and your family. You can only love him wrongly if you love him *in place of* God. But if you receive him *as a gift from God*, in all of his wonder and beauty and sweetness and fragility, then you cannot love him too much or prize him too highly, and you should feel no shred of guilt because you love him as you do and long for his health and desperately want to cling to him and know him and spend time with him for as long as you can.

So I just want to encourage you and your wife to plunge headlong into the gift. Savor every moment with that baby. Touch him, hold him, caress him, let the love that you feel for him surge through you. Let it provoke you to tears and sadness and that gut-wrenching feeling that you would do absolutely *anything* to make your son whole. Let your love for your little boy take you beyond the pain and sorrow to the indestructible joy of the God who gives good gifts *and is not threatened by them.*

It's as if God is saying to you, "You don't know how intense my love is for you, how deep my affections are for you. So I'm going to show you. I'm going to stretch your heart to the breaking point. It will feel like you are dying. But if you go with me, into the love, into the pain, into the sorrow and longing and desire, then when all is said and done, you will know that "as a father has compassion on his children, so does the Lord have compassion on you."

That is what integrated joy looks like when the precious gift is being removed.[12] It's the opposite of detached and aloof. It's what delivers us from the lie that says, "If you truly love God, you won't wail and moan. If you really trusted his goodness, you'd resist all this weeping." Integrated joy banishes such stoicism to the outer darkness. It dispenses with the mistaken notion that God is honored when we act as if our hearts are not screaming in anguish at how much we miss our father or husband or sister or child.

Integrated joy frees us from false guilt, the kind born from the misguided belief that the way to magnify the value of God is by pretending that his gifts are not really as enjoyable as we find them. Instead, right enjoyment of the gifts gives full vent to the delight (or the corresponding anguish), knowing that no matter how wonderful we discover God's gifts to be, he himself is better still.

Integrated joy frees us to grieve like biblical figures. Job's absolute trust in God's sovereign goodness toward him did not lead him to stoically take the loss of everything he found precious. He did not treat the loss of his children lightly. He tore his robe. He shaved his head. He fell on the ground. He grieved and wept and worshiped through tears.

The psalms are filled with intense emotion in the midst of all kinds of suffering. The psalmists wrestle with God in the midst of opposition, in horrific loss, in the maddening silence of heaven. And they really wrestle and agonize in prayer. They claim God's promises, appeal to God's character, call for God's justice, and demand God's ear.

And let us not forget Jesus. Man of sorrows and acquainted with grief. Weeping over Jerusalem. Deeply moved in his spirit by the grief of Mary and Martha. Shedding troubled tears at the tomb of Lazarus, minutes before he would raise him from the dead.

No, biblical grief is not detached. It is not aloof and above it all. Born from integrated joy, biblical grief does not suffer the loss of precious gifts lightly. The experience of suffering is grievous. It produces real sorrow and anguish. It rages against the darkness and the void, against this cursed world, full of death and loss, and against the Devil and his host who do nothing but steal, kill, and destroy.

But however much our grief may wail and rage, biblical grief never curses the Lord, who gives and takes away according to his good and wise purposes. Integrated joy is transformed into lamentation and grief when precious things are pulled from our arms. And, in so doing, even horrific suffering and loss expand our soul, stretching our heart beyond what we think it can bear so that we rest most deeply in the God who will ever and always be our portion.[13]

Gratitude Always and for Everything

Sometimes poets can say in verse what feels impossible in prose. A song that communicates the heart of this chapter is "Gratitude" by Nichole Nordeman. In the song, she does a tremendous job of pushing on the Pauline admonition: "giving thanks always and for everything" (Eph. 5:20). The song is filled with prayers and supplications for God to send rain on the thirsty ground, to give daily bread to fill our bellies, and to grant peace in a war-torn world. But again and again the song returns to the truth that God may not answer these prayers as we'd like. He might choose to provide in other, harder, more trying ways. But if he does, we will still "give thanks to You with gratitude, for lessons learned in how to trust in You."[14]

True gratitude remains, even when the gift is withheld. Gratitude gladly receives *whatever* God supplies, taking the good with cheerfulness and the hardship with a deep sense of sorrowful-yet-always-rejoicing. Gratitude knows that God is honored in the glad reception of wonderful gifts and in the deep, unshakeable satisfaction in God when the wonderful gifts are gone. And gratitude loves to display the worth and value of the giver of all good gifts and all severe mercies.

This was Paul's discovery in his own trials and tribulations. In the midst of demonic harassment, Paul pleaded with God to remove his thorn in the flesh, to deliver him from some unbearable weakness (2 Cor. 12:7–8). Notice that it wasn't wrong to ask for relief. Christians are not masochists who delight in pain for its own sake. But despite Paul's earnest plea, God responded by denying his immediate request and drawing attention to the spiritual fruit overflowing from Paul's life as a result of his affliction. "My grace is sufficient for you, for my power is made perfect in weakness" (2 Cor. 12:9). And Paul responds not by denying the reality of the weakness or the pain of the torment but by boasting gladly in his weakness, so that Christ's power rested on him and displayed the supreme worth of Jesus in and through Paul's hardship and affliction.

How Integrated Joy Faces Death

Losing one of God's magnificent gifts can break our hearts. Losing multiple gifts, as Job did, can bring us to our knees in anguish. But what will we do when we are faced with the loss of *all* good things? What will we do when the reality of death lands on us, the reality that we and all the created delights we love are vapor, breath, fading grass? What will we say and do when we are about to lose all the created beams of glory that warm our hearts and bring us joy?

On our deathbed, integrated joy seeks to magnify God, whether in life or in death (Phil. 1:20), by enjoying him supremely, by knowing deep in our bones that all these gifts have simply been "the far off and momentary coruscations of a Being at whose right hand are pleasures forevermore."[15] Integrated delight in God's gifts knows that Christ is the joy of all our joys, the pleasure at the heart of every pleasure, and that death simply opens up new vistas for knowing and enjoying *him*. For this reason, integrated joy desires to depart and be with Christ, because that is far better (Phil. 1:24). Integrated joy is anchored through the experiential knowledge that the steadfast love of the Lord is better than life (Ps. 63:3). Integrated joy labors to see living as Christ, to enjoy Christ in everything and everything in Christ, and, therefore, integrated joy embraces the loss of every good gift in death *as gain* (Phil. 1:21).

But even here, the integration doesn't end. Paul regards the soul's sinless, bodiless presence with Christ as far superior to an embodied existence that is marred by corruption, indwelling sin, and death. Being in heaven with Jesus *without* a physical body is better than being on a fallen earth *with* a decaying body, even with the Spirit dwelling within. Being there without a body is better than being here with sin and pain. But Paul's ultimate hope transcended both of these options:

> For we know that if the tent that is our earthly home is destroyed, we have a building from God, a house not made with hands, eternal in the heavens. For in this tent we groan, longing to put on our heavenly dwelling, if indeed by putting it on we may not be found naked. For while we are still in this tent, we groan, being burdened—not that we would be unclothed, but that we would be further clothed, so that

what is mortal may be swallowed up by life. He who has prepared us for this very thing is God, who has given us the Spirit as a guarantee. (2 Cor. 5:1–5)

Three options are presented here. We can be clothed with an earthly tent (i.e., body), subject to decay and death and remaining sin. We can be unclothed (i.e., bodiless), but with Jesus, which is better than option one. Or we can be further clothed in an immortal, incorruptible resurrection body, and it is this last option that is our ultimate hope, the hope that is guaranteed to us by the Holy Spirit.

God is preparing us to be spiritual *and* embodied men and women. That is, God is preparing us to live in bodies that are enlivened and transformed by the Holy Spirit, just as Jesus's was at his resurrection. The last Adam is a life-giving Spirit, and we must bear his image as Holy Spirit–transformed and –embodied people (1 Cor. 15:45–49).

The implications of this future hope are far-reaching. It means that when we say good-bye to our earthly delights at death, we are really saying, "See you later." We regard death as gain, first because we are going to be with Christ right then, and then because one day we'll hear a trumpet blast from an archangel and find ourselves restored to our earthly bodies and unleashed to use them in ways that we can't comprehend yet.

Death takes away our earthly delights, and then resurrection restores them in spades. Nothing good will ever be finally lost. It's not just that all the best joys here *point* to joys there, but that many of the best joys here will actually *be* there, only glorified, transfigured, and heightened beyond our imagination. This means that even our conception of our future hope is colored by comparative and integrated approaches to God's gifts. As we eagerly await the new heavens and the new earth, we ought to soberly and seriously ask questions such as:

> If you could have heaven, with no sickness, and with all the friends you ever had on earth, and all the food you ever liked, and all the leisure activities you ever enjoyed, and all the natural beauties you ever saw, all the physical pleasures you ever tasted, and no human conflict or natural disasters, could you be satisfied with heaven, if Christ was not there?[16]

And if our answer is yes, then we ought to fear for the state of our souls. Christ is not glorified in our enjoyment of his gifts apart from his presence. To desire a Christless heaven is to commit a subtle and suicidal form of idolatry, one that will not commend us to God on the last day.

But if we've been born again, and if we know in our bones that we could never be satisfied in the best heaven without Jesus, then we expand our vision of our ultimate hope by eagerly anticipating the health and food and friends and family and natural beauty and cultural achievements and harmonious relationships that will be present in the new heavens and the new earth, and we do so precisely because we know that God will be present and revealing himself *through* all these created and renewed realities in ways that we simply can't fathom.[17]

In other words, God is not teaching us integrated enjoyment *here* so that we can ditch it when we arrive *there*. After all, "what the soul cries out for is the resurrection of the senses."[18] When we pass through the stable door and leave Narnia behind, we are entering true Narnia. We are bidding farewell to the Shadowlands and finding our true home. To put it in practical terms, when we get to heaven, we'll still need and want things such as hugs. And not merely hugs from Jesus himself (as wonderful as those will no doubt be). In fact, we'll be able to receive a hug from a friend *as a hug from Jesus* in ways that remain mysterious to us now. Heavenly integration exceeds the human mind's capacity to know. "What no eye has seen, nor ear heard . . . what God has prepared for those who love him" (1 Cor. 2:9).

What Is Our Great Reward?

The fullness of this heavenly hope is described beautifully in the book of Hebrews, where the author provides a clear definition of authentic faith:

> Without faith it is impossible to please him, for whoever would draw near to God must believe that he exists and that he rewards those who seek him. (11:6)

So faith is coming to God who exists for the reward he offers. But what is this reward? Read each passage below carefully, noting what we are called to hope for *and* the type of earthly lifestyle that this hope produces.

> You had compassion on those in prison, and you joyfully accepted the plundering of your property, since you knew that you yourselves had *a better possession and an abiding one.* Therefore do not throw away your confidence, which has *a great reward.* (10:34–35)

> He was looking forward to *the city that has foundations,* whose designer and builder is God. (11:10)

> People who speak thus make it clear that they are seeking a *homeland.* If they had been thinking of that land from which they had gone out, they would have had opportunity to return. But as it is, they desire *a better country, that is, a heavenly one.* Therefore God is not ashamed to be called their God, for he has prepared for them *a city.* (11:14–16)

> By faith Moses, when he was grown up, refused to be called the son of Pharaoh's daughter, choosing rather to be mistreated with the people of God than to enjoy the fleeting pleasures of sin. He considered the reproach of Christ greater wealth than the treasures of Egypt, for he was looking to *the reward.* (11:24–26)

> Some were tortured, refusing to accept release, so that they might rise again to *a better life.* (11:35)

> For they disciplined us for a short time as it seemed best to them, but he disciplines for our good, that we may *share in his holiness.* (12:10)

> Strive for peace with everyone, and for the holiness without which no one will *see the Lord.* (12:14)

> But you have come to *Mount Zion* and to *the city of the living God,* the heavenly Jerusalem, and to *innumerable angels* in festal gathering, and to *the assembly of the firstborn* who are enrolled in heaven, and to *God, the judge of all,* and to *the spirits of the righteous made perfect,* and to *Jesus,* the mediator of a new covenant, and to the sprinkled blood that speaks a better word than the blood of Abel. (12:22–24)

> Therefore let us be grateful for receiving *a kingdom that cannot be shaken*, and thus let us offer to God acceptable worship, with reverence and awe. (12:28)

> So Jesus also suffered outside the gate in order to sanctify the people through his own blood. Therefore let us go to him outside the camp and bear the reproach he endured. For here we have no lasting city, but we seek *the city that is to come*. (13:12–14)

So what is our hope and reward? What enables us to gladly embrace the loss of our property and leave our homeland to go where God calls us? What empowers us to forgo earthly treasures and fleeting sin, to endure torture for the sake of Christ, and to welcome God's painful discipline? What inspires us to live in peace with others and to reject sexual immorality and ungodliness and to worship God rightly with reverence and awe? What frees us to leave behind the comforts of earthly cities and venture outside the camp to suffer reproach with Jesus?

One thing. One multilayered, complex, and magnificent thing. We can say that ultimately it is God himself, but Hebrews presses us to say more. What sustains us in the darkest times and unleashes the greatest sacrifices in the cause of love is *the holy and abiding presence of God with his perfected and transformed and embodied people in his unshakeable and glorious kingdom city for all eternity, world without end, Amen.*

This is our hope. These are the *pleasures* (plural!) forevermore that sit at God's right hand. Heaven truly is a world of love—supreme love for the triune God, expanding love for redeemed people, and increasing love for a renewed creation. And it's our hope in the fullness of God's glory that sustains us through suffering and persecution, hardship and sickness, horrific loss and grievous death.

12

Embrace Your Creatureliness

Gratitude is happiness doubled by wonder.

G. K. Chesterton

What then shall we say to these things? If God is for us, who can be against us? He who did not spare his own Son but gave him up for us all, how will he not also with him graciously give us all things?

Romans 8:31–32

The chief insight of Christian Hedonism is that we don't have to choose between a passion for God's glory and a passion for our joy. As John Piper says, "Let your passion be single." They are the same passion. The thesis of this book is that we don't have to choose between a love for God and a love for his gifts and that this remains true even when we lose good gifts or give them up for his sake.

The sixteenth psalm contains many of the truths we've explored in this book, and we can refresh ourselves with them by a brief walk through this wonderful song:

> Preserve me, O God, for in you I take refuge.
> I say to the Lord, "You are my Lord;
>   I have no good apart from you." (vv. 1–2)

The Things of Earth

The Lord, Yahweh, is my Lord and sovereign, and he is the author and source of every good thing I have. There can be no separation of the giver from his gifts, for apart from him there is no good for me.

> As for the saints in the land, they are the excellent ones,
>> in whom is all my delight. (v. 3)

Because I don't enjoy any good thing apart from God, all of my joy can be placed in his excellent saints. There are no limits to my delight in God's people. All my joy, all my delight, all my affection is in them, because all my good is in God.

> The sorrows of those who run after another god shall multiply;
>> their drink offerings of blood I will not pour out
>> or take their names on my lips. (v. 4)

My supreme and full love for God and his gifts means that I reject all false gods, all sorrowful and destructive separation of gifts from the giver. I resist the impulse to even name such idolatries with my lips.

> The LORD is my chosen portion and my cup;
>> you hold my lot.
> The lines have fallen for me in pleasant places;
>> indeed, I have a beautiful inheritance. (vv. 5–6)

God is my portion, my cup, and my lot. Like the Levites (Num. 18:20), God is my inheritance, surpassing all of his earthly gifts with his beautiful presence and provision.

> I bless the LORD who gives me counsel;
>> in the night also my heart instructs me.
> I have set the Lord always before me;
>> because he is at my right hand, I shall not be shaken. (vv. 7–8)

Even with God as my portion, I bless him and thank him for his gifts, such as his counsel and wisdom. What's more, God is always before me, always in my field of vision, even when I devote myself to fulfilling his commands and instruction. Because he is supreme in my life, I am not shaken when crisis, tragedy, or suffering come. When earth gives way and waters foam, when shadows fall on hearth and home, when nations rage and kingdoms mock, then I stand on God the rock.

> Therefore my heart is glad, and my whole being rejoices;
>   my flesh also dwells secure.
> For you will not abandon my soul to Sheol,
>   or let your holy one see corruption. (vv. 9–10)

Because of God's place in my life, I am free to rejoice with heart and soul and body. There is a deep security and stability and freedom, knowing that my fundamental allegiance is to him. And this security cannot be stolen by death. Sheol cannot rob me of joy, since God has promised us deliverance from the grave and guaranteed it by raising his Son as the firstfruits of the resurrection harvest (Acts 2:24–33; 13:32–39; 1 Cor. 15:20–23). Thus we can rejoice, be glad, and dwell secure, because nothing good will ever finally be lost.

> You make known to me the path of life;
>   in your presence there is fullness of joy;
>   at your right hand are pleasures forevermore. (v. 11)

So we see that God shows us the way that we are to live: placing the Lord before us as our Lord, our portion, our inheritance, and then enjoying and delighting in whatever he gives, whether delightful saints, his wise guidance, or any other good that we can conceive. We always dwell *coram Deo*, before his face. It is in his glorious presence alone that we find fullness of joy, and this fullness is granted to us in all of the various pleasures that his right hand bestows, both now and forevermore.

Embrace Your Creatureliness

At the heart of this book is the call to embrace your creatureliness. And the heart of creatureliness is receptivity. God is fundamentally a giver. Within the Trinity, the members of the Godhead fully and completely give themselves to each other. In relation to creation, he himself gives to all men life and breath and everything. He opens his hand and satisfies the desire of every living thing. God so loved the world that he gave his only Son to us, and the Father so delights in his Son that he gives us to him. The Father and Son together give us the Holy Spirit. The Spirit gives us comfort and grace and power and himself in our hearts and in our midst as his everlasting dwelling place. Yes, God is fundamentally a giver.

Therefore, to be a creature is to be a receiver. "What do you have that you did not receive?" (1 Cor. 4:7). The great privilege of man is to receive everything that God gives in all the ways that he gives it, and then to know it and enjoy it and delight in it and sing about it, and to know *him* in it and to enjoy *him* in it and to sing about *him* in it. All things are truly ours—"whether Paul or Apollos or Cephas or the world or life or death or the present or the future—all are yours, and you are Christ's, and Christ is God's" (1 Cor. 3:21–23).

So embrace your creatureliness. Don't seek to *be* God. Instead, embrace the glorious limitations and boundaries that God has placed on you as a character in his story. Embrace the fact that creation is a magic glass, the kind that allows you to see God more clearly the thicker it becomes. Embrace time and space as glorious and wise features of creaturely existence. Embrace your body and your five senses and the wonders that they can perceive and receive in the world. Embrace your heart and your mind, your ability to think and feel, your understanding and your will, that amazing image of the triune God that he has embedded in your soul. Anchor yourself in a supreme, full, and expanding love for God and then let your enjoyment of his gifts run wild.

And then seek to be *like* God—generous, overflowing, lavish. Share your time, talent, and treasure with those near and far as a way of spreading a passion for God's supremacy in all the things you have gladly received from him through Jesus Christ.

And, as a final exhortation, let me commend to you a life of gratitude. Gratitude is the proper response to an abundance of gifts. Gratitude is the posture of the soul that most readily increases receptivity. Gratitude demands humility, since only those who acknowledge their dependence, their need, and their delight in the goodness and kindness of another can be grateful. Give thanks always and for everything. And be specific. To that end, let me offer some fresh thanksgiving to God for his manifold kindness to me.

I'm thankful for cool autumn days and the brilliant colors that ride on them; for my wife's diligent efforts to care for me and our boys, especially when it's hard; for the college guys who help me with yard work; for my in-laws who will be visiting for the next week or so; for nine years of splendor and grace in marriage; that God owns the cattle on a thousand hills; that I get to teach and invest my life at Bethlehem College and Seminary; that I have two pillows to sleep with at night, one under my head and one between my knees; that the kingdom advances when I'm faithful at my post; for Narnia and the North; for the gifts, talents, and success of others; for Parkway Pizza and Oatmeal Stout; for the ability to think and remember; that God governs the affairs of men, including mine; that Jesus paid it all.

So if you are awash in a sea of God's gifts, dive in and savor them. Relish all there is to relish in them as a means of expanding your mind and heart to know God more deeply. Receive God's gifts gladly, give thanks for them, and then be as generous with others as God has been with you. And if you are in the midst of losing something or someone precious to you, don't detach. Press in. God is your only comfort, and he is present in your loss in ways you cannot fathom if you run from the desire and the longing and the pain.

All you have is Christ,

1) whether you have him in all the good gifts that he lavishes on you;
2) or whether you have him in all the gifts that you gladly receive and then freely give away in the cause of love;
3) or whether you only have him in the loss of everything else that is precious to you.

May the Father of lights, who knows how to give good gifts to his children, teach you the secret of facing plenty and hunger, abundance and need, being brought low or being raised up. May he grant you the grace to do all good things, receive all good things, lose all good things, and endure all hard things through Christ, who gives you strength.

Notes

Introduction

1. For a book-length refutation of the prosperity gospel, see David Jones and Russell Woodbridge, *Health, Wealth, and Happiness: Has the Prosperity Gospel Overshadowed the Gospel of Christ?* (Grand Rapids, MI: Kregel, 2010).
2. John Piper writes, "Christian Hedonism is a philosophy of life built on the following five convictions: (1) The longing to be happy is a universal human experience, and it is good, not sinful. (2) We should never try to deny or resist our longing to be happy, as though it were a bad impulse. Instead, we should seek to intensify this longing and nourish it with whatever will provide the deepest and most enduring satisfaction. (3) The deepest and most enduring happiness is found only in God. Not from God, but in God. (4) The happiness we find in God reaches its consummation when it is shared with others in the manifold ways of love. (5) To the extent that we try to abandon the pursuit of our own pleasure, we fail to honor God and love people. Or, to put it positively: The pursuit of pleasure is a necessary part of all worship and virtue. That is: *The chief end of man is to glorify God* by *enjoying Him forever.*" *Desiring God: Meditations of a Christian Hedonist*, rev. ed. (Sisters, OR: Multnomah, 2011), 28.
3. John Piper, "Boasting Only in the Cross," http://www.desiringgod.org/conference -messages/boasting-only-in-the-cross (accessed February 11, 2014).
4. Arcing is a method of visually representing the logical relationships and flow of thought of a biblical passage. For more information, visit http://www.biblearc.com.
5. These posts include "Piperian Hedonism 3.0," http://dougwils.com/s7-engaging -the-culture/piperian-hedonism-30.html; "A Full Tank of Gas and Lots of Wyoming Ahead," http://dougwils.com/s7-engaging-the-culture/a-full-tank-of-gas-and-lots-of -wyoming-ahead.html; and "The Barkity Barkity Midnight Dog," http://dougwils .com/s7-engaging-the-culture/the-barkity-barkity-midnight-dog.html (accessed July 22, 2014).
6. To be sure, John Piper has addressed a number of these issues in his books. See *Desiring God*, chap. 6; *The Pleasures of God: Meditations on God's Delight in Being God* (Sisters, OR: Multnomah, 2000), chap. 3; *When I Don't Desire God: How to Fight for Joy* (Wheaton, IL: Crossway, 2004), chap. 11.

Chapter 1: The Glory of the Triune God

1. Wayne Grudem, *Systematic Theology* (Grand Rapids, MI: Zondervan, 1996), 231. Kevin DeYoung offers a fuller exposition in seven statements: "(1) There is only one God. (2) The Father is God. (3) The Son is God. (4) The Holy Spirit is God. (5) The Father is not the Son. (6) The Son is not the Holy Spirit. (7) The Holy Spirit is not

the Father." "The Doctrine of the Trinity: No Christianity Without It," *The Gospel Coalition Blog*, http://thegospelcoalition.org/blogs/kevindeyoung/2011/09/28/the -doctrine-of-the-trinity-no-christianity-without-it/ (accessed February 11, 2014).

2. C. S. Lewis, *Mere Christianity* (New York: HarperCollins, 2009), 154.

3. Ralph Smith, *Paradox and Truth: Understanding Van Til on the Trinity* (Moscow, ID: Canon, 1998), 109–10. In categorizing models as either oneness or threeness, I'm not intending to weigh in on any of the contemporary discussion of the history and development of Trinitarian theology. It's merely a simple and intuitive categorization. Academic discussions of the Trinity are important and can, in their own way, be highly entertaining (especially when they take on the character of junior high food fights). For my own part, I've been helped by the work of Robert Letham, *The Holy Trinity: In Scripture, History, Theology, and Worship* (Phillipsburg, NJ: P&R, 2004); Stephen Holmes, *The Quest for the Trinity: The Doctrine of God in Scripture, History, and Modernity* (Downers Grove, IL: InterVarsity, 2012); and Stephen Holmes, *God of Grace and God of Glory: An Account of the Theology of Jonathan Edwards* (Grand Rapids, MI: Eerdmans, 2001).

4. E.g., Jonathan Edwards, after seeking to shed light on the Trinity through various models, wrote: "But I don't pretend fully to explain how these things are and I am sensible a hundred other objections may be made and puzzling doubts and questions raised that I can't solve. I am far from pretending to explaining the Trinity so as to render it no longer a mystery. I think it to be the highest and deepest of all Divine mysteries still, notwithstanding anything that I have said or conceived about it." Later he wrote, "I am far from affording this as any explication of this mystery, that unfolds and renews the mysteriousness and incomprehensibleness of it, for I am sensible that however by what has been said some difficulties are lessened, others that are new appear, and the number of those things that appear mysterious, wonderful and incomprehensible, is increased by it. I offer it only as a farther manifestation of what of Divine truth the Word of God exhibits to the view of our minds concerning this great mystery." Jonathan Edwards, "Discourse on the Trinity," in *Writings on the Trinity, Grace, and Faith*, vol. 21, *The Works of Jonathan Edwards*, ed. Sang Hyun Lee (New Haven, CT: Yale University Press, 2003), 134.

5. Ibid., and John Piper, *The Pleasures of God: Meditations on God's Delight in Being God* (Sisters, OR: Multnomah, 2000), chap. 1. For a fantastic and accessible introduction to the doctrine of the Trinity, see Michael Reeves, *Delighting in the Trinity: An Introduction to the Christian Faith* (Downers Grove, IL: InterVarsity, 2012).

6. C. S. Lewis shares Edwards's understanding of the Holy Spirit as the personal bond between the Father and Son: "The union between the Father and Son is such a live concrete thing that this union itself is also a Person. . . . What grows out of the joint life of the Father and Son is a real Person, is in fact the Third of the three Persons who are God. . . . God is love, and that love works through men—especially through the whole community of Christians. But this spirit of love is, from all eternity, a love going on between the Father and the Son." *Mere Christianity* (New York: HarperCollins, 2001), 175.

7. Some object to Edwards's psychological analogy on the grounds that it seems to depersonalize the Spirit. By describing the Spirit as God's love for God, have we not turned the Spirit into a force or energy rather than a person with understanding and will? After all, love is an action, not a person. The simplest response is to note that we don't seem to have the same problem when the Bible identifies the Son as God's Word

(John 1:1). We don't normally think of words as being distinct persons who can think and act, yet the Bible is comfortable speaking of the Word as a person (and hopefully we are too). Thus, I'd suggest that we make the same mental adjustments with respect to the personhood of the Spirit that we make when we regard the eternal Word of God as a distinct, divine person. After all, the same biblical author who identifies the Word with God ("The Word was God," John 1:1) also identifies love with God ("God is love," 1 John 4:8). For a further explanation, see Edwards, "Discourse on the Trinity," and Piper, *The Pleasures of God*, 42–45. For a scholarly exposition and assessment of Edwards's view of the Trinity, see Kyle Strobel, *Jonathan Edwards's Theology: A Reinterpretation* (New York: T&T Clark, 2013), 21–72.

8. In linking the Son with God's wisdom and knowledge and the Spirit with God's love and joy, I'm not implying that the Son does not love or that the Spirit does not have knowledge. As we'll see, the doctrine of perichoresis, which refers to the mutual indwelling of the divine persons, enables us to both link God's knowledge and love with the Son and Spirit, respectively, and yet maintain with the Scriptures that all members of the Godhead share everything they have and are, including their knowledge and love. For a discussion of perichoresis, see Letham, *The Holy Trinity*, 178–80, 381–83; and Thomas Torrance, *The Christian Doctrine of God* (New York: T&T Clark, 2001), 168–202.

9. C. S. Lewis, *The Weight of Glory: and Other Addresses* (New York: Macmillan, 1949), 43, emphasis original.

10. Careful readers will note the surprising absence of any explicit reference to the Holy Spirit in Jesus's prayer in John 17. However, the psychological model of the Trinity that we explored earlier in the chapter suggests that the Spirit is not completely absent in this passage. If we are right to link the Holy Spirit to God's love and joy in particular, then Jesus does refer to the Holy Spirit in his prayer. In 17:13 Jesus notes that the purpose of what he's said to the disciples is "that they may have my joy fulfilled in themselves." Not just any joy, but the joy of the Son of God himself (cf. John 15:11). In 17:26 Jesus again testifies to his purpose in revealing the Father's name: "that the love with which you have loved me may be in them, and I in them." Again, Jesus's revelation doesn't place just any old love within us, but the Father's own love for the Son. And what (or who) is the Son's joy, the Father's love? Might it not be the Holy Spirit?

11. In saying that our knowledge of God is simply God's knowledge in us, I don't mean to imply that we know *in the same way* that God knows. God is God, and we are creatures, and there is a fundamental gap (what theologians call "the Creator-creature distinction") that cannot be bridged. Thus, when God gives us knowledge of himself, it is his own knowledge but appropriate to our creaturely frame.

12. Lewis, *Mere Christianity*, 176.

Chapter 2: The Author and His Story

1. Jonathan Edwards, "God Is Everywhere Present," in *The Blessing of God: Previously Unpublished Sermons of Jonathan Edwards*, ed. Michael D. McMullen (Nashville, TN: Broadman, 2003), chap. 6.

2. John Piper helpfully summarizes: "This 'all things' includes the fall of sparrows (Matt. 10:29), the rolling of dice (Prov. 16:33), the slaughter of his people (Ps. 44:11), the decisions of kings (Prov. 21:1), the failing of sight (Ex. 4:11), the sickness of

children (2 Sam. 12:15), the loss and gain of money (1 Sam. 2:7), the suffering of saints (1 Pet. 4:19), the completion of travel plans (James 4:15), the persecution of Christians (Heb. 12:4–7), the repentance of souls (2 Tim. 2:25), the gift of faith (Phil. 1:29), the pursuit of holiness (Phil. 3:12–13), the growth of believers (Heb. 6:3), the giving of life and the taking in death (1 Sam. 2:6), and the crucifixion of his Son (Acts 4:27–28)." "Why I Do Not Say, 'God Did Not Cause the Calamity, but He Can Use It for Good,'" sermon, http://www.desiringgod.org/articles/why-i-do-not-say-god-did -not-cause-the-calamity-but-he-can-use-it-for-good (accessed February 11, 2014).

3. Though he doesn't use the imagery that I do, Herman Bavinck highlights this same two-step process in the execution of creation: "The world was first conceived by God and thereupon came into being by his omnipotent speech; after receiving its existence, it does not exist apart from him or in opposition to him, but continues to rest in his spirit." *Reformed Dogmatics, Vol. 2: God and Creation*, ed. John Bolt, trans. John Vriend (Grand Rapids, MI: Baker Academic, 2004), 262.

4. I was first introduced to the author-story analogy in a philosophy of religion class with Dr. Hugh McCann at Texas A&M University. McCann has developed the author-story analogy from the perspective of philosophical theology in his own writings. See Hugh McCann, "Divine Providence," in *The Stanford Encyclopedia of Philosophy* (Winter 2012), http://plato.stanford.edu/entries/providence-divine/ (accessed July 22, 2014). C. S. Lewis utilizes this analogy in his essay "The Seeing Eye," in his *Christian Reflections* (Grand Rapids, MI: Eerdmans, 1967), 167–76. For other explorations of the author-story analogy, see Wayne Grudem, *Systematic Theology* (Grand Rapids, MI: Zondervan, 2000), 321–22; John Frame, *The Doctrine of God* (Phillipsburg, NJ: P&R, 2002), 156–59, 174–82; and Tim Keller, *The Reason for God* (New York: Dutton, 2008), 122–23 (Keller is building on Lewis). N. D. Wilson makes extensive use of the author-story analogy in *Notes from the Tilt-A-Whirl: Wide-Eyed Wonder in God's Spoken World* (Nashville, TN: Thomas Nelson, 2009).

5. Wilson, *Notes from the Tilt-A-Whirl*, 23–24.

6. In Gen. 50:20, the pronoun "it" is feminine in Hebrew, which means that it must have a feminine antecedent (Hebrew, like Greek, Latin, and Spanish, has gendered nouns and pronouns). The only feminine word that precedes the pronoun is the Hebrew word *ra'ah*, which is translated "evil." Thus, if we substitute the noun for the pronoun and make it explicit, the verse reads, "You meant evil against me, but God meant evil for good." In making the grammar explicit, it's important to note that God is not evil when he means "evil for good." How he is able to ordain evil and yet remain unsullied is mysterious to us, though I hope the author-story analogy provides one fruitful way of imagining how this is possible, even if questions still remain.

7. Augustine, *The Trinity*, ed. Edmund Hill (New York: New City Press, 2012), 97. The full quotation emphasizes the painful stretching involved in pressing into God: "People who seek God, and stretch their minds as far as human weakness is able toward an understanding of the trinity, must surely experience the strain of trying to fix their gaze on *light inaccessible* (1 Tim. 6:16), and the difficulties presented by the holy scriptures in their multifarious diversity of form, which are designed, so it seems to me, to wear Adam down and let Christ's glorious grace shine through."

8. For more extended application of this paradigm to the problem of evil, see my article "Confronting the Problem(s) of Evil: Biblical, Philosophical, and Emotional Reflections on a Perpetual Question," http://www.desiringgod.org/resource-library /articles/confronting-the-problem-s-of-evil (accessed February 11, 2014). For a com-

plementary treatment of the problem of evil, see Martin Cothran, "How Literature Solves the Problem of Evil," *Circe* http://mag.circeinstitute.org/6_howlitsolvesthe problemofevil.html (accessed February 11, 2014). Cothran helpfully draws out the way that story and narrative overcome the apparent absurdity of evil, which is what gives the problem its existential force: "What most disturbs us about evil is not that it presents a logical problem. In fact, what most disturbs us about evil is not evil itself. What most disturbs us about it is its seeming absurdity. . . . What we fear is not evil per se, but metaphysical chaos. What scares us is not bad things; what scares us, to use the words of William Butler Yeats, is that 'things fall apart—the center cannot hold.'" Cothran argues that this is why story and song provide the most adequate response to evil—they provide a larger narratival and moral order in which evil makes sense, and is thus endurable: "While his Comforters bring him reasons, God brings the news of the poetic order of the world. God's words mean more to Job than those of his comforters because the world is more like a poem than a syllogism."

9. The two lenses correspond to what theologians have historically called God's "will of decree" and his "will of command," or his "sovereign will" and his "moral will." For a fuller explanation of this distinction, see John Piper, "Are There Two Wills in God?," http://www.desiringgod.org/articles/are-there-two-wills-in-god (accessed February 11, 2014).

10. Douglas K. Stuart, *Exodus* (Nashville, TN: Broadman, 2006), 121.

11. In my experience, Calvinists tend to emphasize that God is the transcendent author of the story, whereas Arminians (and open theists) emphasize that God is an immanent character within the story. My proposal is that we don't have to choose between these two paradigms (since the Bible bears witness to both), nor should we somehow privilege one perspective over the other. In the same way that the triune God is equally three and equally one (so that neither one takes absolute priority over the other), so also his transcendence and immanence—his authorship and his charactership—are equally ultimate. My hope is that Calvinists will not allow their true belief in God's glorious sovereignty to undermine the reality of God's relational interaction (his weeping, his repentance, his changing his mind). In the same vein, I hope that Arminians will not allow their right embrace of God's authentic relationality within creation to keep them from acknowledging and delighting in God's absolute sovereignty over all things.

Chapter 3: Creation as Communication

1. Maltbie D. Babcock, "This Is My Father's World," 1901.

2. C. S. Lewis, *Letters to Malcolm: Chiefly on Prayer* (New York: Harcourt, Brace, & World, 1964), 75.

3. Jonathan Edwards, *Typological Writings*, vol. 11, *The Works of Jonathan Edwards*, ed. Wallace E. Anderson, Mason I. Lowance, and David H. Watters (New Haven, CT: Yale University Press, 1993), 152.

4. Ken Myers, "Epiphany Lecture 1: Introduction," http://www.canonwired.com /epiphany-lectures/ (accessed February 11, 2014). Elsewhere Myers notes that modern Christianity and modern secularism share a common assumption about God's relation to creation: "Modern Christians have often assumed that they could relate to God apart from any kind of deliberate relation to creation. And modern seculars

assume that they can relate to nature without recognizing or honoring the creator in any way. For both sides, creation tends to be raw material, meaningless stuff awaiting human creativity to achieve its significance. . . . Where the scriptures present creation as an epiphany, modern culture sees creation as a pile of raw materials, natural resources, inert meaningless stuff. The world is commonly regarded as material to which we do something, not a source from which we receive something." Ken Myers, "Creation and the Ordered Imagination," chapel lecture, Dallas Theological Seminary, http://dev.dts.edu/media/play/creation-and-the-ordered-imagination -myers-ken/ (accessed February 11, 2014).

5. Edwards, *Works*, vol. 11, 150.

6. Ibid., 151.

7. In his inimitable way, Doug Wilson expresses just how wide these divine lessons are: "I believe that the kingdom of God is like an endless river, like a sawtooth mountain range, like whole milk, like a cultivated plain, like a marble city with gardens, like a marbled steak on the grill, like aged cheese, like smart phones, like a high mountain meadow, like the laughter of family at the table, like the way of a man with a maid, like a moonlit ocean, and like a warrior crying high defiance. The kingdom of God is like everything" (http://dougwils.com/s16-theology/an-odd-credo.html). In that same spirit, let me add my own: I believe that the kingdom of God is like a moonless night with a starry sky in the middle of nowhere, like a lively conversation, like swordfights on the back deck, like a Sunday afternoon nap, like shared tears that bring relief, like sliced jalapeños, like aged wine on the lees, like a case of the giggles, like melting snow in March, like Mozart's Concerto no. 20 in D, like a mother's embrace, like a father's approving smile, like the knowing grin of an older brother with a twinkle in his eye. The kingdom of God is righteousness, peace, and joy in the Holy Spirit.

8. Peter Leithart echoes this view of creation in an article at the Trinity House website: "All created things were made by God, designed after His Wisdom and Logos. As such, it is communication from God about God (Psalm 19). God made rocks, and in making them (we may surmise) intended them to be useful to display some of His glory. God created human beings in His image, and in so doing designed them to be suitable icons of His character. God oversaw the formation of human families and polities, and as He did so, He directed them so that a 'father' and a 'king' depict in various ways how Yahweh relates to His creation, to human beings, and to His people in particular. God created everything to communicate of Himself. That is the nature and purpose of everything created. If that is what created things *are*, and if God is the Creator who knows and governs His universe, then created things are designed to speak of Him." Peter Leithart, "Relations, Uncreated and Created," http:// trinityhouseinstitute.com/relations-uncreated-and-created/ (accessed February 11, 2014). From this, Leithart rightly draws out an implication about the use of human language (including the Bible) to speak about God: "Scripture also assumes that God speaks human. Because God designed creation and humanity to communicate something of Himself, He can speak in ordinary human language about Himself. God has revealed Himself in human language, that human language has been preserved in the Bible, and it is ordinary human language. Therefore, ordinary human language is adequate for communicating the reality of God to us. Of course, there is mystery at every point, but why should we expect anything else? We want to talk about an infinite, incomprehensible God and creatures made in His image."

9. In stressing that creation reveals God, it's important to underline that it does so by also revealing more about creation. In other words, we shouldn't isolate every aspect of creation in order to see how each part displays God. Instead, we ought to view creation as a web of intertwining threads. Each thread helps us to understand the other threads, and then the web itself, with all its woven relationships, reveals God to us more fully. To use Psalm 19 again, "The heavens declare the glory of God"—it's true. But they do so because the sun is like a bridegroom is like a warrior. In other words, Psalm 19 doesn't just reveal *God* to us through the heavens; it also reveals something about marriage and war and the sun (and so on and so on), and it's the swirl of images that enables us to see God's glory more clearly.

10. In a discussion of the great hope promised to the faithful in Christ, C. S. Lewis notes how this diversity of imagery guards us from error: "The variation of the promises does not mean that anything other than God will be our ultimate bliss; but because God is more than a Person, and lest we should imagine the joy of His presence too exclusively in terms of our present poor experience of personal love, with all its narrowness and strain and monotony, a dozen changing images, correcting and relieving each other, are supplied." Lewis, *The Weight of Glory*, 35. In *The Problem of Pain*, Lewis writes about the request for a loving God, using vivid and concrete imagery: "The great spirit you so lightly invoked, the 'lord of terrible aspect,' is present: not a senile benevolence that drowsily wishes you to be happy in your own way, not the cold philanthropy of a conscientious magistrate, nor the care of a host who feels responsible for the comfort of his guests, but the consuming fire Himself, the Love that made the worlds, persistent as an artist's love for his work and despotic as a man's love for his dog, provident and venerable as a father's love for a child, jealous, inexorable, exacting as love between the sexes." C. S. Lewis, *The Problem of Pain* (New York: HarperCollins, 2001), 39–40. In saying this, Lewis is simply living according to his own advice and seeking to rescue our thoughts about God from "the abyss of abstraction." C. S. Lewis, *Miracles* (New York: HarperCollins, 1947), 144.

11. C. S. Lewis, *God in the Dock: Essays on Theology and Ethics* (Grand Rapids, MI: Eerdmans, 1970), 212–15.

12. John Piper, *When I Don't Desire God: How to Fight for Joy* (Wheaton, IL: Crossway, 2004), 185.

13. Ibid.

14. Lewis, *Letters to Malcolm*, 70.

15. Ibid., 74. Lewis goes on to say, "One is always fighting on at least two fronts. When one is among Pantheists one must emphasize the distinctness, and relative independence, of the creatures. Among Deists . . . one must emphasize the divine presence in my neighbor, my dog, my cabbage-patch."

16. Some readers may wonder whether I'm arguing for some sort of panentheism, the belief that the world exists in God. While I would want to carefully guard against errors, I do believe that some sort of panentheism is exegetically demanded by passages such as Acts 17:26 ("*In him* we live and move and have our being") and Col. 1:16 ("In him all things hold together"). To return to the analogy from chapter 2, creation exists in God in the same way that an author's story exists in his mind. The story is not to be identified with the author, but the story is, in some real sense, *in* the author.

17. Lewis, *Letters to Malcolm*, 89, emphasis added.

18. Ibid., emphasis added.

19. Ibid.

20. Lewis, *Weight of Glory*, 44.
21. I'm grateful to Toby Sumpter and Peter Leithart for proposing these interpretations. What's more, I don't think that they are mutually exclusive. See "Un-naked God," http://www.leithart.com/2010/12/16/un-naked-god/; and "Bridal Glory," http://www.leithart.com/2010/12/17/bridal-glory/ (both accessed February 11, 2014).
22. Douglas Wilson, "Creation Is Thick, I Tell You," http://dougwils.com/s7-engaging-the-culture/creation-is-thick-i-tell-you.html (accessed February 11, 2014).
23. Lewis, *God in the Dock*, 29. He expresses the same sentiment when he writes, "The doctrine I understand to be something like this: There is an activity of God displayed throughout creation, a wholesale activity let us say which men refuse to recognize. The miracles done by God incarnate, living as a man in Palestine, perform the very same things as the wholesale activity, but at a different speed and on a smaller scale. One of their chief purposes is that men, having seen a thing done by personal power on the small scale, may recognize, when they see the same thing done on the large scale, that the power behind it is also personal."
24. My brief discussion of incarnation and discarnation owes much to the work of Michael Ward, particularly his *Planet Narnia: The Seven Heavens in the Imagination of C. S. Lewis* (New York: Oxford University Press, 2008). Ward shows how Lewis imaginatively constructed each of the Narnian chronicles to communicate certain spiritual symbols (represented by the seven medieval planets). The qualities associated with each planet are concentrated in the character of Aslan in the respective book. However, these same qualities are also dispersed throughout the book itself, forming the environment, ambience, and air that we breathe in each story. Ward thus highlights how Lewis was imitating the vision of God's revelation and incarnation that he sets forth in *Miracles*.

Chapter 4: Created to Be a Creature

1. C. S. Lewis, *Mere Christianity* (New York: HarperCollins, 2009), 64.
2. N. D. Wilson, *Notes from the Tilt-a-Whirl* (Nashville, TN: Thomas Nelson, 2009), 43.
3. Through the writings of Peter Leithart I first became aware of the deep theological importance of embracing finitude. In his book *Deep Comedy* (Moscow, ID: Canon Press, 2006), Leithart devotes his attention to exposing and demolishing what he calls "tragic metaphysics." He writes, "Within the category of 'tragic metaphysics,' . . . I also include philosophies that treat finitude, temporality, bodiliness, and limitation as philosophical and practical *problems* that must be either transcended or grudgingly accepted. Any metaphysics that treats 'becoming' as a problem (which is to say, most metaphysical systems in history) is basically and inherently tragic. Such philosophies are tragic because they assess the world as if it were designed to frustrate human life and inhibit human flourishing. They are tragic because they believe the world has been designed to prevent man from realizing himself. Tragic metaphysics issues in a tragic ethics that kicks against the pricks of createdness, either resentfully or joyfully or resignedly. Gnosticism is one of the key illustrations of tragic metaphysics, for it sees creation as a tragedy if not a travesty. Ultimately, these systems are tragic because they refuse to recognize the world as a gift and to give thanks. They are tragic because they systematize the Satanic desire to be as God" (p. 38). The present book might be seen as an attempt to erect considerable

biblical and theological defenses against any whiff of tragic metaphysics and the accompanying tragic ethics.

4. In saying that the prohibition in the garden was temporary, I'm suggesting that God always intended for Adam and Eve to eat from the tree of the knowledge of good and evil. The prohibition was the central part of Adam and Eve's probation, their period of testing in which God forbade them to eat something delightful and good in order to see whether they would trust and obey God above all else. In Scripture, "the knowledge of good and evil" is a way of describing mature and royal wisdom. As William Wilder writes, "The tree is a tree of *wisdom*, because in the Bible 'knowing good and evil' (or some approximation of that phrase) refers to the kind of wise discernment and discrimination exercised by mature and capable adults." William Wilder, "Illumination and Investiture," *Westminster Theological Journal* 68 (2006): 51. A few examples will establish this point. In Gen. 3:6, the woman recognizes that the tree is "desirable to make one wise." Thus, in the immediate context, the biblical author links the knowledge of good and evil with wisdom. In addition, Deut. 1:39 indicates that knowing good and evil is the mark of adulthood and maturity, because little children are specifically said to be lacking it. Isa. 7:16 contains a similar construction ("before the boy knows how to refuse the evil and choose the good") with the added nuance that the knowledge of good and evil involves discrimination and discernment between the two. 2 Sam. 14:17 and 14:20 draw the connection between discerning good and evil and wisdom, as the woman from Tekoa flatters David as one who is like an angel of God in that he discerns good and evil (14:17) and possesses wisdom (14:20). In addition, "her description of David as '*like* the angel of God' reminds us of God's words to his angelic host at the end of Gen 3: 'See, the man has now become *like* one of us, knowing good and evil'" (p. 55). In 1 Kings 3:9 Solomon prays, "Give your servant therefore an understanding mind to govern your people, that I may discern between good and evil, for who is able to govern this your great people?" Prior to his request, Solomon describes himself as a little child (v. 7), further proof that the knowledge of good and evil marks mature adults. Moreover, God answers his prayer by giving him "a wise and discerning mind" (v. 12). Thus, we see the connection between the knowledge of good and evil and royal wisdom. Finally, the author to the Hebrews rebukes his readers for remaining as children, infants in the faith, rather than moving on to maturity and becoming teachers "who have their powers of discernment trained by constant practice to distinguish good from evil" (Heb. 5:14). From these texts, we may conclude that the knowledge of good and evil is a metonymy for the wisdom that characterizes mature adults and particularly kings. Such knowledge is not inherently sinful, since both God and angels (Gen. 3:22; 2 Sam. 14:17–20) possess it. The goodness of the knowledge of good and evil suggests that God intended for Adam and Eve to eventually eat from the tree. John Walton argues that the prohibition was a matter of timing: "God's prohibition of the tree need not lead us to conclude that there was something wrong with what the tree gave (remember, everything was created 'good'). Rather than God's putting the tree there simply to test Adam and Eve, it is more in keeping with his character to understand that the tree would have use in the future. When the time was right, the first couple would be able to eat from it. One can compare this to the temptation of Christ, when Satan offered him all the kingdoms of the world if Jesus would bow down to him (Luke 4:5–7). There was nothing wrong with Christ's ruling all the kingdoms of the world—it was his destiny. The temptation involved bypassing appropriate

process and timing, seizing them through deviant means." *Genesis*, NIV Application Commentary (Grand Rapids, MI: Zondervan, 2001), 205–6. C. S. Lewis portrayed the prohibition in this way in his novel *Perelandra* (New York: Scribner, 2003).

5. I stress human companionship in general and not marriage in particular because I believe this passage relates to more than the husband and wife relationship. The biblical author is fundamentally speaking to the centrality and glory of marriage. However, marriage is not the only way to address man's solitude. The unmarried are not alone in the way this passage speaks of alone. All of us enter this world into relationships. We're born into a family. More importantly, we're born *again* into a family, the church. God meets our need for human companionship not only through a spouse; he also supplies it through friends, neighbors, family, and his people.

6. See Gregory K. Beale, *We Become What We Worship: A Biblical Theology of Idolatry* (Downers Grove, IL: IVP Academic, 2008), 128; and Gregory K. Beale, *The Temple and the Church's Mission: A Biblical Theology of the Dwelling Place of God* (Downers Grove, IL: InterVarsity, 2004), 66–121.

7. Further evidence that Adam was to guard the garden comes in Gen. 3:23 where the cherubim with the flaming sword replaces Adam as the one who keeps or guards (same word as Gen. 2:15) the way to the tree of life.

8. An imperfect analogy for this type of derived but inherent value might be found in Jesus's words concerning his relationship to the Father in John 5: "For as the Father has life in himself, so he has granted the Son also to have life in himself" (v. 26). The Father has "life in himself," and so does the Son. But the Son's "life in himself" is a gift from the Father. It is, in a sense, derived. He really has it, but he has it as an eternal gift.

9. Further biblical evidence for the principle of proportionate regard may be found in those places where God tells us that we are to desire his Word more than much fine gold (Ps. 19:10; cf. Ps. 119:72, 127; Prov. 8:10).

10. Christopher Wright discusses this scale of values in Israel's legal code in his *Old Testament Ethics for the People of God* (Downers Grove, IL: InterVarsity, 2004), 305–14.

11. Jonathan Edwards, "The End for which God Created the World," in John Piper, *God's Passion for His Glory* (Wheaton, IL: Crossway, 1998), 141.

12. Ibid., 143.

13. Ibid., 141, emphasis original.

14. Jonathan Edwards, *The End for which God Created the World* (Boston: S. Kneeland, 1765), 17–18.

15. Jonathan Edwards, "The End for which God Created the World," in Piper, *God's Passion*, 93.

16. John Piper, "Let Your Passion Be Single," http://www.desiringgod.org/conference -messages/let-your-passion-be-single?lang=en (accessed November 30, 2013).

17. I've chosen my words carefully. Following Edwards, I want to affirm that God does value things according to their value, but not because he is conforming to some external standard. The principle of proportionate regard is *descriptive* with respect to God, not *prescriptive*. For more on this distinction, see Walter Schultz, "Jonathan Edwards's *End of Creation*: An Exposition and Defense," *Journal of the Evangelical Theological Society* 49/2 (2006): 247–71.

18. This paragraph assumes a distinction between natural inability and moral inability. Natural inability means that there is some physical or creaturely constraint placed upon me so that I cannot obey *even if I want to*. Moral inability, on the other hand,

means that I am unable to obey *precisely because* I don't want to. When the Bible says that the fleshly mind *cannot* submit to God's law (Rom. 8:7), it is referring to moral inability. Natural ability is a prerequisite for moral accountability; moral ability is not. The fact that we are so wicked that we cannot respond to God on our own does not absolve us from guilt; it increases it. For more on this distinction, see John Piper, "A Response to J. I. Packer on the So-Called Antinomy Between the Sovereignty of God and Human Responsibility," http://www.desiringgod.org/articles/a-response-to -ji-packer-on-the-so-called-antinomy-between-the-sovereignty-of-god-and-human -responsibility (accessed February 18, 2014).

19. Technically, the first of the Ten Commandments commands that we should worship God *exclusively*. "No other gods before me" means "no other gods in my presence." But given that we worship what we love most, "no other gods before me" is the same as saying "no other loves above me." Worshiping God exclusively means loving God supremely.

20. Mary E. Byrne, "Be Thou My Vision," 1905, emphasis added.

21. For a helpful treatment of what it means to give give God our all, see Jason De-Rouchie, "Love God with Your Everything," http://www.desiringgod.org/blog /posts/love-god-with-your-everything (accessed July 22, 2014).

22. Jonathan Edwards, "The End for Which God Created the World," in Piper, *God's Passion*, 159, emphasis added. Attentive readers will identify a deep connection between this passage and the discussion of the Trinity in chap. 1. An increasing knowledge of God, love to God, and joy in God in creatures is simply another way of describing God's communication of his Trinitarian fullness.

23. Ibid., 159–61, emphases original. Readers familiar with the mathematical concept of an asymptote will more easily grasp Edwards's argument. An asymptote describes the relationship between a curve and a line in which the distance between the curve and the line approaches zero as they tend to infinity. The curve gets closer and closer to the line without ever actually touching the line. For Edwards, this is what heaven is—an ever-increasing union with the infinite God.

Chapter 5: The Gospel Solution to Idolatry

1. Jonathan Edwards, "The End for which God Created the World," in John Piper, *God's Passion for His Glory* (Wheaton, IL: Crossway, 1998), 143.

2. Hugh Evan Hopkins, *Charles Simeon of Cambridge* (Grand Rapids, MI: Eerdmans, 1977), 203.

3. Augustine, *The Confessions of St. Augustine*, in *Documents of the Christian Church*, ed. Henry Bettenson (London: Oxford University Press, 1967), 54.

4. Dante depicts precisely this sort of idolatry and mind-set in his description of the cleansing punishment of the greedy and avaricious in *Purgatorio* 19.118–23: "For as our eyes were never raised on high but fixed themselves upon the things of earth, here justice humbles them to touch the ground. As avarice quenched the love we should have borne for all good things, and made us lose our labor, so justice holds us here within its clench." The greedy fixed their eyes on the things of earth and never sought the things above. As a result, greed and covetousness destroyed the love of all good things. As C. S. Lewis was fond of reminding us, "If you put first things first, you get second things thrown in. Put second things first, and you lose both first and second things." C. S. Lewis, "Letter to Dom Bede Griffiths," in *Collected Letters of C.*

S. *Lewis*, vol. 3, ed. Walter Hooper (New York: HarperCollins, 2009), 228. Set your mind above and receive the good things below as well. Set your mind below, and every good thing turns to chalk in your mouth.

5. I'm grateful to my friend David Mathis for drawing my attention to these passages, especially the differences between *phroneo* and *logizomai*.

6. This is Timothy Keller's definition of idolatry in his book *Counterfeit Gods: The Empty Promises of Money, Sex, and Power, and the Only Hope That Matters* (New York: Dutton, 2009).

7. Jonathan Edwards, *Charity and Its Fruits* (Carlisle, PA: Banner of Truth, 2005), 157–58.

8. Ibid.

9. John Calvin, *Institutes of the Christian Religion*, ed. and trans. Henry Beveridge (Peabody, MA: Hendrickson, 2008), 2.2.15. In this passage, Calvin is especially commending the study of the liberal arts, including the writings of pagans. Echoing Phil. 4:8 he says, "Shall we deem anything to be noble and praiseworthy, without tracing it to the hand of God?" (ibid). Elsewhere he exhorts us to dwell long upon the works of God so that we might see his attributes reflected in them as in a mirror: "Undoubtedly were one to attempt to speak in due terms of the inestimable wisdom, power, justice, and goodness of God, in the formation of the world, no grace or splendour of diction could equal the greatness of the subject. Still there can be no doubt that the Lord would have us constantly occupied with such holy meditation, in order that, while we contemplate the immense treasures of wisdom and goodness exhibited in the creatures as in so many mirrors, we may not only run our eye over them with a hasty, and, as it were, evanescent glance, but dwell long upon them, seriously and faithfully turn them in our minds, and every now and then bring them to recollection." Ibid., 1.14.21.

10. I intentionally included Big Macs and Twinkies in the list. One of the besetting sins of our day is food-fussing, the attempt to resurrect some kind of food laws, whether they be all-natural, organic, paleo, gluten-free, or what have you. While there is no problem in having food preferences (I myself am not a fan of raw onions, bubble gum, or coffee), there is a serious problem in ascribing moral value to your food preferences. Making food choices based on food allergies or other responses to food is perfectly legitimate, but imposing those choices on others (or judging others for making different choices) is not. While a full treatment of food-fussing is beyond the scope of this book, all Christians would do well to memorize, digest, and embody Mark 7:19, 1 Cor. 8:8, and 1 Cor. 10:31–33. In the first, Jesus declares all foods clean. All of them. *All of them*, which means the attempt to treat some foods as functionally unclean is contrary to Christ, however distasteful or dissatisfying they may be to you. The second reads, "Food will not commend us to God. We are no worse off if we do not eat, and no better off if we do." Your kale and arugula salad won't commend you to God. And your neighbor's greasy burger and large Diet Coke won't condemn him. God does not care about what you eat, provided you do so with gratitude in your heart (see 1 Tim. 4:4–5). Finally, we all know that 1 Cor. 10:31 commands us to eat and drink to the glory of God. What we don't often recognize is that Paul primarily has in mind our attitude toward others, not our attitude toward the food itself. The following verse reads, "Give no offense to Jews or to Greeks or to the church of God, just as I try to please everyone in everything I do, not seeking my own advantage, but that of many, that they may be saved" (v. 32). We glorify God in

eating when we refuse to make dietary choices a barrier to fellowship. So thank God for the food, love your neighbor in your eating, and quit your fussing.

11. 1 Tim. 4:4–5 is one of the only verses in the Bible that potheads have memorized (the other is Gen. 1:29–30). They ask the perfectly reasonable question as to why all marijuana use is forbidden, given that everything created by God is good. The simplest response is to note that the goodness of creation doesn't keep it from being abused. God gave wine to gladden the heart of man (Ps. 104:15) and still forbids drunkenness (Eph. 5:18). The sinfulness of recreational marijuana use is not owing to the evil of the Cannabis plant, but to the inevitable intoxication that results from ingesting the drug. Eph. 5:18 forbids us to be drunk on wine, and it is a legitimate application of the text to forbid intoxication with beer, whiskey, and rubbing alcohol as well. The difference between most forms of alcohol and marijuana is that weed smoking is inherently intoxicating and impairing. On the other hand, there may be a legitimate medicinal use for marijuana in pain relief, and thus we can preserve its God-designed benefit, if imbibed for medical reasons and with proper oversight (in the same way we do for narcotics). For more on the question of marijuana use, see the appendix in Douglas Wilson, *Future Men* (Moscow, ID: Canon Press, 2012), 173–83.

12. I'm grateful to my friend Jason Meyer, who drew attention to this demonic contrast in a sermon on this passage.

13. John Piper's sermon "Boasting Only in the Cross" is well worth a listen. It was the first sermon that I ever heard from Piper, and it was absolutely life-changing for me in college. http://www.desiringgod.org/conference-messages/boasting-only-in-the-cross (accessed July 22, 2014).

14. See Richard Gaffin, *Resurrection and Redemption* (Phillipsburg, NJ: P&R, 1987).

15. C. S. Lewis, *Miracles* (New York: HarperCollins, 2001), 266.

Chapter 6: Rhythms of Godwardness

1. Pete Seeger, *Turn! Turn! Turn! (to Everything There Is a Season)*, Columbia Records, 1965.

2. Thus, the primary difference between them is in our intentions, in what our minds are attending to at any given moment. Kevin Vanhoozer helpfully identifies intention as the "directedness of one's mind, the miner's lamp that focuses wherever we look," in *Is There a Meaning in This Text?: The Bible, the Reader, and the Morality of Literary Knowledge*, anniversary ed. (Grand Rapids, MI: Zondervan, 2009), 246, 252. Vanhoozer's entire discussion of intention is valuable and fits with my own thoughts here.

3. That this is a biblical way to think can be illustrated by the fact that loving God with everything we have (Matt. 22:37–40) is not at odds with loving our neighbors as ourselves. What's more, in Philippians 2, Paul celebrates Timothy's love and holiness by describing him as the only one who is "genuinely concerned for your welfare" (lit. "the things concerning you"). In the next verse, he says that others seek their own interests (lit. "the things of themselves"), but Timothy seeks those of Jesus Christ (lit. "the things of Jesus Christ"); i.e., Timothy pursues the things of Christ *by* being concerned for the things of the Philippians. Or, more precisely, the things of Christ simply *are* the Philippians and their needs and welfare. Therefore, if we are to show genuine godwardness, we will often find ourselves manward in the moment.

4. Richard Baxter, *The Practical Works of Richard Baxter, Vol. 1: A Christian Directory* (Morgan, PA: Soli Deo Gloria, 2000), 266.

5. The best treatment of fasting that I'm aware of is John Piper, *A Hunger for God: Desiring God through Fasting and Prayer* (Wheaton, IL: Crossway, 2013).

6. C. S. Lewis, *Letters to Malcolm: Chiefly on Prayer* (New York: Harcourt, Brace, & World, 1964), 90–91.

7. Helen Lemmel, "Turn Your Eyes upon Jesus," 1922.

8. Jonathan Edwards, *Letters and Personal Writings*, vol. 16, *The Works of Jonathan Edwards*, ed. Wallace E. Anderson, Mason I. Lowance, and David H. Watters (New Haven, CT: Yale University Press, 1993), 793–94.

9. George Herbert, "The Elixir," http://www.poetryfoundation.org/poem/173627 (accessed July 22, 2014).

10. Martin Luther once expressed a similar sentiment about daily tasks: "Now observe that when that clever harlot, our natural reason (which the pagans followed in trying to be most clever), takes a look at married life, she turns up her nose and says, 'Alas, must I rock the baby, wash its diapers, make its bed, smell its stench, stay up nights with it, take care of it when it cries, heal its rashes and sores, and on top of that care for my wife, provide for her, labor at my trade, take care of this and take care of that, do this and do that, endure this and endure that, and whatever else of bitterness and drudgery married life involves? What, should I make such a prisoner of myself? O you poor, wretched fellow, have you taken a wife? Fie, fie upon such wretchedness and bitterness! It is better to remain free and lead a peaceful, carefree life; I will become a priest or a nun and compel my children to do likewise.' What then does Christian faith say to this? It opens its eyes, looks upon all these insignificant, distasteful, and despised duties in the Spirit, and is aware that they are all adorned with divine approval as with the costliest gold and jewels. It says, 'O God, because I am certain that Thou hast created me as a man and hast from my body begotten this child, I also know for a certainty that it meets with Thy perfect pleasure. I confess to Thee that I am not worthy to rock the little babe or wash its diapers or to be entrusted with the care of the child and its mother. How is it that I, without any merit, have come to this distinction of being certain that I am serving Thy creature and Thy most precious will? O how gladly will I do so, though the duties should be even more insignificant and despised! Neither frost nor heat, neither drudgery nor labor, will distress or dissuade me, for I am certain that it is thus pleasing in Thy sight.' A wife too should regard her duties in the same light, as she suckles the child, rocks and bathes it, and cares for it in other ways; and as she busies herself with other duties and renders help and obedience to her husband. These are truly golden and noble works. . . . Now you tell me, when a father goes ahead and washes diapers or performs some other mean task for his child, and someone ridicules him as an effeminate fool, though that father is acting in the spirit just described and in Christian faith, my dear fellow you tell me, which of the two is most keenly ridiculing the other? God, with all His angels and creatures, is smiling, not because that father is washing diapers, but because he is doing so in Christian faith. Those who sneer at him and see only the task but not the faith are ridiculing God with all His creatures, as the biggest fool on earth. Indeed, they are only ridiculing themselves; with all their cleverness they are nothing but devil's fools." Martin Luther, "The Estate of Marriage," in *Martin Luther's Basic Theological Writings*, 2nd ed., ed. Timothy F. Lull (Minneapolis: Augsburg Fortress, 2005), 158–59.

11. B. B. Warfield, *The Religious Life of Theological Students* (Phillipsburg, NJ: Presbyterian and Reformed, 1911), 182.

12. Self-examination and self-forgetfulness provide another example of the use of anchor points. Self-examination has a crucial role in the Christian life (2 Cor. 13:5). We ought to regularly ask God to search us and know us, to test us and know our anxious thoughts, to expose any offensive ways in our lives (Ps. 139:23–24). However, once we've honestly laid ourselves open to God's searchlight and done our own humble probing, we ought to move away from self-examination and seek to live a self-forgetful life. Jonathan Edwards expressed this well in relation to assurance of salvation when he wrote, "It is not God's design that men should obtain assurance in any other way, than by mortifying corruption, increasing in grace, and obtaining the lively exercises of it. And although self-examination be a duty of great use and importance, and by no means to be neglected; yet it is not the *principal* means, by which the saints do get satisfaction of their good estate. Assurance is not to be obtained so much by *self-examination,* as by *action.*" *Religious Affections* (Carlisle, PA: Banner of Truth, 2001), 123. Self-examination is like the comparative approach to God and his gifts (see chap. 5) and like our times of direct godwardness. It plays a vital role in rooting and anchoring us in God and his gospel, but it is designed to push us out into the world God made, where we integrate our joy in God and his gifts and self-forgetfully and indirectly pursue God through all the ways that he gives himself to us in his creation.

13. The direct quote is, "I believe in Christianity as I believe that the Sun has risen, not only because I see it, but because by it I see everything else." See C. S. Lewis, "Is Theology Poetry?," in *The Weight of Glory: and Other Addresses* (New York: Macmillan, 1949), 140.

14. Peter Leithart helpfully comments on this passage: "Everything that the light shines on becomes a reflector of light, that being the only way it can become visible at all. Everything that receives light becomes a lamp, and, conversely, if something doesn't receive light, it is not a light." http://www.firstthings.com/blogs/leithart/2014/02/ontology-of-light.

15. E.g., the Bible often speaks of the immense benefit of regular, scheduled times of prayer (Isa. 62:6–7; 1 Chron. 16:37–42; often "day and night" or "morning and evening" as in Ps. 88:1–2, 9, 13; Neh.1:6; Luke 18:7; Col. 1:9; or "evening, morning, and at noon" as in Ps. 55:17; Dan. 6:10); as well as the cultivated practice of spontaneously and continually turning to God in prayer whenever an opportunity arises (2 Chron. 20:1–30; Eph. 6:18–20; Col. 4:12–13; 1 Thess. 5:17). I'm grateful to my colleague Justin Woyak for drawing my attention to this theme in Scripture and, more importantly, for practicing it himself and encouraging others to do likewise.

Chapter 7: Naming the World

1. You could extend this point even to an apple plucked right from the tree. While God certainly created its capacities, most of our food has been bred and modified by shrewd farmers (or smart men in white lab coats). With the possible exception of the heavens, it would be difficult to find any realm of pure nature, any part of creation that is untouched by human activity.

2. For a fuller treatment of culture and culture making, see David Bruce Hegeman, *Plowing in Hope: Toward a Biblical Theology of Culture* (Moscow, ID: Canon Press,

1999); Andy Crouch, *Culture-Making: Recovering Our Creative Calling* (Downers Grove, IL: InterVarsity, 2008); and Henry Van Til, *The Calvinist Conception of Culture* (Grand Rapids, MI: Baker, 1959). For a wonderful answer to the question of pursuing cultural activities even as people stand on the brink of hell, see C. S. Lewis's essay "Learning in Wartime," in *The Weight of Glory: And Other Addresses* (New York: HarperCollins, 2001).

3. Hegeman, *Plowing in Hope*, 34.
4. Van Til, *Calvinist Conception of Culture*, xvii.
5. Robert Farrar Capon, *The Supper of the Lamb: A Culinary Reflection* (Garden City, NY: Doubleday, 1969), 189.
6. I'm grateful to John Piper for inspiring the overall direction of these thoughts in his message "What God Made Is Good—And Must Be Sanctified: C. S. Lewis and St. Paul on the Use of Creation," http://www.desiringgod.org/conference-messages/what-god-made-is-good-and-must-be-sanctified-c-s-lewis-and-st-paul-on-the-use-of-creation (accessed July 23, 2014).
7. C. S. Lewis, *Reflections on the Psalms* (New York: Harcourt, Brace, 1958), 95.
8. Steve Jeffery, "A Biblical Case for Classical Education," unpublished manuscript.
9. The connection between wisdom and kingship is clearly established in Prov. 8:15–16, when wisdom exclaims, "By me kings reign, and rulers decree what is just; by me princes rule, and nobles, all who govern justly."
10. Both Abraham and Moses are referred to as the friend of God (Ex. 33:11; 2 Chron. 20:7; Isa. 41:8; James 2:23), which may also explain Jesus's words to his disciples in John 15:15: "No longer do I call you servants, for the servant does not know what his master is doing; but I have called you friends, for all that I have heard from my Father I have made known to you." Similarly, God makes known to Abraham his plans for destroying Sodom and Gomorrah (Gen. 18:17–19). God also consulted with Moses, "face to face, as a man speaks to his friend" (Ex. 33:11). In the latter two cases, the consultation involves a back-and-forth, a negotiation of sorts between God and his human representative (cf. Ex. 32:7–14; 33:12–23).
11. Israel's history manifests this progression through the dominant institution at any given time. From Moses to Samuel, the priesthood is the dominant institution. From Saul to the exile, the kingship rises to prominence. From the exile until the time of Christ, the prophets are dominant (with John the Baptist being the final prophet before Christ). This threefold division approximates Matthew's division of Israel's history in his genealogy of Jesus: Abraham to David, David to the exile, the exile to Christ. However, in describing one institution as dominant, I'm not suggesting that the others are absent. Moses was a prophet (Deuteronomy 18) who lived during the era when the priesthood was the main institution. Samuel was a priest who fulfilled a kingly role as a judge as well as spoke God's word to the king. Elijah and Elisha were prophets who arose during the time of the kingship (though they came at the end of the northern kingdom). And, of course, there were priests during the kingly and prophetic eras. Nevertheless, there still appears to be a progression in terms of prominence.
12. "Language is a God-given capacity that enables human beings to relate to God, the world, and one another. Specifically, language involves a kind of relating with God, the world, and others that yields personal knowledge. Language, that is, should be seen as the most important means of communication and communion. In Genesis 2, for example, God and Adam relate by means of language. Adam also relates to

his world by using language to name the animals (Gen. 2:19–20), an extraordinary scene that shows how humans make the distinctions and connections that both invent and discover the world." Kevin J. Vanhoozer, *Is There a Meaning in This Text?: The Bible, the Reader, and the Morality of Literary Knowledge* (Grand Rapids, MI: Zondervan, 1998), 205. Peter Leithart underscores the way that art is a kind of discovery-through-transfiguration: "The artist is always transfiguring, but this transfiguration is an attempt to get at dimensions of what's really there, not an abandonment of what's really there, even when the artist is aiming at fantasy. Art attempts to highlight patterns, correspondences, dimensions to reality that are usually missed in our everyday experience, and to force us to look again at the sunflower or the pipe or the chair. As the Russian formalists say, one of the purposes of art is to defamiliarize the familiar." "Art," http://www.firstthings.com/blogs/leithart/2005/09/art/ (accessed February 25, 2014).

13. J. R. R. Tolkien beautifully captures the progress and completion of creation through human naming in his poem "Mythopoieia": "Yet trees are not 'trees', until so named and seen / and never were so named, till those had been / who speech's involuted breath unfurled, / faint echo and dim picture of the world, / but neither record nor a photograph, / being divination, judgement, and a laugh / response of those that felt astir within / by deep monition movements that were kin / to life and death of trees, of beasts, of stars." (http://home.agh.edu.pl/~evermind/jrrtolkien/mythopoeia.htm, accessed July 22, 2014). The physical oak tree doesn't become what it's meant to be until man names it and sees it in light of its name. Man's complex naming is an echo and dim picture of the world but one that is no mere record or photograph. Naming is part conjuring, part verdict, part humor—a human response to reality stirred up by the lively movements of the same Spirit that breathed life into creation.

14. Notice that the name of the female sex (*ishshah*) is rooted in the past, in the woman's origin, whereas the first woman's personal name (Eve) is oriented to her future as the mother of all humanity.

15. The fact that Adam names woman on the basis of observed characteristics and relationships leaves open the possibility (and I would contend, likelihood) that names for things might have improved as Adam and Eve grew in knowledge and maturity about the world and their place in it; i.e., as time passed and their relationship deepened, it is quite possible that Adam would have given his wife a new name in order to reflect new traits or significant experiences. We see this sort of progression elsewhere in Scripture when God changes Abram's name to Abraham ("exalted father" to "father of many") and Jacob's name to Israel ("he takes by the heel" to "he strives with God") on the basis of new promises from God or significant events in the life of the patriarchs. In both cases, the name is changed to reflect observable characteristics and relationships.

16. "It follows that in Genesis 2 Adam was imitating God in the process of naming." Vern Poythress, *In the Beginning Was the Word: Language—A God-Centered Approach* (Wheaton, IL: Crossway, 2009), 30.

17. These six italicized verbs correspond to the six habits of heart and mind that John Piper has commended as essential to all education: "We aim to enable and to motivate the student to *observe* his subject matter accurately and thoroughly, to *understand* clearly what he has observed, to *evaluate* fairly what he has understood by deciding what is true and valuable, to *feel* intensely according to the value of what he has evaluated, to *apply* wisely and helpfully in life what he understands and feels, and

to *express* in speech and writing and deeds what he has seen, understood, felt, and applied in such a way that its accuracy, clarity, truth, value, and helpfulness can be known and enjoyed by others." John Piper, "The Earth Is the Lord's: The Supremacy of Christ in Christian Learning." http://www.desiringgod.org/resource-library /conference-messages/the-earth-is-the-lords-the-supremacy-of-christ-in-christian -learning (accessed August 20, 2013), emphasis original.

18. "If indeed God spoke to create the world, then the world from its beginning, and down to its roots, is structured by God's language. Language is not an alien imposition on the world but the very key to its being and its meaning. And if God governs the world even today through his word, then language, God's language, is also the deepest key to history and to the development of events." Poythress, *In the Beginning Was the Word*, 24.

19. Vanhoozer, *Is There a Meaning in This Text?*, 20. Later he writes, "Hermeneutics is relevant not only to the interpretation of the Bible, but to all of life, insofar as everything from a Brahms symphony to a baby's cry is a 'text,' that is, an expression of human life that calls for interpretation." Ibid., 23.

20. I'm grateful to Alastair Roberts and James Jordan, on whom I'm dependent for many of the connections in this section. See Alastair Roberts, "The Authority of Scripture: From Priests to Prophets," http://alastair.adversaria.co.uk/?p=198=1 (accessed February 25, 2014).

21. Solomon's proverbs are attempts to generalize about observed patterns in the world, examples of inductive reasoning in the pursuit of wisdom. Solomon recognizes that God is communicating always and everywhere, and so he says, "Go to the ant, O sluggard; / consider her ways, and be wise. / Without having any chief, / officer, or ruler, / she prepares her bread in summer / and gathers her food in harvest" (Prov. 6:6–8). Jesus commends a similar sort of wise reading of nature when he teaches us to fight anxiety by considering the birds of the air and the lilies of the field (Matt. 6:25–33).

22. "In relation to God, the Prophet was a confidant, one with whom the LORD consulted and discussed his plans. But in relation to the world, the Prophet was preeminently a speaker. His task was to persuade, to use words in a powerful and compelling way, to change people's minds and so to change the world." Jeffery, "A Biblical Case for Classical Education." Likewise, Poythress underscores the relationship between fellowship with God and creativity in speech: "The key to creativity is fellowship with God, who is the unique Creator. . . . Through Jesus we have our fellowship restored with God (2 Cor. 5:18). Then we can be creative, in imitation of God's creativity. We are stimulated because we begin to understand God, and the vastness of God's mind opens up new directions and new thoughts. We blossom as whole people, who are no longer slaves to sin (Rom. 6:20–21). And if we blossom as whole people, we blossom as speakers as well. We learn to be creative in what we say, because through renewal in the Holy Spirit we become creative in what we think." *In the Beginning Was the Word*, 47.

23. In Genesis 2, this includes the prohibition about the tree but also presumably God's description of Adam's origin, so that Adam recognizes that he (*adam*) was taken from the dust of the ground (*adamah*), and then imitates God. Theologians refer to this as "special revelation."

24. Thus Adam must consider the animals, examining them and reflecting on how they reflect the wisdom, grace, and character of God. As Poythress says, "God gives us moral rules for living, as summarized in the Ten Commandments. But his command-

ments call for application to our specific circumstances, and in the application we need God's wisdom to be insightful about the circumstances, and to be creative in exercising love. Human creativity, rightly understood, does not produce tension with God's rules but acts in harmony with the rules in reaching out to new situations and needs." *In the Beginning Was the Word*, 43. Theologians refer to this as "general revelation."

25. In calling human activity and culture making a kind of revelation, I don't mean to place it on the level of Scripture. Scripture alone is free from error and therefore functions as the standard by which we evaluate truth in every other area of reality. Rather, I mean that culture making can be included under the category of general revelation, since human beings and their acts are as much a part of God's revelatory creation as the heavens are. My point is that God *means* something through human activity. Sometimes, what God means and what we mean blend together, as when a preacher faithfully preaches God's Word or a father delights in his children. Other times God means something different from what the human agents mean, as when God means the slavery of Joseph for good, whereas his brothers meant it for evil (Gen. 50:20).

26. C. S. Lewis, *Mere Christianity* (New York: HarperCollins, 2009), 127.

27. In speaking of "the presence of evil in culture," the word "culture" refers to the human activity of culture making as well as to the cultural products (texts, artifacts, clothing, buildings, etc.). What's more, strictly speaking, evil doesn't reside in the artifacts; that is, sin isn't in "the stuff." Sin is always a matter of the people and their thoughts, dispositions, intentions, and actions. In other words, to speak of the presence of evil and sin in culture is to speak of the intentions of the human (and demonic) agents who communicate through culture making. To put it another way, insofar as the products of culture are considered bare artifacts—as material stuff—there is no evil in them. But insofar as those products are communicating the intentions of God's image bearers, they can be morally evaluated.

28. Thus, we can recognize the complexity of delighting in a fallen creation. Thinking of the use of lions in Scripture allows us to flesh out the picture even more, seeing the layers at work in God's world. A lion chasing down and slaughtering a gazelle is clearly an instance of natural evil, of predation and violence. Nevertheless, Judah is likened to a lion, whose hand is on the neck of his enemies (Gen. 49:8–9). Jacob compares the king of beasts to the kingly tribe, who will rule the peoples (Gen. 49:10–11). So seeing a lion slaughter a gazelle can remind us of the greatness of Jesus, the Lion of Judah who conquers his enemies, and can lead us to worship him. What's more, Prov. 28:1 encourages us to become like lions in their boldness. At the same time, the Devil "prowls around like a roaring lion, seeking someone to devour" (1 Pet. 5:8), and the enemies of David are young lions, "eager to tear" and "lurking in ambush" (Ps. 17:12). Thus, Christ is a lion, producing bold and righteous lions, and the Devil is a lion, producing violent and wicked lions. So we see the surprising and profound ways that natural evil can instruct us in the ways of God.

29. The need to depict evil in books, movies, and music creates particular challenges for Christian culture makers. The problem is complex, but to identify one dimension of the problem, there is a difference between reading about the fact of adultery (as in the story of David and Bathsheba) and acting out the scene for a film. What's more, some evil actions can be imitated without sin (as when a man shoots a gun loaded with blanks at another in a film), whereas others can't be (you can't properly

pretend to have sex on camera without engaging in some form of action that other people should not watch). For a perceptive analysis of the problem, see Douglas Wilson, "On Not Being Scabrous," http://dougwils.com/s7-engaging-the-culture/on -not-being-scabrous.html (accessed February 25, 2014).

30. Nathan's parable in 2 Samuel 12 provides a clear example of the way that fiction can awaken godly affections and (in this case) repentance from real sin. Jesus's parables seem designed to accomplish a similar feat.

31. When talking in terms of rebellious culture, it's important to note that sin and evil remain, even when we are speaking of Christian culture making. Between the fall and the last trumpet, there are no sinless cultures and no perfect culture making. However, while sin may pervade all human culture, it does not do so equally or identically. Our cultural activities can be more or less obedient to God, at both the individual and the corporate level.

32. N. D. Wilson and Douglas Wilson, *The Rhetoric Companion* (Moscow, ID: Canon Press, 2011), 8.

33. In commending thanksgiving, I don't want to give the impression that all our cultural enjoyment must include high-level analysis of theological themes in the book or the movie. Sometimes, we simply need to give thanks for enjoying a short rest, a bit of recreation, a taste of Sabbath.

34. J. R. R. Tolkien, "On Fairy Stories" in *The Tolkien Reader* (New York: Del Rey, 1986), 73.

Chapter 8: Desiring Not-God

1. Paul seemed to view his love for people in precisely these terms. In Phil. 1:7–8 Paul describes how he holds the Philippians in his heart, because they are fellow partakers of God's grace, and describes his longing for the Philippians' welfare as yearning for them "with the affection of Christ Jesus." Paul's affection for his fellow believers was an instance and expression of Christ's affection for them, spurring Paul to pray (vv. 9–11) and encourage the Philippians in the faith (v. 6).

Chapter 9: Sacrifice, Self-Denial, and Generosity

1. C. S. Lewis, "Some Thoughts," in *God in the Dock* (Grand Rapids, MI: Eerdmans, 1970), 147.

2. Ibid., 149.

3. Charles Williams describes the relationship between rejection and reception, between enjoyment and renunciation, in terms of perichoresis or coinherence: "Rejection was to be rejection but not denial, as reception was to be reception, but not subservience. Both methods, the Affirmative Way and the Negative Way, were to co-exist; one might also say, to co-inhere, since each was to be the key of the other." Quoted in Gilbert Meilaender, *A Taste for the Other: The Social and Ethical Thought of C. S. Lewis* (Grand Rapids, MI: Eerdmans, 1978), 32–33.

4. C. S. Lewis, *The Weight of Glory: and Other Addresses* (New York: Macmillan, 1949), 1.

5. Ibid., 1.

6. The greatness of what we receive back is also emphasized by the change in conjunction. When describing what's given up, Jesus uses the word "or": "house *or* brothers *or* sisters." When describing what is received back, Jesus uses the word "and": houses *and* brothers *and* sisters." I take this to mean that even when you give up one of the items on the list, you still receive back more than what you lost. You may leave

only your house for the gospel, but God still returns to you "houses and brothers and sisters and lands."

7. See John Piper, *Desiring God: Meditations of a Christian Hedonist*, rev. ed. (Sisters, OR: Multnomah, 2011), 239–40.

8. C. S. Lewis, *The Screwtape Letters* (New York: Simon & Schuster, 1996), 59.

9. Richard Baxter, *The Practical Works of Richard Baxter, vol. 1: The Christian Directory* (Morgan, PA: Soli Deo Gloria, 2000), 214–18.

10. For a devastating critique of the prosperity gospel, see John Piper, *Let the Nations Be Glad*, 3rd ed. (Grand Rapids, MI: Baker, 2010), 15–32. Piper defines the prosperity gospel as "a teaching that emphasizes God's aim to make believers healthy and wealthy in this life, while it overlooks or minimizes the dangers of wealth, the biblical call to a wartime mindset, and the necessity and purposes of suffering" (p. 19).

11. Grammatically, the connection between the two responses to God's provision is even more direct. Verse 18 is in fact a continuation of the sentence begun in v. 17. The last of the three commands in v. 17 is to set our hope on God. Everything after that is a description of the God on whom we've set our hope. This God richly provides us with everything. We are then given four purposes for God's rich provision: (1) to enjoy it; (2) to do good with it; (3) to be rich in good works; (4) to be generous and sharing. Thus it would seem that we cannot obey Paul's exhortation in this passage if we do not gladly receive from God everything he richly provides and then fulfill his kingdom purposes for that provision.

12. Incidentally, this is why guilt is such a terrible motivation for giving; if all the good things in your life simply make you feel guilty, why on earth would you want to spread that wretched sentiment by giving things to others?

13. This explosion of generosity is not optional. It's what prevents us from (mis)using the truth that all of creation reveals God to justify our indulgence of our every desire, no matter how extravagant. It's what keeps us from hoarding God's gifts for ourselves, rationalizing our luxurious lifestyle and lavish vacations and expensive purchases on the grounds that we're simply trying to enjoy God in everything. But the thrust of the New Testament is on gladly spending what we've been given for the sake of others. God gives to us that we might be fruitful with his gifts, that they might be enjoyed in the meeting of our needs, and then spent in service of his gospel purposes in the world. As we saw in chap. 4, gifts are for our enjoyment, and they are provision for mission. To pursue one at the expense of the other is to do violence to what God has joined together. It truly is more blessed to give than to receive, and thus we know God more fully in gladly giving than we do in selfishly hoarding.

14. Peter Leithart helpfully underscores the connection between gratefully receiving what God gives and wisely using what God gives to serve others: "For the apostle Paul, gratitude is expressed not so much in giving return gifts as in faithful use of the gifts given. Christians respond gratefully to the Spirit by using his gifts to serve the common good of Christ's body. Meister Eckhart captured this point when he said that fruitfulness in the gift is the most perfect form of gratitude. In place of a closed and narrow circle of generous giver and grateful recipient, Paul and Eckhart envision a dissemination of the gift." Peter Leithart, "The Dark Side of Gratitude," http://www.firstthings.com/web-exclusives/2012/08/the-dark-side-of-gratitude (accessed February 25, 2014).

15. Prov. 3:9–10 underscores God's way of granting abundance in response to our faithfulness with what he's given. "Honor the LORD with your wealth / and with the

firstfruits of all your produce; / then your barns will be filled with plenty, / and your vats will be bursting with wine." Giving the firstfruits to God does not diminish our supply; it increases it. Similarly, glad-hearted generosity does not deplete our resources but rather calls forth the greater generosity of God, who fills our barns that we might have enough and give abundantly.

16. This is my summary of comments by Nancy Leigh DeMoss in her excellent book, *Choosing Gratitude: Your Journey to Joy* (Chicago: Moody, 2009), 38–43.

Chapter 10: When Wartime Goes Wrong

1. John Piper, *Let the Nations Be Glad*, 3rd ed. (Grand Rapids, MI: Baker, 2010), 65.
2. Ibid., 68.
3. Ibid., 125.
4. John Piper, *Brothers, We Are Not Professionals* (Nashville, TN: Broadman, 2013), 203–4.
5. To underscore the point made earlier, my main concern is not with the amount of what's given. And I certainly don't mean to suggest that we should give our children or spouses everything they ask for. We have limited resources, after all. The key issue is that once we've decided to give, we must be all in with the gift. Our hearts must be *with* those to whom we give. No two-faced, guilt-ridden, manipulative giving. Instead, we wrestle with the complexities of our situation and the strategic use of our limited resources and then act in faith with a clean conscience and a cheerful heart.
6. There are a number of excellent books on economics from a Christian vantage point. Some of those that have been the most helpful to me are Jay Richards, *Money, Greed, and God: Why Capitalism Is the Solution and Not the Problem* (New York: HarperOne, 2009); and R. C. Sproul Jr., *Economics for Everybody: Applying Biblical Principles to Work, Wealth, and the World* (Sanford, FL: Reformation Trust, 2012). Other helpful books that don't necessarily adopt a Christian perspective include Thomas Sowell, *Basic Economics: A Common Sense Guide to the Economy*, 3rd ed. (New York: Basic, 2007); and James Gwartney, Richard Stroup, Dwight Lee, and Tawni Ferrarini, *Common Sense Economics: What Everyone Should Know about Wealth and Poverty* (New York: St. Martins, 2010).

Chapter 11: Suffering, Death, and the Loss of Good Gifts

1. John Piper, "Making Known the Manifold Wisdom of God through Prison and Prayer," http://www.desiringgod.org/conference-messages/making-known-the-manifold-wisdom-of-god-through-prison-and-prayer (accessed February 18, 2014).
2. Jason DeRouchie, "Shepherding Wind and One Wise Shepherd: Grasping for Breath in Ecclesiastes," *The Southern Baptist Journal of Theology* 15.3 (2011): 4–25.
3. DeRouchie argues that *hebel*, the Hebrew word that the ESV translates as "vanity," ought to be rendered as "enigma." By this, he means "that life 'under the sun' is frustratingly perplexing, puzzling, or incomprehensible, though still with meaning and significance." Ibid., 10. Thus he rejects the notion that Ecclesiastes is arguing that life is completely worthless, meaningless, or hopeless. Instead, it is filled with puzzles, both good and bad, and that our finite and fallen minds are incapable of fully grasping the way that the world works.
4. Ibid., 14.
5. Ibid., 14–15.

6. Ibid., 15.
7. Jordan Kauflin, "All I Have Is Christ," Sovereign Grace Music (2008).
8. Graham Kendrick, "Knowing You (All I Once Held Dear)," Make Way Music (2008).
9. Martin Luther, "A Mighty Fortress Is Our God," 1529.
10. Echoing Job 13:15, Shane Barnard and Shane Everett express this glorious and heartbreaking sentiment well: "Though You slay me, / Yet I will praise you. / Though you take from me, / I will bless your name. / Though you ruin me, / Still I will worship, / Sing a song to the one who's all I need." Shane Barnard and Shane Everett, "Though You Slay Me," (Brentwood, TN: Fair Trade Services, 2013).
11. "Spiritual Appetites Need No Bounds," in *The Puritan Pulpit American Series: Jonathan Edwards*, ed. Don Kistler (Morgan, PA: Soli Deo Gloria, 2004), 223–35.
12. In saying that we cannot love gifts too much, I'm trying to steer away from thinking of our love for God and love for his gifts in merely quantitative and comparative terms. Relatively speaking, it is possible to love God's gifts too much, as when we prefer them over him. But in truth, the person who loves God's gifts too much doesn't love the gifts enough. The glutton is someone who doesn't love food enough. If he loved food enough, he would allow food to be food instead of making food into a god. Thus, once supreme, full, and expanding love for God has oriented our affections, it unleashes our lesser loves to be as intense and high and powerful as they can be, since their intensity only serves to increase our love for the giver of all good things.
13. In an earlier chapter, I spoke of the way that the Bible expands our minds by pulling us in opposite directions and that we must embrace the mystery and refuse to allow one truth to cancel out another. This is no less true of our emotional lives. One of the seemingly impossible commands in the Bible is found in Rom. 12:15: "Rejoice with those who rejoice, weep with those who weep." The gospel lays both of these commands upon us. Those who suffer are called to add their joy to the joy of the blessed. Those who receive favor must join the grieving in the midst of their sorrow. And we must do so without allowing one emotion to tyrannize the other. The glad-hearted must not lord their blessings over the afflicted. The hurting must not allow their pain to drown out real joy when it's given from God. Love must be genuine (Rom. 12:9), and we must endeavor to live in harmony with one another (Rom. 12:16). Practically speaking, this means that our lives will be characterized by the same heart as the apostle Paul, who lived "as sorrowful, yet always rejoicing" (2 Cor. 6:10). It also means that wisdom and propriety will govern our joy and sorrow, so that we move with the rhythms of Eccles. 3:4: "[There is] a time to weep, and a time to laugh." And the only way that we'll make any progress in getting these rhythms right is if we are open and honest in communicating with one another and if we are trusting in the grace of God to be sufficient for our every need. It is grace that enables the sorrowful to rejoice in the joy of others, especially when they receive something that we desperately want or have tragically lost. It is grace that enables the joyful to bear with the suffering of the grief-stricken, especially when our hearts are bursting with gladness. Grace must reign, love must cover a multitude of sins, wounds, and thoughtlessness, and Christ must do what is impossible for us.
14. Nichole Nordeman, "Gratitude," 2002.
15. C. S. Lewis, *Letters to Malcolm: Chiefly on Prayer* (New York: Harcourt Brace, 1964), 90.
16. John Piper, *God Is the Gospel* (Wheaton, IL: Crossway, 2005), 15.
17. In his beautiful poem "Mythopoieia," J. R. R. Tolkien offers a suggestion for how the enjoyment of heaven will not be restricted to God alone, apart from the new

heavens and new earth: "In Paradise perchance the eye may stray / from gazing upon everlasting Day / to see the day illumined, and renew / from mirrored truth the likeness of the True." J. R. R. Tolkien, *Tree and Leaf: Including "Mythopoieia"* (New York: HarperCollins, 2001), http://home.agh.edu.pl/~evermind/jrrtolkien /mythopoeia.htm (accessed July 22, 2014). In heaven we will behold God with fresh and unstained eyes and thus will find our deepest joy in him. However, even there our eyes may stray from looking directly at God, who is the everlasting day, and see all that the day illumines—all the family and friends and angels and created glories and human activities. And in seeing the light of God reflected and refracted in this created mirror, our vision of God himself will be renewed and enhanced. Even in heaven, Tolkien suggests, we will ride the rhythms of direct and indirect godward-ness, spiraling forever upward in the Great Dance.

18. Lewis, *Letters to Malcolm*, 121.

General Index

Scripture Index

James

1:17	114
2:23	252
4:2	51
4:4	96
4:15	240

1 Peter

4:19	240
5:8	148, 255

2 Peter

1:4	42

1 John

2:15–17	96
3:24	38
4:8	239
4:12–13	38

Revelation

1:16	65
5:5	149
20:14	57
21:2	65